ities

DATE DUE			
GAYLORD N-2			PRINTED IN U.S.A.

Resources for the Study of Anthropology

Edited by
James A. Clifton

Peasants in Cities:
Readings in
The Anthropology of
Urbanization

Edited by
William Mangin

Houghton Mifflin Company · Boston
New York · Atlanta · Geneva, Illinois · Dallas · Palo Alto

Printed in the U.S.A.

Contents

Foreword

For decades anthropology has worn the public image of that science concerned exclusively with the isolated, exotic little community of "primitive" people. Much less appreciated has been the long anthropological tradition — one growing very much in scale and emphasis — of the description and analysis of complex societies and of the study of such associated phenomena as socioeconomic development, industrialization, and urbanization. In this set of readings Professor Mangin, who is an authority on urban anthropology, particularly of Latin America, brings together a variety of anthropological statements on the transformation of life styles as rural (or peasant, or tribal, or primitive) peoples take up residence in the cities of the world. Here are the hopes and aspirations and the manners of adaptation of such folk, the newer urbanites, whether they be Latin American, African, or Asian. In his perceptive and strongly felt introductory essay Professor Mangin makes it clear that anthropological observation in this field of urban studies can hardly proceed in the absence of anthropological involvement. For the urban anthropologist the inhabitants of Morocco's growing slum towns or of Rio's *favelas* cannot remain objects of detached and studious interest; they must also become subjects of anthropological responsibility.

JAMES A. CLIFTON

Preface

Peasants have been studied and written about by novelists, poets, academics, journalists, and bureaucrats for at least a century. The authors in this volume are mostly academics, including eleven anthropologists, two architects (Turner and Awad), and two journalists (Lelyveld and Nwoga). Anthropological interest in peasants (folk societies) is as old as the field itself and has been reflected, mostly, in specific studies of peasant communities. A frequent criticism of the studies deals with their failure to place peasant villages within the context of the political states in which they are located. Eric Wolf, an anthropologist, in his books *Peasants* (1966) and *Peasant Wars of the Twentieth Century* (1969) shows that peasants can be understood only as members of national states, and many aspects of peasant life, for example the wars he describes in Mexico, Russia, China, Vietnam, and Cuba, have to be viewed in terms of how the power holders of the state interact in the international arena. Two recent collections of readings (Potter, Diaz, and Foster, 1967; Bock, 1969) attest to the increasing attention anthropologists are giving to the relationship between peasant societies and state institutions. An important aspect of the involvement of peasants with national institutions, and one that has received all too little emphasis, is the massive migration to and settlement in cities by peasants all over the world.

Robert Redfield said, "The peasant is a rural native whose long established order of life takes important account of the city" (1953:31). The present collection of readings deals with peasants who have taken important account of the city by moving to it. The impression from the selections, including even Lelyveld's somewhat frightening picture of Calcutta, is that peasants show considerable initiative and creativity in coping with the urban situation. The impression may reflect my own bias, but after a thorough survey of the literature I think that the impression is justified in terms of the results of the vast majority of empirical studies, that is, studies where the investigator spent time living with or observing peasants in cities. All of the contributors to this volume have done first hand field work and, with the exception of John Turner's general article on squatter settlements, the selections are specific case studies.

When I began to collect the material I thought my major problem would be to find enough high quality articles on the subject. Compared to other areas of social science the material is, in fact, scanty, but there is a surprising amount of good literature about peasants in cities. In deciding what to omit I have had to be quite arbitrary. I left out Europe and the United States and gave more space to Africa and Latin America than to Asia. I also left out some of the more generally available works such as those of Oscar Lewis on Mexico (1959), Kenneth Little on Sierra Leone (1965), Janet Abu-Lughod on Egypt (1967), Aprodicio Laquian on the Philippines (1968), Lisa Peattie on Venezuela (1968), to mention a few. Four of the articles, those by Doughty, Beuchler, Bryce-Laporte, and Southall, are published here for the first time. They, as well as the other essays in the book, deal with various adaptations of peasants to city problems through modifying familial, religious, and political institutions of the countryside and adopting new patterns when necessary.

Acknowledgments

I would like to thank the following publishers for permission to reprint articles and chapters from their publications: *America Indigena,* American Universities Field Staff, *Architectural Design,* Bishop Museum Press, Ethnographic and Folk Culture Society, *Journal of the American Institute of Planners,* The New York Times Company, *Nickel Review,* Oxford University Press, Royal Geographical Society, *Sociologus, Trans-action,* and *Transition.* I would also like to thank the following authors for their cooperation in the preparation of this text: Hassan Awad, Frank Bonilla, Edward M. Bruner, Roy Simón Bryce-Laporte, Hans C. Buechler, Douglas S. Butterworth, Paul L. Doughty, Harold A. Gould, J. Clyde Mitchell, Leonard Plotnicov, Aidan Southall, and John C. Turner.

I also wish to thank Rosa Jo Donohue for her invaluable assistance in the many tasks involved in putting together a reader.

Acknowledgments

Introduction

Two unkind questions could be asked about the title of the present collection of readings, but I don't think the problems implied in the questions affect the choice of selections or my intent in bringing them together. The questions are, "What is a peasant?" and "What is a city?"

There are many definitions of peasants (Wolf, 1966), but most agree that peasants are relatively poor rural people who usually live by farming, producing for their own subsistence as well as for trade and tribute within a market and political system centered in cities. Karl Marx in *The 18th Brumaire of Louis Bonaparte* said that French peasants were as alike and as badly organized as potatoes in a sack. Many social scientists would agree. Many others, however, have found considerable variety within peasant communities and have also reported high degrees of organization. There is probably more similarity among peasant societies than among the hunting and gathering societies studied by anthropologists. On the other hand, there is also a great deal of cultural variety among rural peasants from Thailand, Japan, India, Pakistan, Iran, Egypt, Rumania, Finland, Italy, Ireland, Jamaica, Brazil, and the Andes. In that they are all exploited in similar ways by local, national, and foreign interests more powerful than they, peasants are alike. In many other areas of behavior, religion, family and kinship, child training, sexual behavior, aggression, technological skill, acceptance of change, world view, and so on, peasant groups are quite different from one another.

Almost all hunters and gatherers, "the primitives," have come into contact with the direct influence of powerful national states during the last one hundred years and have suffered from this contact. The European expansion into their territories pushed the primitives ruthlessly out of the way as did the Chinese, Japanese, and Malay expansions. The "new" states of Indonesia and Brazil seem no more solicitous for the cultural, economic, or social integrity, or even personal safety of the tribal hunters of New Guinea and the Amazon than were the Dutch, English, Australians, and Portuguese before them. All have used military repression, as have most national states with the ability and opportunity. The driving off, and often the killing off, of the primitives has been pushed and applauded as much by the peasantry as by their leaders. The nineteenth century American saying, "The only good Indian is a dead Indian," has its counterpart in most of the world. Even the North and South Vietnamese are agreed on the driving off of the Montagnards. In spite of the nature of the contact the primitives have been remarkably tenacious about survival. Some of them have become peasants. Many of them have just moved further and further back into undesirable land. Some are on reservations. Many have moved into cities and into industrial work. Jivaro Indians of Ecuador work successfully in oil fields. Many Eskimos and American Indians are highly skilled mechanics and machine workers, though many others seem to have great difficulty adjusting to cities. The selections in this book deal with more traditional peasants whose contact with the city has been much more extensive and long-standing. But keep in mind that even the black native Australians, for some reason called "aborigines" by the Europeans, have begun to move into cattle and sheep ranches and cities, and one of them has recently become a world's boxing champion.

Having bypassed the problem of what a peasant is, I come to what a city is. I am tempted to leave it by saying that, "A city is a place that when you are in it you know, especially if you are downtown," but I suppose that is too frivolous. For our purposes, however, it is enough to say that a city is a place where a large number of people live close together and say they are living in a city. The people involved in the selections in this book moved from sparsely populated rural areas or small towns to large cities — cities by anyone's definition.

Since all definitions of peasants involve contact with cities, we can say that peasants have been coming to cities since there have been peasants and cities. Rural people have been visiting and settling in cities for centuries, retaining many patterns of behavior, changing others. They have created new institutions and adapted old ones. People with all sorts of subsistence patterns, land tenure systems, kinship systems, and world views have done well in large and small cities all over the world. Some have done better than others, and the stories of new arrivals being fleeced by crafty older residents, overstaying their welcomes in the homes of city relatives, attempting ludicrous adaptations of rural institutions, or being sought after as tractable low-paid workers are as familiar in Lima, Johannesburg, and Calcutta, as they are in Moscow, London, and Chicago. In recent years in many parts of the world, because of the ease of transportation and communication (particularly the diffusion of movies and cheap transistor radios), urban ways of life have become familiar in the countryside. Many of the readers of this book are first, second, or third generation descendents of peasants who moved from the rural area of their own country to cities in the United States. Many others of us are first and second generation descendents of people who moved from country to city within the United States. It might be worth the time to explore your own past to gain an additional perspective on the people in this book. Ask parents and grandparents what the move was like, and perhaps ask other relatives and neighbors how urbanized the countryside has become.

In East and South Africa, a "Dear Abbie" syndicated newspaper column appears under the title "Tell me, Josephine." The letter writers, for the most part, appear to be young men and women from the country trying to reconcile rural, village, ethnic, or tribal customs to city demands and to relate customs of widely different ethnic or tribal groups to each other. The writers of the following two letters are trying to do both. The first one is trying to reconcile his culture with that of his wife, who comes from a matrilineal group. In the second the man appears to be trying to choose between loyalty to his mother's brother and his obligation to pay a bride price when he marries. Josephine's answers, similar to most of her others, try to bridge the gap but always on the side of adapting the traditional to modernization, westernization, and the new marketplace:

Q. During the course of my marriage I find my wife belongs to a tribe which is maternal. When we divorce or one of us dies, our children will belong to her brothers. I rushed into marriage without learning of this custom.

I am afraid that if we divorce, I shall go to my village quite old and helpless while my wife's brothers will get every help possible from my children. So where should I get children to support me? My tribe does not do this.

I find some difficulty in divorcing her now, before the children come, because I love her very much and she does the same to me. But what about this awful custom? When I mention my fears she tries to bluff me by saying her brothers will let me get my children, but I don't believe it. What have you to say before I sadly act?

A. That it would be foolish to break up a happy marriage for fear of an old custom that may no longer be practiced when you are old. Do not think of divorce, many people live happily together all their lives. Also, you may die before your wife. If you are good to your children they will not desert you in your old age. Twenty years from now, these customs may have died out completely.

Q. My uncle who is a charcoal-burner was taken to Native Court and told to pay 15 pounds for damaging two virgins.

He has written to me that according to our custom I must get money for him, and send it quickly to the Northern Province or he will go to prison. This will take all my savings which I had planned to use for marriage in two years. So must I send him the money?

A. If you wish to keep tribal custom, then you are obliged to help your uncle.

If you do not care about tribal custom any more and do not intend to visit your family in the rural areas again, then no-one can make you pay. Only you can decide.

I presume that according to the same custom you will inherit your uncle's property when he dies (Josephine 1964:72–73, 92–93).

Except for the kinship problems involved here, the same general type of advice is sought and given, although not always as directly and publicly, in other parts of Africa as well as in other parts of the world.

Anthropologists have tended to like primitives and village peasants and dislike acculturation and the involvement of "their" people with cities and with national and international politics. Sociologists in the United States also have manifested their small-town and rural bias and dislike of cities. In fact, despite its urban character, the whole Western world has shared an anti-city bias for many years. For anthropologists the neglect of cities has been influenced also by their preference for the study of whole communities or cultures. We now realize that it was quite presumptuous to think that a foreign anthropologist could know an entire culture after only a year or two of field work in one small area, but it is still true that it is easier to get a wholistic view of a small homogeneous village than of a complex modern city.

The neglect of cities has been encouraged further by our preference for theories of dynamic equivalence, dating from Pareto, Henderson, Parsons, Malinowski, Radcliffe-Brown, and others. These theories present rather static models and make it difficult to account for change even when things are changing before one's eyes. The avoidance of national political issues has many of the same roots as the avoidance of cities, as well as problems of sponsorship, both local and in the investigator's own country. The studies of isolated villages have been less sensitive politically than those of displaced peasant migrants, city slum dwellers, political decision-making, and so on. A number of anthropologists recently have begun to work in cities. These include Landsberger (1968) and others who have studied peasant political movements. In fact, the last few years have seen hundreds of articles about cities.

The present selections try to combine some general analytical views with an emphasis on what happens to the individual people who move to the city and are caught up in economic and political forces beyond their understanding or, more often, beyond their control. In view of the tremendous body of literature attesting to the destructive nature of the contact of peasants with cities, the remarkable thing is the efficient way so many peasants have adapted and contributed to city development. In many cases, it is hard to see how they could have done better.

There is probably some personal bias in the selection of articles about Latin America and Africa in greater numbers than articles from Asia and the Middle East. I know the literature of those areas better. I also feel that a concentration of a few articles on one or two regions, for example Nigeria and the Andes, will provide the reader with a better idea of the complexity of each local situation.

The cultural behavior of most rich people is different in many ways from that of most poor people in the United States or in any other society. Much of this is due primarily to the difference in wealth and access to power. The persistence of much cultural behavior in a particular class has been demonstrated over and over by social scientists, novelists, newspapermen, and others. In fact, most of the popular theories of cultural development are cyclical models of a rather static kind. Oscar Lewis (1966b), in a comment on the misuse of the phrase culture of poverty, says that he uses it as a "label for a specific conceptual model that describes in positive terms a subculture of Western society with its own structure and rationale, a way of life handed on from generation to generation along family lines." He then goes on to talk of "the intolerable repetitiousness and the iron entrenchment of (the) lifeways" of those in the culture of poverty. In the same sense almost any culture shows inexorable repetitiousness and entrenched lifeways. The objection to such cyclical theories as Lewis's is that they do not account for change, yet change is more the rule than stability in any observation of a culture over time.

There are things that poor people in modern industrial states — whether capitalist, socialist, or whatever—have in common with each other. Like the rich, the poor demonstrate persistence of much cultural behavior. However, in terms of cultural views of the world, ideal family and kinship patterns, aspirations, values, and even body movements and language habits, the poor of a country have more in common with the rest of their country (or culture) than they have with the poor of another country (or culture). The British poor described by Booth (1902) were more like the British middle and upper classes than they were like the poor of Istanbul or Naples. The poor of Appalachia and Harlem are more like the "average American" in cultural values and responses than they are like the poor of China, Viet Nam, or Germany. The poor of Mexico and Puerto Rico (San Juan and New York varieties) described by Lewis have more in common culturally with the general population of Mexicans and Puerto Ricans than they do with the poor of France or Pakistan. Poor Negroes in the United States are more like middle class black and white Americans, even granting the black power rhetoric, than they are like the poor of Ghana, Egypt, or Mexico.

The presence of different cultural groups within a national state complicates the question. In the Andes, for example, the rich and poor are more like each other and less like rich or poor Mestizo or White Peruvians, Bolivians, or Ecuadoreans. Judging from the literature a similar situation applies to much of Africa in that in relation to many important identifications, values, beliefs, and views of the world, rich and poor Ibos, for example, are more like each other than they are like rich and poor Hausa-speakers or Yorubas. It would also appear that in many countries of the world the small, often alien, upper class people have less in common with the rest of the members of the country than they have with comparable upper classes, for example, the elites of Peru and Spain. But even in such situations the language community is crucial, and it would be difficult to argue the similarities between the upper classes of Peru and Vietnam, even though there are some superficial resemblances.

If the differences are cultural and racial, as in the Andes, Guatemala, Nigeria, or among the Indians in North America, the combination of cultural persistence and racial visibility makes the problem of assimilation very difficult. The interplay between control, repressive force, toleration of cultural and racial diversity, opportunities for autonomous behavior, and perceptions of the realizability of desirable goals for self or children are more important than poverty itself in discussing the behavior of poor people, or, in some cases, in simply identifying people living in poverty.

Poverty is a relative concept: relative to place, time, and to one's reference group. The London or New York poor of generations ago are very different from today's poor in regard to what material things and what services they had. However they were in about the same situation, or perhaps a worse one, in relation to their total society and with regard to their hopes for the future. Poverty is not an absolute amount or percentage of wealth. As Miller and Rein wrote (1964), "It is a moving escalator, reflecting the values of a society. . . . The recent tendency in American society has been to raise the absolute level while increasing inequality. The percentage of the total pie going to the bottom twenty per cent has declined slightly in the post-World War II period." Michael Harrington documented the extent of poverty in our affluent society in *The Other America* (1962). He went further than Miller and Rein by showing that even in absolute terms there are hundreds of thousands of poor people in the United States. I still maintain, though, that the comparison with others who have more and the lack of opportunities to change one's position are the major factors that lead to what Oscar Lewis calls the "culture of poverty."[1]

The Siriono of Eastern Bolivia and the Penan of Borneo are cultures whose people are constantly seeking enough food to get through the week, but these groups are isolated from others for most of the time, and all have more or less the same opportunity to share in the good things of the society. Thus, though these societies live, in comparison to the rest of the world, in conditions of abject poverty, they all manage to live a satisfying, integrated, nonalienated life.

The Siriono, since coming into extensive contact with Bolivians and foreign missionaries, have become demoralized welfare dependents, as have many Alaskan Eskimos after extensive contact with Americans and foreign missionaries, but that does not negate the point. I would not go so far as to say that conditions are idyllic in primitive hunting bands because no man exploits another, but the concept of exploitation is necessary to explain the culture of poverty. The concepts of reference group and relative deprivation (Merton and Kitt, 1950) are useful in explaining the development of the attitudes of the culture of poverty. A Northwest Coast Indian tribe could lose over half its members to famine or disease without bemoaning their poverty or disadvantage since they were all, more or less, in the same situation, and they also had no rhetoric of the rightness of equality.

The long history of the development of slums and ghettos (Clinard, 1966) shows that such developments vary tremendously among themselves in terms of organization, morale, and internal cultural integration. My impression is that the high end of the scale on the latter items is associated with availability of models and possibility of success in either the general society or in the slum, or in both. In many places both routes have been open to at least a few members of the slum group. In the studies of a Boston Italian neighborhood twenty years apart by Whyte (1943a) and Gans (1962) the remarkable cultural persistence is accompanied by the possibility of choosing local or city-wide routes to cultural success. The recreation of the shtetl in the Eastern European Jewish ghettos (Zborowski and Herzog, (1952) provided fewer opportunities for movement in the general societies but considerable satisfaction within the local cultural setting. The voluminous literature, including hundreds of excellent novels and stories from all over the world, on the adaptation of agricultural peasant groups to urban and industrial life shows, again, remarkable persistence of peasant village patterns, cultural values, and beliefs—two, three, or even four generations after the initial migration away from the peasant community.

Erasmus (1967) has suggested that the upper limits of peasantry go beyond those described by Eric Wolf (1966), and he cites some evidence from Bolivia, Mexico, and Venezuela concerning the disappearance of peasant economic features such as the disposal of surplus through religious fiestas under the impact of land reform and outside capitalization of the rural sector. Without adopting a Redfield-Tonnies approach to societies as polar types with rural-sacred at one end and urban-secular at the other and without pushing the importance of peasant characteristics in slums and ghettos, I think that many peasants in cities carry with them much of their rural culture and pass some of it on to their children. In the urban United States many of us are first, second, and third generation peasants.

The Concept of Culture

Anthropologists have studied primitives and peasants, most of whom are "poor" when compared with rich or even most poor Westerners, but few of whom are in the culture of poverty. What is emphasized in most anthropological studies and ignored in most discussions of the culture of poverty is the integrated and interrelated nature of cultural patterns and the intimate relationship of man's social and biological behavior. Anthropology, first of all, studies man as a part of nature, rather than man apart from, above, or against nature. Man is seen as a mammal, a primate, a part of the evolution of life in the narrow and fragile biosphere. What people do in cultures generally makes internal sense. The patterns of behavior meet the needs of survival and, if you will excuse excessive reification, these patterns hang together. People see themselves in nature in different ways. Most North American Indians apparently saw themselves as essentially part of the natural scene. Western Man, on the other hand, sees himself as mastering nature and mastering his biological drives. He sees himself as more important than other forms of life that exist to serve him. This is a fundamental part of the Judaeo-Christian tradition. It is a short step to the Social Darwinistic view so common in the Western world that non-Western Man, particularly nonwhite man, deserves (or deserved) his colonial or lower class status or he would not have it. His natural role is to serve Western Man or, in the more enlightened view, to emulate him.

Anthropology is concerned always with the unity and variability in man's behavior. Unity is based on man's biological makeup and its relationship to his basic social needs, such as the necessity of care for children for a prolonged time or for pregnant and nursing mothers or the necessity for mutual aid in providing food, shelter, and defense. Variability is based on the thousands of different ways men have worked out responses to these biological and biosocial needs in different cultural settings.

Biological needs are met in many complex ways. Each society becomes very attached to its own solutions, however, and tends to value them above those of other societies. The solutions often are given a sacred character, and deviations from them within the society are punished, while the practice of other societies are laughed at, disapproved of, or where possible, often punished.

Anthropology has been principally a Western science, and social anthropology, with a few recent notable exceptions in Latin America and Africa, has developed in England, Germany, France, and the United States. In teaching American students it is not difficult to interest them in studying the customs of Eskimos and Andean peasants. However, it *is* difficult to introduce the idea that their own customs can be studied in the same manner. The vast majority of the students are white, and it often turns out that even in the relatively unimportant area (biologically speaking) of racial differences they are able to study the customs of the black minority much more readily than those of the white majority. There is no reason to think that this situation is unusual. Probably most people would react the same way to examining their own behavior. In my own experience, for example, I have found that North Americans can often be objective about the abuse of Indians by white Peruvians, but they can seldom see the abuse of Negroes by white North Americans in an objective way. I also have found, in teaching in Peru, that Peruvians can be more or less objective about race relations in the United States but are almost never able to take a detached view of Peruvian racial problems. It is much the same with other peoples' poverty.

The major elements in definitions of culture are that it is learned by a man as a member of a society and it is shared and transmitted by the members of a society. There is also general agreement that cultures develop as a response to human needs—biological and social—and that, in one way or another, practically all cultural behavior is related to those needs. If we take a wide enough definition of human needs, it is hard to argue with that position. All societies have to solve the same problems of feeding, housing, and clothing their members; protecting them against each other and outsiders; raising and teaching children; caring for mothers during the period of intensive infant care; controlling aggression and sexual behavior; relating their members to the world and the universe; and motivating their members to repeat the process each generation.

The argument is circular if it says simply that societies have to do these things because they do them. It is, however, difficult to imagine a society surviving *without* doing them. It is equally difficult, as Dorothy Lee (1959) has pointed out, to imagine a society surviving only doing those things. Every society elaborates some kind of activity, apparently for its own sake. Eskimos, even in a situation of food scarcity, eat as much as they can at one sitting. Trobriand Islanders spend months growing as many yams as they can only to let them rot in sacred storehouses. Kwakiutl Indians accumulated vast quantities of oil and blankets in order to burn them in competitive ceremonies. The United States spends about one billion dollars a month on bombing and ravaging the territory of one of its allies in order to protect that ally's integrity yet will not approve a few million dollars a year to save its own cities. In all of these cases an outsider has trouble relating the behavior to survival or to human needs, but in each case the people in question have some kind of explanation that fits an internal logic. Some cultures, generally those shared by small numbers of people in relative isolation, have more or less internally consistent patterns. The Eskimos, before extensive contact with Europeans, seemed to have little dissent on what ought to be done in every situation over a wide area and a long period of time. Developing cultures of relatively new national states (for example Yugoslavia, Nigeria, India, the United States, South Africa) and other larger, pluralistic cultures have considerable dissent over cultural values and are constantly analyzing and explaining in an attempt to reconcile the cultures incorporated in the state to one another.

Each society has its own version of culture, unique to itself and to a particular moment in time. Sioux, Zuni, Trobriand, French, Vietnamese, and American cultures differ among themselves and differ within themselves over time. Cultures are constantly changing in some respects and are remarkably conservative in others. DeToqueville said some things about attitudes and social groupings in the United States one hundred years ago that are pertinent and accurate today. However, in the realm of technology, urbanization, and international relations there have been enormous changes. English culture today is not the same as English culture eight hundred years ago. In some ways, of course, it is, but it has changed in many major ways. A reasonable analogy would be with language. The English spoken eight hundred years ago is unintelligible to a present day English speaker, but it sounds familiar to him and is relatively easy to learn.

Most people think that their culture is the best one. Most patterns of inculcating culture stress its uniqueness and superiority to others. Some people are remarkably receptive to new patterns of behavior, some are remarkably resistant, some stress missionizing and proselytizing, some are quite content with no spreading, some are very secretive and hide many of their customs from others. Pueblo Indians have been killed for revealing religious and social patterns to outsiders. No culture, however, has ever willingly decided to abandon all, or even a significantly large number, of its practices in favor of another's. Except for a few places where conquerors have eliminated all the members, as in Tasmania or in the case of some North and South American Indian groups after the coming of Europeans, or where the members have been forcibly taken from their societies and families in great numbers as in Negro slavery in North

America, cultures have retained continuity and, where there have been great technological and social changes, have adjusted their value systems and patterns to the new conditions.

Poverty and Culture

In 1943 Whyte pointed out that there was a high degree of social organization in a Boston slum and that most people who had studied slums had focused on poverty and reform to the exclusion of the social life of slum dwellers (Whyte, 1943a). During the last twenty-five years there have been many good studies of social life[2] in slums, but the emphasis is still on poverty and reform. There is nothing wrong with that emphasis, but it does tend to avoid some basic questions relating to function and change. Since the writers are middle class representatives of the politically powerful bloc in the society, the reforms generally call for "them" to be more like "us." Whyte says, in reference to Booth's study of the London poor, "Booth applied without question the standards of middle and upper class society to his lower class population." He goes on to say that Booth's terms "good" and "evil" had been replaced in 1943 by terms like "interstitial" and "disorganization." Now we have "marginal," "family deterioration," "cyclical poverty," and "the culture of poverty." The concepts (particularly Lewis's) are much more sophisticated than the older ideas of social disorganization, but the reform is still to be of the lower class, the poor, the blacks, with some saying they should reform themselves and others saying the affluent classes should help. Few say that the more powerful, controlling part of the culture should change, or that the total social structure needs changing.[3]

I believe that the presence of diversity, the opportunity for autonomous behavior that reflects some control over one's destiny, and the possibility of realizing a portion of the desirable goals of a society are not associated with the culture of poverty as described by Lewis. I suggest that in efficient, tightly controlled, industrial states such as Russia and the United States, diversity and autonomous behavior on the part of groups of people, especially poor and relatively powerless people, is much more difficult than in politically unstable, "developing" societies. In such industrial societies, however, particularly in the United States and Western Europe, there is a much greater possibility of large numbers of people realizing a fair portion of the desirable goals of the society through institutionalized ways. However, when a large segment of the population in such a society is blocked from access to goals as well as from moving on its own, for example Negroes and Indians in the United States, pressure and repression can be expected. If diversity is tolerated, and racially or culturally visible groups are allowed access to goals, if only at middle and lower levels, it is possible for different groups to coexist within the same national state. If the differences are racial, as in Brazil, the problems can be handled with minimal disruption in the affluent parts of the country. If the differences are cultural, as in the United States with white immigrant groups, in Belgium with Fleming and Walloons, and in India with dozens of different groups, cultures show remarkable persistence, but usually those people who *want* to can pass into a "national" culture.

Folk Culture, Peasant World View, and the Culture of Poverty

Robert Redfield in his noted book *The Folk Culture of Yucatan* (1941) discussed the idea that culture change in Yucatan could be studied by looking simultaneously at a large capital city, a small provincial city, a peasant village, and an isolated Mayan speaking Indian community. He also assumed that the same sort of study could be done elsewhere in the world. The four types of social organization were thought to represent not only differences within the area but differences over time. That is, the Indian community was said to be changing more slowly than the others and thus was thought to represent an earlier period in time. The other communities along the line were said to follow sequentially, with the capital city, Merida in the case of Yucatan, being the most modern and the most rapidly changing. The idea has been criticized, and it doesn't work as well outside of Yucatan, nor does it really explain the situation in Yucatan itself. There is, however, a logic to the idea, and it was around long before Redfield.

Redfield's scheme tends to reify change, as though change were some kind of object or person that moves from place to place, and it imposes an order on behavior that does not exist in fact. We know, for example, that a Mayan speaking Indian from Tusik can learn Spanish, go to school in a neighboring town, go to college in Merida, and even become a graduate student in New York. And he can do it all before he is twenty-five. In other words, it does not always take four hundred years for the kinds of change generally observed between Tusik and Merida. People move around more and faster now than ever before. Peasant and primitive culture patterns are found in cities. And city patterns, spread by radio, movies, administrators, schools, tourists, armies, and so forth, are found in the most remote rural areas, jungles, deserts, and mountains. By the same token some of the features of the folk society described by Redfield, that is, face-to-face contact between members of a community, social relations governed by kinship rather than impersonal laws, blending of religious, medical, and political institutions, and so on, can also be found in large cities, as many of the selections in this book demonstrate. The same kind of continuity seems to be present with regard to a concept of peasants developed by Foster.

George Foster, an anthropologist with extensive experience in Spain and Latin America, has developed an idea about the peasant world view that he calls the image of limited good. He applies it to peasants throughout the world and has amassed an impressive body of supporting data (Foster, 1965a, b). He describes the limited good orientation this way:

> I mean that broad areas of peasant behavior are patterned in such fashion as to suggest that peasants view their social, economic, and natural universes — their total environment — as one in which all of the desired things in life such as land, wealth, health, friendship and love, manliness and honor, respect and status, power and influence, security and safety, exist in finite quantity and are always in short supply, as far as the peasant is concerned. Not only do these and all other "good things" exist in finite and limited quantities, but in addition there is no way directly in peasant power to increase the available quantities (Foster, 1965b, p. 296).

He says that "an individual or a family can improve a position only at the expense of others" (Foster, 1965b, p. 297). He also points out the importance of envy in influencing economic and social relationships among peasants. It will be apparent to the reader that the condition described is by no means confined to peasants, and to a student of peasant society it will be apparent that it is by no means the only way to look at peasant communities. A much more common block to economic progress is the impingement of outside forces — landlords, government officials, lawyers, armies, foreign investors — on peasants. Peasant suspicion of community members and the subsequent internal hostility and abuse cannot compare with the abuse and robbery from outside. Much of our foreign aid prescriptive literature emphasizes the considerations mentioned by Foster, and much of it is correct. Many peasant communities are quite conservative and resistant to change. On the other hand, a story recounted by Marvin Harris (1964) about Ecuador, one that could be found easily in many other places and one that fits my own experiences in the field as much as Foster's pictures, presents another type of explanation for slow changes. Harris points out that a type of Merino sheep superior to the local variety was introduced into an Indian peasant community in Ecuador. When the local people overcame their initial suspicion and adopted the sheep, wool production improved to such an extent that the local mestizos came in and stole the sheep.

There is no conflict between the two positions. The argument is on the level of the present discussion of aggression in man that has so captured the popular book and magazine market. Aggression is common enough in man. But so is cooperation. It is not one or the other. There is variation among peasant communities, even between neighboring ones sharing the same culture. Nash (1964) has compared two neighboring communities in Mexico and found that one "is much more acculturated, much more receptive to Ladinos, works in closer harmony with the Instituto (a Mexican government bureau), and in general is a less defensive and hostile community in relation to the outside world." Similar differences between communities have been noted from all over. Each case raises questions of aspiration levels, differential calling forth of existing themes in the culture, the availability of locally defined success goals, and different kinds of economic and social relationships with local and national political forces.

If local patterns are upset by encroachment from outside, natural disasters, or the introduction of new desirable goals by local or outside leaders, change often occurs. Change is, in fact, much more the norm in human societies than stability. The Latin American experience in this regard does not seem very different from much of the third world. Some peasant communities retreat in the face of pressure (Algería, 1941; Castillo, Castillo, and Revilla, 1964; Wallis, 1953). Some develop new patterns, incorporating themselves into industrial urban life through migration and education. Some acculturate strategically (Kubler, 1946; Mangin, 1957) and develop new patterns of coping with change through reacting defensively against the state or the outside world. There have been a few nativistic movements in the Andes and in Latin America in general, and there have been numerous "social bandits and primitive rebels" of the type described by Hobsbawm (1965). These movements have been unsuccessful for the most part because, as Hobsbawm points out in his illustrations from Sicily and Andalusia, political organization and strategy have been less important than manipulative charisma and anarchistic appeals. Migration to cities has been the most successful adaptation for peasants under pressure. Rotondo and I found in Lima, Peru the same envy and distrust among peasant migrants that was noted by Foster, but we also noted much more cooperation, pride in achievement, and support for local leaders.

Many of the selections in this book show peasants adapting to cities and contributing to national development. It is also true that changes are occurring in rural areas. As Foster says,

> Those who have known peasant villages over a period of years have seen how the old sanctions begin to lose their power. . . . The problem of the new countries is to create economic and social conditions in which this latent energy and talent is not quickly brought up against absolute limits, so that it is nipped in the bud. This is, of course, the danger of new expectations . . . outrunning the creation of opportunities (1965b, p. 310).

I would agree. And I would suggest that fear and jealousy of other's individual progress and the personal envy described by Foster are less important in retarding change than external economic and political conditions. It is not, in most cases, "the fault" of the peasants that they do not often attain economic and social progress.

Oscar Lewis's much discussed concept of the culture of poverty, as ingenious and descriptive as Foster's image of limited good, can also be charged with overemphasizing internal conditions, personality factors, and the like, and underemphasizing external economic conditions. At times he seems to be saying that it is their own fault that the poor are poor. He says that the culture of poverty develops when a highly stratified society is breaking down or being replaced by another, for example, during the change from feudalism to capitalism or at the time of the industrial revolution. It may also come out of an imperial conquest where the conquered are kept subservient through force for several generations (Lewis, 1961, pp. xxiv). He goes on to say:

> The economic traits which are most characteristic of the culture of poverty include the constant struggle for survival, unemployment and underemployment, low wages, a miscellany of unskilled occupations, child labor, the absence of food reserves in the home. . . .
> Some of the social and psychological characteristics include living in crowded quarters, a lack of privacy, gregariousness, a high incidence of alcoholism, frequent use of physical violence in the training of children, wife beating, early initiation into sex, free unions or consensual marriages, a relatively high incidence of the abandonment of mothers and children, a trend toward mother-centered families and a much greater knowledge of maternal relatives, the predominance of the nuclear family, a strong predisposition to authoritarianism, and a great emphasis upon family solidarity—an ideal only rarely achieved (Lewis, 1961, pp. xxvi–xxvii).

However, Lewis also states that many aspects of the culture of poverty are attempts to solve survival problems when existing state agencies are unable or unwilling to do so.

He stresses the cyclical nature of the culture of poverty, that is, the passing down of the patterns from one generation to the next. Undoubtedly there is something in his view, as there is in Foster's. My point in this discussion is not to say that they are wrong, but to point out that other things are taking place outside of peasant communities and outside of the culture of poverty that are as important as, if not more important than, local social and personality problems are in maintaining the economic depression of people in the situations they describe. It is to the advantage of commercial interests and the middle classes, as well as to some peasant leaders and professional leaders of the poor, to maintain social systems with large numbers of peasants and poor people on the bottom rungs.

It is becoming more difficult to count on the same low level of aspiration among peasants because of the revolution in communications and in the ease of travel. There is an increasing awareness, also, that if increasing millions of people are brought into the pattern of high consumption characteristic of the world's upper and middle classes, the resultant situation will throw out of control the already critically dangerous threat to the ecological balance that allows man to survive on earth. That argument, however, no matter how persuasive scientifically, has been hard to sell to affluent consumers. It is almost impossible to sell to people who have been shut out of any participation in the short term bonanzas of the technological revolution. The issue, however, is too complex to be dealt with here, and I bring it up only as a necessary backdrop for the continuation of the discussion of poverty, peasants, and migration to cities.

Poverty implies involuntary deprivation in relation to some known standard. A poor farmer who speaks a national language of radio and the press, for example a Peruvian Spanish speaking mestizo, can be living in poverty by his own and by society's standards, while a non-Spanish speaking Indian from a closed community and with much less in the way of material wealth, can be disregarded by "society" and yet see himself relatively well off as compared to his peers. When rural people migrate to cities, however, the type of limited aspiration encountered in the closed community can rarely continue for more than a generation. At the risk of appearing contradictory, it is also a fact that even in many of the rural closed communities most of the people are well aware of the disparities in wealth that exist in their areas, and they have deep resentment towards local patrons and officials. The conditions are often so oppressive, for example in the Peruvian sierra, that migrants to urban areas, although appearing to be in an appalling economic state, are often pleased with the relative improvement in their status. The realization of certain goals such as acquiring property in a squatter invasion, getting children into school, or, above all, getting steady work, can more than overcome substandard living conditions, low pay, poor quality education, and so forth for a time. There is data supporting this from Peru (Mangin and Turner, 1968; Turner, 1965), Mexico (Butterworth, 1962), Chile (Goldrich, 1965), and Venezuela (Peattie, 1968), and I have had personal conversations with anthropologists that provided indications that the same situation exists in Guatemala, Colombia, and Bolivia (Mangin, 1967a). The children and grandchildren of the migrants, however, inevitably do have higher aspirations and are not satisfied with the same conditions.

The migrants often exhibit, in addition to the traits enumerated by Lewis, the envious behavior Foster attributes to the image of the limited good. But, as in the case of Foster, blocked access to opportunities would seem to account for the phenomenon as much as internal dynamics and intergenerational passing down of a culture of poverty. As John C. Turner and I and many Peace Corps volunteers noted in Lima, when changing access to opportunity through community organization and presentation of new possibilities for gaining political power, whether from inside or outside the community, from political, religious, foreign, or domestic groups, most communities responded by widespread participation. New leaders arose, internal fights crystallized, cooperation occurred, morale improved, and people acted. What appeared to be apathy often turned out to have been a strong, resentful feeling that there was no chance. The moves towards organization were often short-lived and unsuccessful. At times they left the communities more divided and alienated. However, at times they had the reverse effect. The differences in morale between squatter settlement dwellers and slum dwellers in Lima is impressive to even casual visitors and seems to me to be largely due to the fact that the squatter settlements were formed by organized invasions, have internal community organization with elections, and reward talent, initiative and courage (Mangin, 1965). The slum dwellers are basically the same kinds of people as the squatter settlement dwellers with regard to status characteristics. That is, many of them are young rural migrants from the mountains. However, the slum dwellers do not view the future in the same way the people of squatter settlements do. They exhibit more depression and alienation according to Rotondo (1959).

Vicos has skirted disaster for fourteen years, but now that the residents own the place morale has improved and new action is taking place. They have bought a truck and new land. They even expelled the Peace Corps for a few months and allowed them back in only under very strict conditions (Patch, 1964). The Maryknoll Catholic Church credit cooperatives have shown remarkable growth and responsibility in the face of dire predictions that the Puno Indians did not have any savings and would never be able to understand books and pay back loans. There have been almost no defaults; people turned out to have years of hoarded capital (wisely hidden since the chances of its being stolen by Mestizos were great), and credit and bookkeeping are well within the capacity of the members. The Peruvian *Cooperación Popular* program of forming community development teams of university students to work with highland peasants has been successful, particularly considering the pessimistic outlook held by so many prior to its beginning in 1964. *Accion* in Venezuela, the Colombian program of community development, and similar Chilean and Mexican programs have had successes and failures but, more often than not, the failure of technical assistance and community development programs have been due to political factors above the community level rather than to internal exhibitions of envy and the sense of being trapped in a persistent culture of poverty.

Urbanization, Industrialization, and Peasants

The cities of the world are growing at a rapid rate and much of the growth is directly attributable to rural migration. Peasant communities, however, continue to exist in a stable relationship with cities much as they have for centuries. They change and adopt new patterns, again as they always have. Provincial cities are now growing in many countries at a faster rate than the large capital cities, and peasants and rural people are attracted to industrial and other jobs in these cities. Industries have also moved to rural areas, and the names of giant American, European, and Japanese companies are known from Katanga in the Congo to La Paz in the Bolivian Andes. Some employers train workers; others look for trained workers. There is a large volume of articles and books on industrialization and its effects on migration and peasants. Some employers prefer peasant workers. Kahl, in a study of industrial workers in Mexico (1960), says, "Thus a man from a peasant background who moves into semiskilled factory labor feels that he is lucky to have such a good job; a man from an urban middle class background who moves into the intermediate ranks of industry as a foreman feels blocked, but one who becomes an engineer feels satisfied and anticipates a steadily improving future." The experience described may not be universal, but it is common. Many peasants work to earn money for specific purposes back in their own communities, for example, for fiestas or for the purchase of agricultural equipment, and are more interested in money than working conditions. Others who migrate to work decide to stay in the industrial center. These people adopt a wider view of their jobs and join unions to improve working conditions, secure fringe benefits and higher wages. The situation is complex and varies from country to country and zone to zone.

Urbanization is older in history than industrialization, and the two can proceed independently. The Western experience is not always descriptive of other areas, and no part of the third world is free to develop its own industrial pattern without influence from the industrial states of the East and West. Industrialization and technological advance do not always progress forever upward. Many towns in the world, much as seven towns known to me from the Callejon de Huaylas, a mountain valley in Peru, have had electricity and let it go. Industrialization can fail for many reasons. Many of the traditional peasant patterns such as hoarding silver and gold coins, keeping an excess of livestock, unwillingness to switch from subsistence to cash crops, and so forth, are conscious or semi-conscious hedges against inflation. Most of the blocking of land reform is political. The technical problems are minimal. Many of the benefits of foreign owned industry are not felt within the local areas where the plants and mines are located.

The urbanization literature is growing, and I have already referred to some studies of rural to urban migration. The patterns that emerge are similar to those noted by Caplow (1952) for Latin American cities in general:

> The net reproduction rates of urban populations in Latin America, while low in comparison to the surrounding rural districts, are extraordinarily high when compared with urban rates elsewhere in the world. This is presumably related to the survival of familistic social organization to an unusual extent in the urban community. As a result, urban populations in Latin America are often younger than rural populations in Germany, France, or the United States.
>
> Differences in the sex ratio are exceptionally marked, that is, the excess of females in the Latin American city tends to be greater than in cities elsewhere. This must be due in part to the existence of employment opportunities in commerce, light manufacturing, and domestic service, and the relative scarcity of employment in heavy industry or transportation.
>
> Taken together, these factors have produced a remarkably constant rate of growth in certain of the cities. Moreover, it is likely that the relatively high rate of increase of the urban population has had the effect of slowing down the acculturation of immigrants, by reducing the need for demographic circulation. The slow rate of acculturation, in turn, helps to account for the survival of indigenous culture patterns in close proximity to the metropolis, and the failure of many urban culture traits to diffuse through the economically dependent hinterland (pp. 256–257).

Caplow's propositions held up pretty well until recently, and may account, in part, for the frequent observations of slum organization based, apparently, on rural patterns. The spread of "urban" ideas to the hinterland (e.g., Reina, 1964; Goldkind, 1961), and the increasing sophistication of urban migrants leads to different kinds of organization.

There is little reason to think, however, that the situation relative to the unequal distribution of power and wealth in the "underdeveloped" world will change much in countries that do not have revolutions. Judging from the situations in Egypt, Bolivia, and Cuba where there have been revolutions, there are not as many rich people now as there were before the revolutions, but there are probably as many poor people. Lewis says that in Cuba there is poverty but no culture of poverty. The squatter settlements of Peru, Turkey, Athens, Hong Kong, and Brazil have many poor people, but observers see little of the culture of poverty.[4] My own interpretation of the Latin American and United States situations is that the traits mentioned by Lewis, and the phenomenon of apathy and cyclical poverty, are much more tenuous and temporary in both areas than he says. It seems to me that Saul Alinsky is right when he says that there is no such thing as an apathetic group, culture, or class. The political factors that lead to the disparities in wealth and power are much more important than personality and cultural characteristics in thinking about priorities for change. I agree with Valentine (1968) that Lewis has contributed immeasurably to our understanding of family dynamics (particularly in Mexico), but his work on the culture of poverty falls into the widely used body of reform literature mentioned earlier by Whyte (1943a) and, even though it focuses on slum organization, a big improvement on the past, it still suggests that the major problem is not poverty but the culture of poverty.

Nathan Glazer (1965) points out that Tokyo has fewer slums than New York, and by inference less of the culture of poverty, because, even though physical conditions and even relative deprivation are as great in Tokyo, a much smaller proportion of the Tokyo population is defined by the society as a social problem population. He says that, "The chief problems of our slums are social—unemployment, poor education, broken families, crime." He goes on to point out that these problems cannot be solved by building houses for the poor nor by urban renewal. Lewis illustrates this same point when he shows a Puerto Rican family bringing the culture of poverty from a shantytown to a project. I should also point out that Wakefield (1959), Padilla (1958), and Safa (1964) see many more strengths and less of the culture of poverty in Puerto Rico than does Lewis. Safa, particularly, sees the same kind of positive community attitudes and actions in squatter settlements as Turner and I do (Mangin, 1967a, b; Mangin and Turner, 1968). It is not absolutely clear cut, but there is considerable evidence to support further examination of the idea that putting people into government housing has little effect on the culture of poverty, but that if people move on their own—seize land and build their own houses and communities—it has a considerable effect on the culture of poverty.

Ernest Hemingway and F. Scott Fitzgerald are supposed to have had a conversation where Fitzgerald said that the rich were different from us, and Hemingway replied yes, they are richer. The same argument goes on today about the poor. In the United States, on the one hand, William Kvaraceus and Walter Miller (1959) represent a position that the poor are different from us. Ohlin and Cloward (1960) and Albert Cohen (1955) say that they are poorer but have essentially the same hopes and aspirations. Oscar Lewis himself says, in a quick aside in *Children of Sánchez* (1961), that the Mexican middle class fits the description of the culture of poverty except that they are not poor. Writings on working-class America, and much of what one observes of middle-class America seem to me to support the Ohlin-Cohen position. While reading *The Autobiography of Malcolm X* (1966), in spite of the obvious interest in reading about a remarkable man, I was constantly impressed with one thing. Even though he followed a very different route, and in spite of the fact that a lower class black man and a middle class white man see different aspects of America, it was clear to me over and over that he and I (about the same age) were members of the same culture and shared the same, basically urban, American view of the world and of human relationships. If one has access to the goals of his society, he has a larger stake in maintaining it, or, at least, no special interest in attacking it, as long as he feels that the goals are desirable and legitimate.

The Latin American urban squatters who take initiative, defy the police, risk and often lose their property and occasionally the lives of relatives and friends, and who create their own communities and build their own houses in the face of societal opposition, often seem to gain a confidence and strength from the activity that enables them to become a functioning part of the same society that opposed them. They may still be defined as a social problem population by the larger society long after they turn out to be a population that has solved a number of social problems, but since in the majority of cases they are not racially distinguishable from the rest of the population, they are able to pass easily and convert their squatter communities into part of the city.

The major problem of poverty as a subculture in the United States is the problem of large numbers of Negroes concentrated in our cities. As many observers have pointed out, for example Myrdal in *An American Dilemma* (1944) and scores of black power spokesmen today, the problem is a white problem as well as a black one: neither group can "solve" it. Possibly, as Myrdal has recently pointed out, it cannot be solved by both groups together, at least not without the spending of billions of dollars accompanied by drastic attitudinal changes on the part of the white majority. It also probably cannot be solved by black violence and rebellion, American as that may be. And it has only been aggravated by the strange combination of white violence, mostly institutionalized, and white welfare.

Fifteen or twenty years ago James Agee wrote, in the narration to a film called *The Quiet One,* that if we in the United States did not do something about discrimination, unemployment, bad schools, and the resultant family and cultural strains that characterized the lives of Negroes in large cities, we would "create, like mirrors locked face to face, an infinite corridor of despair." He might have said an infinite corridor of anger. In either case, the solution suggested by the film — more individual counselling, provision of male models for disturbed boys, isolated therapeutic centers such as the Wiltwyck School — seem to be beyond our resources. A few

Claude Browns (1966) have come through that route, although it is not too clear what the school had to do with him. The vast majority of Negroes move into the society in an orderly responsible manner, even though they pay a much higher psychological and economic cost than the rest of us. But, in an era of rapid change in many aspects of our culture, change for Negroes who are poor is slower than ever. Low level, hard work jobs that have been handed on by one immigrant group to another, but always handed last to Negroes, are disappearing. In the long run that may not be relevant since many young Negroes do not want those jobs anyway. It is difficult to say to a Negro population well aware of its historical position in relation to whites, "Let bygones be bygones. Just clean those toilets a little longer, and we'll let you in. We mean it this time. After all you don't have much trouble getting into the infantry any more."

Moynihan (1965), speaking for the Liberal Establishment, says we have to concentrate on the Negro family and that the Negro man needs significant employment. One of his few specific suggestions is that Negroes should join the army. It certainly is a socially important job in America, and as larger numbers of whites use the national guard, reserve training, and similar devices to avoid the draft, and as long as we have a war on and longer, we will need blacks in the army. Unless we plan, however, to have a long series of wars fought by a black mercenary army, the military solution is a very limited one. We need basic, radical changes in a very short time. The white culture of poverty is largely confined to old people and what Galbraith has called "pockets of poverty." Caudill (1963) speaks of the Cumberlands as an area where enormous wealth has been drawn out, "but the total losses have exceeded the gains." The Cumberlands is an area where

> the money losses have been equalled or exceeded by the human losses; the mountaineers, once hardy, prolific, and fiercely independent, remain prolific but neither hardy nor independent. Fully half of them are decrepit, sickly dependents on the dole, state, national, or private.

Without the complication of racial prejudice, it is quite obvious that the region could be completely rehabilitated and the people brought into the national culture with no particular strain or loss of pride, and that the total cost, which would turn into an investment in any case, would be less than a month or two of the Vietnamese war. In fact, the Cumberlands present a good example of a systemic problem. In 1967 when a group of mountaineers, aided by a few OEO volunteers, tried to oppose strip mining, probably the most immoral and irresponsible exploitation of men and land in the world, the powers of the state of Kentucky were mobilized, the dissidents threatened, and the volunteers arrested for sedition.

The strip miners hardly lost an hour. The OEO volunteers were not backed up by Washington, nor should anyone expect that they would be. The failures of countless community action programs, black and white, and their subsequent abandonment by Washington after destruction by local and state governments represent similar systemic problems.

Robert Coles (1968) has described the situation for Appalachia in a succinct statement that I see as applying also to black ghettos in the United States, squatter settlements in Peru, and to "the culture of poverty" in general:

> Appalachia is full of ironies, but nothing is more ironic than the fact that America's oldest ethnic group, its white Anglo-Saxon Protestants, live there in poverty as desperate as that experienced by any other impoverished people. It took courage and enterprise to settle the region — and now the region's people are called inert, apathetic, and unresourceful. The region has experienced the severest kind of unemployment as a result of technological change, and yet side by side one sees an almost primitive economy. If ever there was a section of America that needed planned capital investment, federally sustained — as indeed this country has done in other regions of the world with its money — then indeed Appalachia is that region.
>
> In my experience the people of Appalachia do not fit the usual sociological and anthropological descriptions applied to them. By that I mean that their apparent inertia and apathy are reasonable responses to a lack of opportunity and a lack of employment. Given jobs, real jobs, jobs that are not substitutes for work, Appalachian men and women work well and hard. They also can be open, friendly, and generous — even to an outsider like me. What they do not want is a kind of patronizing and condescending sympathy. They are proud and stubborn people who want from this country a share of its wealth. Given that, I don't think we would have any "psychological problems" with the region's citizens (p. 27).

In the face of the existence of the behavior patterns described by Lewis, observers often remark on the strength of character, the ability to maintain dignity and good humor, and the emotional balance of people living in the culture of poverty. Adversity and hostility are faced and borne by masses of people with remarkably little breakdown. Elizabeth Herzog (1966), Robert Coles (1965), Erik Erikson (1965), and others have pointed out the strength, self-discipline, and endurance of Negroes — men, women, and children — under fire in the United States. The South African situation has produced similar dramatic examples. Neira (1964) and I have pointed out similar strengths among the poor people in the land invasions of rural and urban Peru. As yet, no government has taken advantage of these qualities in any conscious way.

The kind of community action represented by the squatters may only be possible in a national state where the government is not in full control. In many of the cases the land squatted on was public land or land in dispute. Building trades unions in most such countries, especially in Latin America, are nonexistent or small, weak, under the control of the governments, or militant and not interested in stopping people from building their own homes. Many construction workers live in squatter settlements and make extra money or build mutual aid capital by working on neighbors' homes. Zoning and housing codes laws may exist in some of the countries, but they are seldom enforced. Repressive police forces exist and are used, but few of the countries with squatters are sure of the loyalty of all branches of the armed forces, and few are willing to risk a full scale attack on hundreds of families in full view of press and television. Also, in spite of the authoritarian nature of many of the regimes, a certain amount of looseness is tolerated as long as it is not in an area of behavior that directly threatens the economic interests and power of the ruling groups. There is no large middle majority with a vested interest in law and order that has the possibility of earning income from every piece of property and every business and labor contract. Interestingly enough, the squatters themselves often adopt extreme versions of nineteenth century capitalism. They begin selling things to each other and make all kinds of restrictive rules about how new members can be admitted to the community. Once they have broken the law and seized their own land, they usually turn out to be conventional, nonrevolutionary, tractable members of the society. But without the looseness, disinterest, and general lack of control, they would never have had the chance.

With a few minor exceptions, no modern state — capitalist, communist, or whatever — has allowed large groups of poor people to work out their own definitions of problems and their own solutions. This may be because it would be too disruptive; I am not suggesting it as an all-purpose solution. Perhaps it is structurally impossible for a state to support conflict against itself. However, the conflict comes anyway, even in benevolent systems. If the hand that is feeding you is the zookeeper's, you probably have to bite it, particularly if it is not feeding you enough. In the countries where large squatter developments have taken place, the governments were not feeding anyone much of anything. That may be the best situation for community action.

In the United States there is limited opportunity for poor people beyond the traditional channels, and many of these channels are closing. Meaningful, satisfying ways to achieve desirable goals are not even in large supply for the middle class. There is considerable discussion as to what are desirable goals. For Negroes, particularly poor Negroes, just when the traditional channels seemed to be available to them, as when Negroes began to gain control of Tammany Hall, the channels became irrelevant. Yet the public voice still says use the traditional channels. It is no wonder that Carmichael's statement that the United States is a racist society meets with little objection among Negroes, even though his plans for changing it do not always meet with the same approval. This racism is nearly as prevalent in the black as in the white community and with more reason. However, in regard to many fundamental views of the world the black poor sound exactly like the white poor and the white middle majority. The solution to white opposition to black voting in Mississippi offered by Malcolm X (1965) is 1000% American:

> So we here in the Organization of Afro-American Unity are with the struggle in Mississippi 1000%. We're with the efforts to register our people in Mississippi to vote 1000%. But we do not go along with anybody telling us to help non-violently. We think that if the government says that Negroes have a right to vote, and then some Negroes come out to vote, and some kind of a Ku Klux Klan is going to put them in the river, and the government doesn't do anything about it, it's time for us to organize and band together and equip ourselves and qualify ourselves to protect ourselves. And once you can protect yourself, you don't have to worry about being hurt . . . (p. 152).

I have heard versions of that all my life, and they have always been in the mainlines of the American tradition. It is a more important and dramatic theme in our culture than the "work hard, send your kids to school, paint your porch, be patient," theme. In thousands of stories, movies and television shows (cowboy, war, and others) the American way is to try to work hard with a quick resort to violence if the work is blocked. If both are blocked, then many manifestations of the culture of poverty appear. But there seems to be evidence, as I have said, that the culture of poverty is not a culture in that it can be thrown off quickly with changes in economic or social opportunities. The changes may be in a constructive manner, as with the changes brought about by squatters, in which case they break the "image of limited good" and "culture of poverty" blocks to development. They may be destructive, as in the Watts and Detroit riots, if no other avenues are open.

Change initiated from the top is necessary in the United States because the top is so powerful and is backed by an enormous and satisfied middle majority with a vested interest in resisting change and with varying degrees of racial prejudice. The technical and financial problems of poverty in the United States could be solved temporarily with one quarter the resources we are now using to carry on the war in Viet Nam. The solutions would have to recognize the crisis and need for fundamental changes in our political, economic, and value systems. That is asking a lot. But culture is a repository of possible patterns of behavior, and we have in our culture many patterns that do allow for change, equality of opportunity, and so forth.

It seems to me that we have a problem in our own society more serious than the culture of poverty. Our culture of poverty, if eliminated or greatly reduced in scope, would still leave a poverty of culture. Indeed, the America of Eric Hoffer gets increasingly difficult to find. We are also in a relationship to the rest of the world where we use resources far in excess of our population's equitable share. Many people in the rest of the world, particularly the "third world," see themselves in relationship to the United States, as members of a culture of poverty. Franz Fanon (1963), who predicts—and recommends—violence against oppressors (broadly defined in racial, colonial, economic, and political terms) by the oppressed (also broadly defined) as the salvation of the oppressed ("The Wretched of the Earth"), appeals to those with an apocalyptic view of human events. He overstates his case on the evilness of the powerful and the goodness of the powerless, but the resentment he describes is certainly present in much of the world. As will be seen in the selections in the book, poor people are remarkably ingenious in coping with the most difficult problems, but the overall context in which the coping occurs is growing more and more frustrating as the world's rural and urban populations continue to grow and wealth and power concentrate in fewer hands.

It is difficult to have any perspective on one's own time. Academic and philosophical pronouncements about these being the best or the worst of times are generally irrelevant and wrong. They may not be as wrong as the statements of journalists and bureaucrats, but they are probably wrong. Prophecies of doom seem to be associated almost permanently with states that have solved the subsistence problem for most of their members. Gibbon says that the prophets were there before the empire "fell," but Rome is still there, and there are more Romans than ever. Edward Sapir, an anthropologist, made a depressing comment in 1924 on American culture. It can be seen in more general terms as a statement about the human condition in an efficient industrial state:

> The transformation of ends is of the greatest cultural importance because it acts as a powerful force for the preservation of culture in levels in which a fragmentary economic functioning of the individual is inevitable. So long as the individual retains a sense of control over the major goods of life, he is able to take his place in the cultural patrimony of his people. Now that the major goods of life have shifted so largely from the realm of immediate to that of remote ends, it becomes a cultural necessity for all who would not be looked upon as disinherited to share in the pursuit of these remoter ends. No harmony and depth of life, no culture, is possible when activity is well-nigh circumscribed by the sphere

of immediate ends and when functioning within that sphere is so fragmentary as to have no inherent intelligibility or interest. Here lies the
grimmest joke of our present American civilization. The vast majority of
us, deprived of any but an insignificant and culturally abortive share in
the satisfaction of the immediate wants of mankind, are further deprived
of both opportunity and stimulation to share in the production of non-
utilitarian values. Part of the time we are dray horses; the rest of the time
we are listless consumers of goods which have received, no least impress of
our personality. In other words, our spiritual selves go hungry, for the
most part, pretty much all of the time.

NOTES

1. Two of the best expositions are Lewis, 1961 and 1964. A revised position is
   Lewis, 1966b. For an earlier view of rural people in the city see Lewis,
   1952. The subject is also treated in somewhat different ways in *Five
   Families* (Lewis, 1959) and in the equally convincing, but considerably
   less representative study of a Puerto Rican family, *La Vida* (Lewis, 1966a).
   For sixteen reviews of *La Vida*, all concerning the culture of poverty, and a
   comment and reply by Lewis, see *Current Anthropology*, 8, 5, December
   1967.

2. The list of slum studies is too long to begin an exhaustive bibliography in
   this context. A few recent titles are: Peattie, 1968; Liebow, 1967; Maria de
   Jesus, 1962; Thomas, 1967; Sexton, 1965; Gans, 1962; Van den Berghe,
   1964; Wilson, 1965; Rubel, 1966; Plotnicov, 1968; Mayer, 1961; and there
   are many others. An equally good, if not better, source of information on
   slums is the vast field of literature, particularly the large number of auto-
   biographical novels.

3. Robert Coles has written about this matter (1968) and it has also been dealt
   with by many Marxist writers. It has become a focus of discussion in relation
   to the culture of poverty and Charles Valentine (1968) deals with the
   matter in detail in his critique of Lewis, Moynihan, Frazier, Matza, Clark,
   Keil, Gladwin, and Liebow.

4. The possibility of observer error, selective perception, or, in many cases,
   selective emphasis is great in this area. I have referred elsewhere (Mangin,
   1967c) to different responses from the same people elicited by Fried and
   myself. In areas such as poverty and disorganization, where there is so
   much room for interpretation based on the personality, background and
   political views of the investigator it is difficult even to arrive at the same
   description of circumstances, to say nothing of what political and social
   changes are necessary, and to say even less of how these changes are to be
   brought about. My own evaluation of most of the studies I have read is that
   the greatest lack is the failure to make political analyses and interpretations
   and the tendency to make psychological ones.

1 ··················

Barriers and Channels for Housing Development in Modernizing Countries

JOHN C. TURNER[1]

Many of the squatter communities of Latin America offer uniquely satisfactory opportunities for low income settlers. They are characterized by "progressive development," by which families build their housing and their community in stages as their resources permit, the more important elements first. The procedures followed by these self-selecting occupant-builder communities, free to act in accordance with their own needs, enable them to synchronize investment in buildings and community facilities with the rhythm of social and economic change. Official housing policies and projects, on the other hand, attempt to telescope the development process by requiring minimum modern standard structures and installations prior to settlement. Such "instant development" procedures aggravate the housing problem by disregarding the economic and social needs of the mass of urban settlers in modernizing countries.

Reprinted by permission of the *Journal of the American Institute of Planners,* (Volume 33, No. 3, 1967).

To suggest that planning and building codes designed to improve and maintain modern housing standards have the opposite effect in many parts of the world may seem heretical. While preparing a paper for the United Nations on the subject (Turner, 1966a), however, I found that experience in many developing countries indicates that they do. The planning concepts derived from the experience of modernized countries are frequently inapplicable under circumstances typical in the modernizing countries. It thus is clear that the question should be discussed widely and openly.

The argument, briefly, is that the principle of "minimum modern standards" is based on three assumptions: that high structural and equipment standards take precedence over high space standards; that households can and should move when their socioeconomic status has changed so that they can afford to have a larger (above minimum) standard dwelling; and that the function of the house is, above all, to provide a hygienic and comfortable shelter. While these assumptions are valid in the United States, Europe, and the USSR, they do not hold true for such countries as Peru, Turkey, and the Philippines.

Observations of what ordinary families in urbanizing countries do, when they are free to act as they will, show that they prefer to live in large unfinished houses — or even large shacks — rather than in small finished ones. As Patrick Geddes wrote half a century ago in India: "I have to remind all concerned (1) that the essential need of a house and family is *room* and (2) that the essential improvement of a house and family is *more room*" (Geddes, 1918, 1:85). The typical family, earning an uncertain wage in an unstable economy which provides little or no social security, depends heavily on property for security — especially while undergoing transition from the status of recently to fully urbanized (Turner, 1966b). For such families, the vast majority in the cities of urbanizing countries, housing is a "vehicle of social change" (United Nations, 1965). Geographic stability is thus often the agent of social mobility than the reverse, which is more generally true in the fully participating sectors of modern society. I have never come across a home-building family in *barriadas* of the kind described in this article that was not building for their children and that did not also hope and expect their children to achieve a higher social status. Charles Abrams, who has observed squatters in every continent, notes that "when tenure seems secure the foundations are made firmer" (Abrams, 1965). Thus squatters are "less worried about what they will build than where they will build it and less concerned about initial standards than about initial layout. *Rancho* houses (squatter houses) will improve with time and with better economic conditions if the *rancheros* are given a stake."[2] Few planners and administrators agree with Abrams yet, but even fewer of the ordinary people would disagree. Secure possession of land where they can live *now* is far more important to them than the promise of a modern house that may never materialize. But given the land and the right circumstances — that is, adequately located, properly planned, and with secure title — experience has shown that development to contemporary standards will surely take place, even if slowly.

The imposition of modern minimum standards on popular urban housing in a transitional economy is an assault on the traditional function of housing as a source of social and economic security and mobility. By requiring a heavy financial outlay initially and by leaving little room for the investment of nonmonetary resources, modern standards delay the processes of urban settlement and resettlement and aid slumlords and land speculators. Unattainable standards increase the demand for and the cost of slum housing and worsen slum conditions. By eliminating all low income and many middle income groups from the market, such standards encourage the tendency to invest in unused building land rather than in housing construction.

In cities where the majority of the population live in slums and cannot build needed houses because they cannot afford the costs of land and construction, it is hardly surprising to find that a great deal of urban settlement and resettlement takes place independently of the legislative and commercial systems. The experiences of certain Peruvian cities are typical of urbanizing countries. During the past twenty-five years the population of Lima has trebled from less than 700,000 in 1940 to an estimated 2,100,000 today. In the same period, the squatter population has grown from an unrecorded and relatively insignificant number in 1940 to a conservative current estimate of twenty-five percent. As in other urbanizing countries, the situation in provincial cities is even more alarming. In Arequipa, the second largest city of Peru with a population of approximately 200,000, fifty percent are reported to be living in the *urbanizaciones populares,* clandestine lower-middle and working-class subdivisions, almost entirely on marginal desert land belonging to the State. In 1960, on the basis of a fairly thorough analysis of a previous census and a sample survey, I estimated that only twenty-two to twenty-three percent of the urban population at that time was then resident in this kind of settlement.

With squatter settlement growth rates of twelve percent or more per annum in Mexico, Turkey, and the Philippines as well as in Peru and many other countries — double that of city growth as a whole — it is hardly exaggerating to say that city development is out of control. During the past two decades the major towns and cities of Peru have trebled in area and population; they now represent approximately thirty percent of the country's total population. Two-thirds of this recent growth, (about ten percent of the population or 1,000,000 people) is composed of squatters who have done more city building in terms of settlement than has been achieved during the previous 400 years.[3] So, in spite of the increasing realization of the necessity for urban planning, and the great need for an orderly infrastructure of economic development, city growth in the urbanizing two-thirds of the world is becoming increasingly chaotic.

> This absence of a central concern for the city's role is related to the deepening crisis that cities in all parts of the world are facing: massive unemployment, squatting and squalor in the developing preindustrial countries; . . . Consequently, the city is a poor habitat, not only for man but for industry and trade. Chaotic in form and destructive socially, the mushrooming urban disarray creates a new impediment to economic growth (Weissman, 1966).

The hypothesis on which the arguments in this article are based is implicit in the claim that the standards required by the authorities (and practiced by institutional and capitalist enterprise) conflict with the demands of the mass of urban settlers. The loss of administrative control over urban settlement and the frequently chaotic conglomerations of inadequate structures which make up the greater part of contemporary city growth in the modernizing countries are a product of the gap between the values and norms required by the governing institutions and those imposed on the people by the circumstances in which they live. The greater the gap between the nature of the officially recognized supply of housing and the nature of the popular demand, and the greater the demand in relation to the police power exercised by the authorities, the greater is the proportion of uncontrolled settlement (Turner, 1966a, IV).

CASE STUDY OF A BARRIADA

The Invasion

The best and perhaps the only way to illustrate these principles is to describe the situations which have lead to their formulation. The following description is a composite case study very largely based on one particular squatter settlement on the outskirts of Lima. Pampa de Cuevas is perhaps the nearest thing to a model *barriada* of its type. Established fairly recently (in 1960), in a more than usually favorable, but otherwise typical location, the settlement has a population of approximately 12,000. Cuevas is one of the type of *barriadas* populated by families moving out of the city slums, where the adults have lived about ten years before moving. Many of them are of recent previous provincial origin, but are not in the lowest income groups and are not without some urban experience (Turner, 1965). This contrasts with another basic *barriada* type, formed by people with very low incomes and living standards, whether the urban-born poor or rural immigrants, and the commercially established tenement slums which have much higher densities and are almost always located near employment centers. Settlements of these latter types serve as "bridgeheads" or urban toe-holds, enabling the very poor to live cheaply and to obtain work more easily by living within walking distance of principal markets and employment areas. Cuevas, which is not within walking distance of either, is an unsatisfactory location for down-and-outs or for ambitious but still very poor migrants. The great majority of its inhabitants are young families with more or less steady incomes. They are poor but represent the average rather than the below average wage-earning sectors and, as the rate of physical improvement of the average dwelling indicates, they have maintained an appreciable rate of upward mobility (Mangin, 1963). I am not, therefore, about to describe a version of the classic shantytown: ". . . the rudest kind of slum, clustering like a dirty beehive around the edges of any principal city in Latin America" where "living almost like animals, the *tugurio's* residents are overwhelmed by animality. Religion, social control, education, domestic life are warped and disfigured" (Schulman, 1966). Cuevas, along with at least two thirds of the *barriadas* of Peru, the majority of the *colonias proletarias* of Mexico City, or of the *Gecekondu* of Ankara, can be more appropriately described as self-improving suburbs than as "slums" (Frieden, 1965; Sewell, 1964).

The history of a settlement must begin with a description of the original settlers and their motives for settlement. As is now clear, the necessity of squatting may occur in quite different circumstances in the same city or at different stages in the life of the same family: The recently arrived migrant may be forced to squat if unable to find or afford other accommodation or, on the other hand, the wage-earning family that cannot afford tolerable accommodation or that desperately needs the security of home-ownership may also be forced to squat if there is no alternative (Turner, 1966b). The great majority of Cuevas settlers were motivated by the desire to escape the tyranny and insecurity of paying high rents for miserably poor conditions. For the average family of five or six with an average monthly income of about $90 (United States dollars) there are only two legal alternatives: to wait until the family's income has risen sufficiently (or until it has accumulated sufficient savings) to buy and build in the lowest-priced subdivisions, or to wait for the chance to get a subsidized government project house. Many families, for reasons explained below, reject the latter alternative, even when they are among the small minority to whom the opportunity is presented. The great majority prefer the illegal alternative of squatting if the prospects of obtaining de facto possession are good, even if very considerable sacrifices must be made to get a plot and to build.

The original Cuevas settlers, about 500 adults from different parts of Lima, formed the "Asociación de Padres de Familia Pro Vivienda," a community association for housing, in December, 1959. Just how this particular group was formed I do not yet know,[4] but the case of El Ermitaño, adjacent to Cuevas, is typical. The Ermitaño association was organized by a self-appointed committee in 1962 which claimed to be the successors of an earlier association that in 1945 had applied to the ministry of Public Works for permission to develop the land the new association intended to invade. Having received no answer, the organizing committee maintained a certain claim to the land, even though it was somewhat tenuous and of a moral rather than legal character. It was enough, however, to guarantee the support of the "Frente Unico de las Barriadas del Peru," — a confederation of *barriada* associations which commanded some political support and lobbying influence. With moral reinforcement and the probability of some political support, a group with access to a good site and with enough members to provide sufficient funds (to defray expenses and to compensate the organizers for their efforts) will be ready and prepared to invade if no other course is open to them.

The Cuevas invasion took place the night of November 17, 1960. The police forced them off the land and the invaders, several hundred men, women, and children, camped along a nearby railway embankment while their leaders negotiated with the authorities. The government was particularly anxious to avoid further invasion at that time because it was about to promulgate a law designed to prevent further invasions and squatting by providing low-cost building land.[5] The owner of the adjacent land, a wealthy man with political influence, was also strongly opposed to the invasion which he saw as a threat to his property. Future events justified his fears. The invaders were allowed, however, as a "temporary measure" to set up an encampment on a part of the land on Christmas Eve, five weeks later.

Either unknown to the authorities, or disregarded by them, the association contracted five topographers (elsewhere reported to have been students of civil engineering) to set out the blocks and individual plots. The plots were to have been 10 by 20 meters (about 2000 square feet), but the majority were in fact only 8 by 16.5 meters. The association paid about $1,000 for the work, which took two months to complete. Ostensibly, the permission granted to the invaders to camp on the land was strictly temporary and was to allow time for the allocation of an alternative site. Over Christmas it was hardly humane — or even politic — to let so many apparently desperately poor families continue to live in the open.

The families themselves, or their leaders, had timed the operation well and had correctly calculated that, once on the land, they would have de facto possession. The invaders, therefore, were prepared to risk their funds for the layout plan and, as soon as it was completed each family transferred its temporary shack (made from woven cane mats wired to a light bamboo frame) to the plot allocated to it by the organizers.

During the first five weeks, the squatters had lived, literally, in the open. Although it was during the summer, when there is no precipitation in the Lima area, camping with no equipment to speak of was a considerable hardship. But given the hope of a building plot of acceptable size on level land reasonably near the city and adjacent to a public transport route, a large number of people were prepared to sit it out indefinitely, rather than return, defeated and demoralized, to the city slums and high rents from from which they had escaped. As soon as the encampment on the site was established, the association organized a school which provided primary education to adults as well as to children, and many set up shops for vermicelli, candles, inca-cola, and other essentials. At first everything, including water, had to be carried up a footpath, but once the families had moved to their own plots an access road was made through the cultivated land which separated the site from the main road in spite of the landowners' protests. Shortly after the invasion many certainly felt themselves to be far better situated than they had been in the slums. Even with such primitive beginnings, a major part of their housing needs were satisfied. In the first place, each family had a fair sized plot of land rent free and with little or no fear of eviction. In terms of space, sunlight, and unpolluted air their shacks were a vast improvement over the dark, unventilated, and crowded rooms on narrow, smelly, and noisy slum courts. There are hardships and expenses in Cuevas, such as having to buy water from doubtful sources at exorbitant rates (usually about 15 U.S. cents per gallon drum). The lack of electric light reduces the opportunity for social life and study and increases a sense of physical insecurity (although there seems to be far less violence in the *barriadas* than in the city itself). On the other hand, the absence of the extremely inadequate number of poorly maintained communal toilets with which the slum courts are equipped is little or no disadvantage when there is plenty of space for individual pit latrines. Transportation cost for the family as a whole is generally greater than before but the extra cost rarely surpasses the saving made on rent as long as there are primary schools and basic shopping facilities in or near the settlement itself. So, even for the minority of families whose cash expenditures are slightly greater than before (through having to buy water or spending more on fares) the net gain in improved conditions is generally appreciable and with regard to personal security it is invariably considerable.

TENURE AND COMMUNITY DEVELOPMENT

As the security provided by the possession of a homesite is the settlers' first concern, top priority is given to action that will consolidate tenure. If there's no way of obtaining title legally and at short notice, and if the precedents show that once settled land of low value is rarely reclaimed, then the surest way of ensuring permanent tenancy is to settle firmly on the land. The squatter associations therefore demand that their members build as soon as they take possession of their allocated plots, so all who can do so, even if it is only to place some foundations. A current anecdote in Lima tells how the government sent bulldozers to clear an invasion of cane matting shacks. The first flimsy shack approached, however, stopped the bulldozer dead in its tracks. It concealed a solidly built structure of reinforced concrete. Though probably no more than a fable, the moral is nonetheless clear.

Apart from building to consolidate tenure — and invest savings before there are further increases in the cost of building materials — there is, of course, the need for a permanent house. The possible sequences of operations and orders of priority between the components of the dwelling structure[6] will be largely determined by the climate and the economic situation or expectations of the settler. Where there is little or no rainfall, as in Lima, it may be more appropriate to enclose the plot with a perimeter wall than to build two or three rooms with permanent roofs. The perimeter wall provides privacy and an improved micro-climate in which the discomforts of a shack are greatly reduced; the family is no longer pestered by neighbors' dogs and children, they are more secure against pilfering, and have, in effect, a spacious living area, even if the rooms are temporary shacks.

During a discussion of priorities of services and structures, one of the leaders of the Cuevas *barriada* argued forcefully for first maintaining perimeter walls until public utilities were installed, then building a bathroom unit, and only after that, beginning the rest of the structure.[7] This man, the secretary of the *barriada* association, felt that it was important to invest first in the improvement and installation of community facilities, then in public utilities, and finally in individual structures. Most *barriada* settlers, however, would give the dwelling structure — the first few rooms anyway — a higher priority than the installation of public utilities. But judging from the results of a series of conversations held in Cuevas, most settlers evidently place as high or even a higher priority on the provision of community facilities or services such as schools, markets, meeting rooms, medical facilities, a parochial center, and a police post than they do on the completion of their own dwelling. These facilities and services, even more than public utilities (with the possible exception of electricity), are a greater asset than a finished house. Observations of what settlers do in fact agitate for and attempt to install, support the statement of the United Nations Ad Hoc Committee on Housing in its report of February 21, 1962: "From the family's perspective, . . . housing is not 'shelter' or 'household facilities' alone, but comprises a number of facilities, services and utilities which link the individual and his family to the community" (United Nations, 1962:1).

While the order in which community services and public utilities have been installed — or attempted — has been partly determined by economic, technical, or administrative practicality, there is a close correspondence between the actual program of operations and the "practical ideal" formulated by the community housing group mentioned above. The indispensible components were provided, albeit crudely, at the very start. Even before the settlers moved onto their own plots they had a water supply, public transportation (at the main road), an elementary school, retail facilities, and basic shelter (in the encampment). In 1962, about eighteen months after the invasion, a permanent primary school, a medical post, a police post, and a chapel had been built. (The latter guaranteed regular visits from priests of a particularly active and highly regarded foreign missionary order.) In the following year a secondary school was established and the area became a separate parish with resident clergy. In 1963 the association also contracted with a private entrepreneur for the installation of electricity. The system was installed and put into operation for a short time with generators powered by a second hand diesel ship's engine. Unfortunately there was a disagreement with the contractor who eventually withdrew his equipment at considerable loss to himself as well as to the inhabitants of Cuevas. Since then the only electricity available has been from small generators installed by individuals who supply current (at about $2.00 per 50 watt lamp per month) to their immediate neighbors. In 1964 the government installed a provisional water supply, but this had not yet been put into operation by the fall of 1965. During 1964 and 1965 the government built several additional schools and a private clinic. A land use survey made in June, 1965[8] revealed a total of 218 retail shops (mostly very modest businesses of more social than economic value) and 14 artisan workshops. Dressmakers', dentists', and electricians' signs, among others, can be seen today. A sample of the dwelling structures surveyed showed that permanent construction had been started on eighty percent of the plots and forty-two percent had walls completed to roof height. Only nine percent, however, had a finished first floor structure and only two percent had started second floor structures.

In 1965 Cuevas became the center of a new municipality incorporating two adjacent settlement areas. In November, 1966 municipal elections were held and, administratively, Cuevas became a fully incorporated part of the city.[9] Physically, however, much remains to be done. No public utilities are operating yet, only a few houses are structurally complete, no roads have been paved, and there is not a single tree because water is not yet piped in.

More serious is the fact that all along the perimeter, creeping up the surrounding hillsides, is a steadily expanding belt of new shacks, many of which are occupied by the poorest sector. This peripheral growth (which in fact started as soon as the area was occupied, probably by those who could not pay the dues or who were late-comers) now threatens the future status and development of the entire settlement. The resident priests estimated that the population of the *barriada* had increased from 9,000 to 12,000 between 1963 and 1965. This is partly accounted for by a normal and healthy increase in the density of the planned area where a proportion of plots remain unoccupied, but part is also due to the ring of "subsquatter settlement." Its existence could well frustrate efforts to bring the rest of the area up to modern standards — which should be only a matter of time — by reducing the status of the neighborhood and the value of the properties. Those with the greatest expectations and social mobility are therefore likely to leave, further downgrading the area and perhaps leaving it to degenerate into a slum before it can develop its potential. Thus, in spite of the remarkable progress that Cuevas (and many other similar areas) has made to date, its future is by no means assured. What happens now depends very much on the nature and the effectiveness of the aid it receives from the municipal and central government authorities.

Whether the settlement as a whole will down-grade the adjacent and as yet undeveloped urban land, or whether its presence will hold potential development in the area at a low level, also remains to be seen. Presumably, Cuevas' influence will depend on the nature of its development. If the community achieves the level it is at present capable of reaching — that of a working and lower middle class neighborhood — there is no reason why adjacent land values or development should be damaged. Both the public and private sectors, therefore, as well as the actual inhabitants, have a considerable vested interest in Cuevas' continued development.

POPULAR VERSUS OFFICIAL HOUSING NORMS

The most striking thing about this type of development is the spontaneous mobilization of human and material resources — spontaneous in the sense that it has taken place independently and even in spite of the public institutions. If governments could induce the same initiative, efforts, and sacrifices for their own housing and urban development policies, both living conditions and the rate of economic growth would be immensely improved.[10] Scarcely less striking is the contrast the spontaneous popular settlement process makes with the "normal" subdivision and construction procedures required by law and practiced by capitalist and state enterprise. If the latter procedures were preferred by squatters and would-be squatters the differences might be dismissed as being the inevitable consequence of the violation of law and the failure of the government to provide low-cost housing. But the more traditional popular procedures are not only a logical response to the economic and social circumstances of modernization, they are actually *preferred* by the great majority of the people concerned.

This fact is less surprising after one has examined the main differences between "popular" and "official" norms in the light of the human situations and experience involved. If we start by comparing the typical programs of operations, the advantages of the popular program are immediately clear: In a society that does not possess, or which cannot mobilize, the necessary material resources to build complete modern minimum standard units for all who need them, each family must wait its turn. Generally, the wait is very long, the best part if not the entire time that the applicants are parents of young children. The squatter's procedure of occupying his plot as soon as he obtains possession, living initially in any sort of shelter he can manage, allows the family to improve its living conditions and to become far more independent at a much earlier and a more active stage of life. Even if they have to pay for the land at commercial rates, the typical family will still jump at the chance to follow this procedure (as a recent clandestine sale of building land adjacent to Cuevas has shown).[11] The sequence of operations subsequent to occupation is also radically different. Official norms give priority to residential construction and the installation of public utilities. The popular procedure is to provide community facilities and services before either dwellings or utilities. Since security of tenure is more important than physical comfort (especially in this favorable climate) and since security of tenure is enhanced by a reduction in the cost of living and the presence of medical and police services, the advantage is clear.

Finally, the disadvantages of orthodox modern "instant" as opposed to initially primitive "progressive" development are considerable, both economically and, once again, from the social security point of view. If capitalization takes place at one fell swoop, it must be financed on the basis of long-term credit. Credit is very scarce in a developing economy and thus the cost of an instantly built, fully or semifinished housing scheme is very great. Even if the interest rates are heavily subsidized by the state (greatly reducing, of course, the number of units the state can finance) the cost of the most economic orthodox housing schemes still impose a long amortization period on the beneficiaries.[12]   A long-term mortgage can also greatly reduce the occupants' security of tenure. The official procedure, therefore, is doubly disadvantageous: it forces the great majority to live in rented slums for many of the years that the need to own a home is greatest, and once a home is obtained they are saddled with a long term debt which threatens the very security which they seek through ownership.

The outstanding physical advantage of "progressive development" over the "instant development" procedure — apart from an early escape from overcrowded and unhealthy slums — is that the families' living areas are generally much larger at an appreciably earlier stage of construction. The progressive developer often provides much more living space than in the average, low-cost instant development scheme. If given the choice, many of the readers of this article would prefer a living area of 700 or 800 square feet enclosed by cane mats lined with newspapers rather than a brick or concrete house half that size and fifteen times the cost. Besides offering more living space, the great majority of *barriada* dwellings have roofed areas of over 1,000 square feet per floor, and virtually all are designed to take a second floor. In one *barriada* begun some twelve years ago, a large proportion of the dwellings have second floors under construction or already habitable. From an analysis of six typical *barriada* dwellings it is evident that after approximately twenty years of construction without any outside financial assistance, a two-story house with a total floor area of over 2,000 square feet can be completed for the same outlay that a government sponsored instant dwelling of half the size or less would cost, even when the administrative overheads and credit financing are heavily subsidized.

It has been stressed that the investment programs naturally reflect both these differences and the advantage of reducing the need for credit to a minimum or of eliminating it altogether. The other vital economic advantage of progressive development is that it permits and stimulates the investment of nonmonetary resources — those that are in most abundant supply in a developing economy. The cause of the great difference in the financial costs of "instant" and "progressive" construction (the former costing at least 100 percent more than the latter) is that the owner-occupier-builder provides other resources in the form of initiative, skills, and time. The time, patience, and bargaining skills of most wage-earning families together with the myriad contacts through workmates, friends, and relatives often results in remarkably good value for precious money spent on materials and on hiring skilled labor. This is true in spite of the fact that substantial help from relatives or even neighbors seems to be quite rare as a spontaneous or traditional attribute of these newly forming communities.

An additional "product" of progressive development is its stimulation of social development through the cultivation and strengthening of the family and of the positive attitudes and relationships to society that the satisfied family acquires. These are qualities which elude quantification but which are, perhaps, the ultimate test of the validity and value of any activity. Anyone who doubts the reality or existence of such "products" has only to spend a little time among people who are working in these ways.

A further very serious problem often created by "instant" housing projects and one that is now receiving the anxious attention of many authorities,[13] is the social stratification and subsequent stagnation of the communities formed. An important difference between the groups formed by officially sponsored projects and squatter settlement communities is that of the criteria and procedures for participant selection. The financial liabilities and sociopolitical risks of projects that depend on the recovery of capital from people with low and uncertain incomes automatically imposes a demand by those responsible for the careful screening of the prospective "beneficiaries." The taxpayers' representatives are likely to require that accommodation be provided only for those who are either financially able to afford the costs involved, or politically acceptable by being the "deserving poor" who most need subsidies. The resultant social groups are stratified either way: if selected on the basis of economic capacity they are narrowly lower-middle-class or, if on the basis of need, they are narrowly lower-class.

In neither case will one get the mix necessary for social change and development. Squatter settlement selection is more orthodox in the commercial sense because no attempt is made to match precisely the consumer and the product.[14] Anyone who decides that he would do well by participating in an invasion is free to do so. A mid-wife, a dentist, or a retailer, for example, might well decide that their livelihood could be ensured by becoming a participant member of a squatter community. In this way the initial socioeconomic composition of the squatter community is far more likely to include the necessary elements for social and economic balance and development than a screened project community. Furthermore, as long as the squatters, as an auto-selected community, experience a reasonably continuous rate of progress, diversification will increase. In an adequately located progressive *barriada* where the basic land use pattern is sufficiently flexible (as the simple gridiron systems generally employed usually are) social diversification will be matched by a growth of industrial and commercial activity. The more there is going on and the more people there are with whom one can have contacts, the more opportunities the poor have of improving their status. The policy of limiting the allocation of housing units in specific projects to specific income groups — and of imposing specific housing types — naturally limits the social mix and inevitably increases the administrative costs both in the short and in the long run. The progressive development procedure virtually eliminates the necessity for direct subsidy, however, and therefore eliminates the motives for socioeconomic selection.

Contrary to the beliefs and arguments of many opponents of "progressive" development, the process provides for relatively high urban densities. It is frequently held that progressive development procedures, which demand one-family housing, is uneconomic because of the immense areas required and the consequent increase in the spread and costs of urban services. In the case of Lima, this argument collapses on close examination. In the first place, during the earlier phases of development, the demand and need for urban services are very limited. Initially, sewers and even water mains are unessential. The difference in time for public transportation, if only a matter of minutes, is negligible in cost terms. An efficient bus service requires very little capital and, in any case, is usually a commercial proposition. By the time sewers and water mains are essential the densities are great enough to justify them. The potential density of the average progressive development settlement, like Cuevas, is 160 persons per acre, in single family dwellings and in structures of no more than two floors. This is assuming that no structures are higher than two stories and that every purely residential property would house an average of one and a half families, a reasonable assumption considering that the majority of second floors are built for children's families or for rent.

If this development procedure is adopted by the planners, and its administration is given over to local authorities, there is no reason why a proportion of land should not be put in public ownership to ensure some flexibility, particularly the attainment of higher densities when circumstances justified them. In the earlier stages, for instance, a market could be a collection of stalls on an open plaza, later to be occupied by shops and apartments. Similarly, cheap one-story rental tenements, municipally owned and administered, could be later replaced by multistory apartments. Land values, in any case, are likely to rise as metropolitan expansion leaves the neighborhood relatively closer to the city core.

Normally the walk-up apartment solution imposes a relatively low density, but in fact there is very little difference between the residential densities of typical walk-up apartment projects and the potential and probable future density of Cuevas.[15] Exceptionally, as in the case of the 7-story walk up, one room apartment blocks of Hong Kong, very high densities can be achieved. Only very rarely, however, are such solutions likely to be socially and politically viable. The more orthodox and socio-economically practical "high-density" developments for families with very low incomes rule out the "progressive development" procedure. In relation to the incomes and amortization capacity of the beneficiaries, low-rise, relatively high density developments require excessively high initial capital outlays. That the financial economies achieved through a slight — or even appreciable — increase in residential density will be sufficient to compensate for the financial and social economies of the "progressive development" procedure is very doubtful. The spatial economy of initially high density residential development (for owner-occupiers) rests on the false assumption that the residences must be fully equipped to modern standards, whatever the economic situation and real needs of the inhabitants or, alternatively, on the so far unjustified fears of excessive land consumption by modern growth.

CONCLUSIONS

The argument for progressive development and against "instant" development based on modern minimum standards can best be summarized by considering the priorities between the basic functions of the dwelling environment in relation to the changing life-situations and consequently changing priorities between the physical components of the environment (Turner, 1966b). It has been argued that the order of priorities between the basic components for popular housing — in the wider sense — are the reverse of those required by official standards. The average lower income family seeking a home in an urban environment wants secure land tenure, community facilities, an adequate dwelling, and utilities in that order. The state offers the exact opposite: a modern (but minimum) house in the first place, some community facilities (generally at later stages), and eventually, title to the property after the mortgage has been paid off. This latter procedure, however, is generally preferred by the middle income groups, whose social and economic security depends far less on home possession than it does on occupation and social status.

Further, in a developing free-market economy, they also have access to insurance as well as to banking services and financial credit seldom available to the lower income sector. Since the socioeconomic security of the middle-income family depends more on the material status of the dwelling they occupy than on actual ownership of it, the "progressive development" concept is, understandably, anathema. The unconscious transference of middle-class values to the designs and plans for the lower classes is, undoubtedly, the main reason for the emotionally loaded opposition of most technicians and administrators to the idea of permitting — still less of encouraging — people to live in an only partially completed environment, and of their apparent blindness to its obvious potential.

The significance of the cultural change that takes place over time and in the same *barriada* location not only confirms this kind of dwelling environment as a vehicle for social and economic development, but also points to the connections between the different demands of various social levels. It is clear that the relative priorities and demands of the low-wage earner and that of the high-wage (or low-salary) earner must be different though not as different as the levels compared above. Preoccupation with material status is as evident in the *barriadas* as it is elsewhere. The typical home-building family, for example, may finish the facade and a "parlor," often to quite high standards and at considerable expense, before the rest of the dwelling is complete. As the family becomes more secure, so will their dependence on the proximity of community services diminish. The pattern of upper-lower or lower-middle income level priorities will be an intermediate link between the lower and the upper-middle priority patterns.[16]

If over-capitalization and the consequent strains on the inhabitants and the state are to be avoided, and if the maximum contribution from the inhabitants is to be obtained in order that the state can serve the greatest number, the interpretation put forward in this article points clearly to the progressive development principles practiced by squatters — and city builders from time immemorial — as against the principles governing housing and urban development policies based on the direct construction of minimum modern standard dwelling units. The modern minimum standard concept, which acts as a barrier to development by attempting to prohibit the intermediate stages, must give way to a concept which uses standards as guides toward the progressive achievement of minimum *goals*.

NOTES

1. The author wishes to acknowledge the support of the Harvard-M.I.T. Joint Center for Urban Studies and the Olivetti Fund for work in part reported in this study.

2. A report made by the author for the United Nations on the housing situation in Arequipa, Peru, with special reference to the squatter settlements, 1959–1960 (unpublished).

3.

	1940 Census	1961 Census	Estimated Growth Rate (per acre)
Cities of over 50,000 inhabitants	675,000	2,556,100	6% (own estimate)
Total population	6,208,000	10,365,000	3.2% (1961 census)

4. Further information will be provided from the field studies recently carried out under the auspices of the Joint Center for Urban Studies of M.I.T.

5. The "Ley de Remodelación, Saneamiento y Legalización de los barrios marginales" Lima, 1961. This law provided for the improvement of *barriadas* of the "progressive development" variety and for the relocation of those incapable of improvement. New low-cost subdivisions were to be provided in order to satisfy the continuing demand for building land.

6. The "components of the dwelling structure" which are subject to different sequences of operations in the construction process in the Lima *barriadas* are: a *cerco* or perimeter wall enclosing the plot; the walls of the first floor (or of the first rooms) with a provisional roof; a permanent (hollow clay tile reinforced concrete slab) roof structure; joinery and metalwork (doors, windows, and window grilles); installations (water supply, domestic drainage, electric light) and fittings; finishes (floor finishes, plastering, and painting); and second story (repeat of the relevant components).

7. The main source for the interpretations of the basic functions of housing, and the priorities between them, are the minutes of a series of meetings between architects (from the National Housing Agency), a U.S. Peace Corps volunteer, a priest resident in the locality (an Englishman), and an average of three *barriada* leaders. The two items discussed were: "In what location should the working-class family live, and why?" and "In the locations selected, what services, utilities, and buildings are required, in what order of priority, and why?"

8. From a survey carried out by Ralph Pattisson, student of architecture at the University of Newcastle, England, while resident in the *barriada* in 1965.

9. Though the legalization process (the administration of the "Ley de barrios marginales") is incomplete, the municipal incorporation of the principal *barriada* districts has proceeded and it is now likely that the newly created municipalities will be largely responsible for subsequent development and legalization.

10. "The unutilized talents of their people constitute the chief waste and future hope of the developing countries. Only a small fraction of these populations participate actively in national life today." United Nations document on *Self Help.* ST/SOA/53.

   "Squatter building is probably the main contributor to the building inventory of the developing nation. It is largely self-help or aided self-help construction. It is financed without government aid" (Charles Abrams, 1966).

11. In July 1965, a large tract of land was bought by an "Associación" which, within the space of one month, has sold every plot (reportedly 800) for $500 — 50 percent cash, the balance in 12 monthly payments — to low-income families with similar status to those that establish the *barriadas*. The plots measure 25 by 60 feet. No services or utilities were included in the agreement and no legally valid title could be given as the subdivision and sales are illegal.

12. Mortgage and credit terms for typical low-cost housing generally provide for a twenty-year amortization period and interest rates of between five and ten percent. Where the loans are made with foreign currencies such low rates (relative to the commercial bank rates generally between fifteen and twenty percent) imply a direct subsidy of about half the financing cost.

13. The "José María Caro" district of Santiago de Chile, with a total low-income population of over 100,000, is an illustrative case. This is discussed in J. C. Turner, *Uncontrolled Urban Settlement* (1966a).

14. The typical agency project is "sold" under circumstances that no free market producer or distributor would dream of imposing: both the buyer and the article are predetermined. Few, if any commercial manufacturers or distributors would care to risk investments on such narrow margins: if the producer wants to decide what to make then he must offer the product on the widest possible market. If he wants to sell to a given sector of the market, then he must produce what that sector demands. Official housing policies commonly attempt to define both and commonly encounter serious consumer problems.

15. Walk-up apartments (one room dwellings) have been built in large numbers in seven-story structures in Hong Kong and, at twelve square feet per person, have achieved very high densities. A typical four-story apartment block project in Peru (Tacna) has a planned density of 160 persons per acre — the potential (and probable future) density of Cuevas.

16. The very low income sector is not discussed in this article. In J. C. Turner, *A New View of the Housing Deficit* (1966b), arguments are put forward to justify the priorities shown on the chart: since the very poor are primarily concerned with feeding themselves and of getting employment, it is argued that they are even more dependent than the wage earners on community facilities (and proximity to sources of employment) but that they are consequently less concerned with stable residence having little or nothing to invest or gain by investment.

ADDENDUM

After this article went to press, my attention was drawn to the U.S. Department of Urban Development publication "The Unfinished but Habitable Home" by William M. Shenkel. This report surveys the existing unfinished house market in the USA — which "In recent years . . . has absorbed a significant share of the housing market" — from 30,000 to 100,000 units a year. The report concludes that the system is economic and should be supported and extended. In principle, it is similar to the procedures discussed in this article, although the savings achieved are proportionately much less — rarely exceeding twenty-five percent. "Unfinished," however, refers mainly to dwellings that lack only the finishes and fittings. On page 73, Shenkel writes: "Four room houses sold with open stud interiors with no interior walls would probably not conform to the minimum property standards. But it is most doubtful that houses unfinished to this point would be regarded as adequate loan security without some provision for early completion of the dwelling." Both the potential economy of "progressive development" and the institutional barriers to its achievement are thus confirmed.

In another very interesting report that has just come to my attention: *A Proposal to Demonstrate Financing and Construction Techniques for Developing Low-Income Housing in Rural California,* by Bellow, Lorenz, Powell and Goldes for the Rural Development Corporation of Los Angeles, the relevance of these principles is further confirmed. Quoting from the 1963 State *Report on Housing in California,* the authors point out that forty percent of farmworker families (of the survey sample) own or were purchasing their own homes in spite of average monthly incomes of only $222.50! Having demonstrated that the demand exists, the report goes on to specific proposals for financing, technical assistance, and designs — illustrating the rather advanced "roof house" and "core house" concepts derived from experience in the developing countries.

2 ·················

Similarities and Differences between Two Types of Peruvian Communities

WILLIAM MANGIN

This paper presents a discussion of social organization in two Peruvian communities.[1] *Vicos* is an agricultural, socially homogeneous community of Quechua speaking Indians located in Ancash in the northern Andean region. It was an hacienda at the time when most of these data were gathered, but this situation has been changed by a program of directed cultural change sponsored by Cornell University and the Peruvian government (Adams and Cumberland, 1960; Holmberg, 1955, 1958; Patch, 1957). It is an old community with a relatively stable population. Some family names have been traced back to 1624 (Vasquez, 1952). *General Benavides,* named for a national hero, is a squatter settlement of provincial migrants located on an arid hillside just outside of the capital city of Lima. It is urban, bilingual, occupationally varied and culturally and

"Similarities and Differences between Two Types of Peruvian Communities" by William Mangin is reprinted from *Sociologus,* XVI:1, 1965, by permission of the author and publisher.

racially heterogeneous (Mangin, 1960a). Cultural change in Peru tends to be from locally-oriented subcultures of the type found in *Vicos* to nationally-oriented subcultures, one type of which is represented in *Benavides.*

Several discussions of class, caste, race, and/or subculture in Peru have been published (Adams, 1953; Arguedas, 1952; Bourricaud, 1954; Hammel, 1961a,b; Mangin, 1955b; Nuñez del Prado, 1951; Rowe, 1947; Simmons, 1952, 1955; Tschopik, 1952; and others). By the criteria used in any of the schemes Vicos can be designated as a community of Indians. Few Indians from this type of community migrate directly to Lima. Individuals leaving Vicos-type communities generally go to small towns or cities of the same mountain valley or to a commercial farm on the coast. They, or more likely their children, may later migrate to Lima. The residents of Benavides are considerably more varied in background. Some have had the migration history just described. Some have come from Indian regions that are in transition to modern national Peruvian, a category referred to by some writers as Cholo. Some others are White, Mestizo or Negro migrants from farms and cities of the coast. These could be called lower class, national Peruvians.

The basic unit of social organization in each community is the nuclear family in a bilateral kinship system. As in most bilateral societies, there is considerable variety in household composition and kingroups. The two communities will be described separately. Vicos is described in the present tense but the period referred to, unless otherwise specified, is 1951–1953. I have returned to Vicos for a week in 1957, a week in 1958, a month in 1960 and for several visits in 1962, 1963 and 1964. Although the hacienda system has changed markedly as a result of the Cornell-Peru project, marriage, family, residence, property ownership and inheritance patterns have remained essentially the same. There is an increasingly large number of Army veterans who speak Spanish and who have formed a cohesive social group not based on kinship, one of the first such groups in Vicos.[2] Benavides is described as of 1957–1959. In short visits in 1960, 1961, 1962, 1963 and 1964, the only obvious changes were an increase in the number of houses, and that many householders had converted their houses from straw to brick construction.

In Vicos the nuclear family, (including a small minority of one-parent families, once nuclear) is found in 356 of 360 households, with household being defined as the group that cooks and eats together. Most "households" occupy a separate house but there is some variation in this, especially in compounds occupied by several families.[3] In seventy-two households there is one person who is not a member of the nuclear family of the head. In twenty-nine households there are two, in twelve there are three, in seven there are four, and there is one with six extra people, i.e.,

200 "extra" individuals in 360 households, the great majority being kinsmen of the household members.

The houses are dispersed over an area about eight miles square. Two hundred five houses are separated by at least one hundred yards (approximately) from the nearest neighbor. Few are much farther apart than one hundred yards. One hundred and seventeen are in compounds of two or more, usually housing a patrilocal extended family, thirty-six are separate from but close to other houses generally occupied by kinsmen.

One hundred fourteen of the nuclear families are patrilocal, 153 are mostly neolocal, although it is not always clear as to whether or not some of them may have been patrilocal at one time. In thirty-nine families the groom had come to live in the household of the father of the bride and to work his land. In these cases there was no male heir to the land and only the children of the women are eligible to inherit, that is, children of the groom by other women have no claim in the land he works and lives on. I have mistakenly referred to these cases elsewhere as matrilocal (Mangin, 1960b). In bilateral societies it is possible to have matrilocal residence, as among many lower class American, British Guianan and Jamaican Negroes (Frazier, 1939; Smith, 1956; Freilich, 1961) but the Vicosino cases represent a device for maintaining male inheritance in the absence of true corporate kin groups where a father has daughters but no sons.[4]

Beyond the nuclear family are three other effective social units. The first, the *casta,* is a formally recognized grouping of patrilineally related families ranging from simple patrilineal extended families to a few fairly strong, land-holding patri-lineages.[5]

There are eighty-four *castas* ranging in size from twenty-two of one nuclear family each to one containing twenty-three and one containing twenty-six nuclear families. A second grouping, the bilateral kindred, is quite important for some individuals. It is not a formally recognized unit and its functions vary with the size of a person's *casta,* the location of his house, the number of available relatives, and the personalities of husband and wife. More important for most than the kindred, and for many than the *casta,* is a third unnamed grouping which overlaps the first two and also may include some nonrelated neighbors, compadres, friends and in many cases a man's wife's sister's husband.[6] This third grouping, sometimes referred to by Vicosinos as "familia" is the group most frequently united for cooperative agriculture, housebuilding and fiestas.

Intergenerational bonds between parents and children tend to be strained and tense. Alternate-generational bonds between grandparents and grandchildren seem to be strong and emotionally close. Intragenerational bonds between siblings, especially brother-sister and sister-sister, are generally close and mutually satisfactory. Brothers occasionally quarrel over land inheritance but father-son conflicts are much more frequent than brother-brother.

Inheritance tends to be patrilineal in that sons usually inherit, although a wife often inherits the house and sometimes the land, and a daughter may inherit in preference to a man's brothers if no sons are in the picture. Land conflicts are a constant feature of Vicos life and the rules for settlement are highly flexible and subject to ad hoc pressures. Legally the hacienda owns all the land, and the people of Vicos are included in the rental contract along with the land, the rocks and the trees. A disinherited son, or a strong lad unwilling to wait for his father to die or give him a field, may acquire a field from the renter of the hacienda, either carved out of a less desirable hacienda field or taken from a nonproductive widow, to keep him as a laborer. The better lands of the hacienda were farmed by the renter, and are now farmed cooperatively for the benefit of the community. The bulk of the poorer lands are held in usufruct by the residents.

Vicos is overwhelmingly endogamous. The incest taboo is strongest within the nuclear family and it extends less strongly to patrilineal relatives and still less strongly to first cousins in general. There are several cases of first cousin marriage but they are not considered good form. When an engagement is formally recognized by the parents of both parties the bride comes to live with the groom in his family's house for about a year. The vast majority of the couples so united marry formally or continue living together as if married formally. There is, however, an option offered at the end of the first year and some individuals decide not to stay together because of incompatibility of the couple, conflict between the wife and the husband's family, no pregnancy, or some other less common reason. Women seldom are involved in more than two such relationships. Some men manage as many as five or six but the general community attitudes toward this practice, although somewhat ambivalent, are primarily negative. This marriage pattern is called *matrimonio de prueba,* or trial marriage, in Spanish. This is not a particularly good translation of the Quechua term *watanacuy.* The Vicosinos enter these relationships as more or less permanent ones which may be dissolved rather than as I'll-see-if-I-like-it affairs (Vasquez, 1952).

Compadrazgo is important at baptism and first haircutting for the compadres, that is the godparents and the parents of the child, and the same individuals are generally chosen for each. The godparents of a marriage establish an important relationship with the bride and groom. Community members are usually chosen, often grandparents for baptism, but some individuals choose Mestizos from neighboring towns, generally for commercial or political reasons.

The individual in Vicos is born into a two-generational family living in the same compound or close-by. He lives with his parents until his marriage, at which time he may establish his own residence or may stay with them. A woman goes to the house of her husband. In some neolocal cases the couple may go to live with one set of parents, usually the groom's, in the parents' old age, or in some cases a parent may come to live with them. In most families, as in Cumming and Schneider's and Bellin's bilateral samples from the U.S. (Bellin, 1960; Cumming and Schneider, 1961), at some time in the family cycle some extra person other than the father, mother and children, is present.

All Vicosinos are farmers, but some earn money as day laborers and a few are carpenters, plasterers, or masons. Some men are mule drivers. Many men are weavers and a few weave for pay. Many men are musicians and make part-time money playing at fiestas. In all, however, the division of labor is chiefly by sex, and work is concentrated in the community or in a Mestizo town about five miles away. Cooperative work is common, but only once or twice a year do the men work together as a community voluntarily. Work on the hacienda fields, now the fields of the community, is done in concert but with sanctions for failure to perform.

There are differences in wealth and status within the hacienda but Vicos, in comparison with the rest of the country, is a one class community (Vasquez, 1955).

In Benavides the nuclear family, including a minority of one-parent families once nuclear, is found in 528 out of 561 households. One hundred fifty-nine households have one or more "extra" persons, overwhelmingly kinsmen. Unlike Vicos there are seventeen individuals living alone.[7] The majority of the houses contain young adults and children. The tenant's council has some screening function in that new arrivals to the squatter-formed settlement are supposed to apply for a lot to the council, and most do. The council tends to reject single women or widows with children as applicants and they get practically no applications from single men or childless single women.

The houses are close together in blocks in the lower section of the barriada, and on paths on the steep hillsides. The most common unit is the isolated nuclear family, but there are some cases of children who have built close to parents, siblings building close to each other, and in-laws of various kinds living near one another. The barriada was founded by an organized invasion in 1954 so the basic residence pattern can be said to be neolocal. There are several cases of married sons and daughters living with parents and of unmarried daughters with children living with parents. Twenty-seven households consist of mother and children, twenty of mother, children, and others. Most of these forty-seven households, plus some of the others with a temporarily residing, easily replaceable male, are essentially matrilineal extended families, a group frequently encountered among migrants to Lima.

The social groupings available beyond the nuclear family are many, and participation varies from not at all to considerable. Most of the heads of families belong to the barriada tenants' association, but few participate actively in it. Extended family groupings are very common and there is considerable visiting back and forth between the barriada and Lima, and some between the barriada and the original home. Regional clubs and informal groupings of friends who have migrated from the same region form an important basis of association, mutual aid, acculturation, etc. (Mangin, 1959), and there are other clubs available to join. For some men friendships formed at work are important. For others unions or political parties provide opportunities for association. The possibilities of non-kinship groupings being important is infinitely greater than in Vicos, but kinship groupings are still the main bases of association for the migrants. *Casta* has no counterpart in Benavides but there is at least one matrifocal "family" with twelve households in the community and three in other parts of Lima.

As in Vicos, parents are frequently ambivalent about their children and there is considerable tension in the parent-child relationship. Parents say, in response to a questionnaire as well as in conversations, that one should sacrifice all for one's children (and to a certain extent they do), but at the same time they restrict their children in many ways and seem to resent the apparent increase in opportunity for their children over themselves. Like the Vicosinos they think that their children should take care of them during their old age but they don't expect that they will. Sibling relationships are strong, and the cooperative relationship noted in the mountains between a man and his wife's sister's husband is also notable in Benavides.

Inheritance, by law and by consensus, should be bilateral, but as of 1959 only two individuals had acquired their lots through inheritance. Most of the property holders either invaded the lot they occupy or acquired it by applying to the tenant's council. Legally the tenant's council has no right to distribute the land and none of the residents has a legal title. The land is owned by the state and the disposition of the considerable portion of public land invaded in this way will be one of the most explosive political issues in Peru for some time to come. Some land has been sold, some houses have been sold or rented, and land conflicts are common, involving lawyers, police, various government bureaus and church organizations. It is probably fairly safe to assume that no prospective government in Peru will feel strong enough to evict the 200,000-plus squatters around Lima, or even the 561 households of Benavides, and there is always the possibility that the 1960 Law of

Barriadas, which provides for the urbanization of the areas guaranteeing the property rights of the residents, will be implemented. As many Peruvians would point out, however, there is also always the possibility that it will not be implemented. Many laws exist in Peru, as well as in most countries, that would be considered models of progressive legislation if they were enforced.

Most all of the couples were married or living together before coming to Benavides. I noted no feeling against marrying someone from the barriada in asking questions about attitudes toward the place. Out of the 561 censused households with a resident mated couple, 338 reported themselves as "married", 131 as *conviviente*, or consensual union, two had one of each, the rest did not reply. There is probably a tendency to over-report marriage, but there is no reason to suppose that a formal marriage makes a union any more stable. An analysis of records of a sample of 65 families indicates that about half of the individuals had had more than one mate. The fact that the couple has an investment in the ownership of a lot and a house probably holds some husbands who might otherwise desert in an urban slum rental. If the husband does desert, particularly if he is a common-law husband, the wife is a good remarriage possibility since she is the "owner" of a house and a lot.

The importance of *compadrazgo* varies with the individual. Most people choose compadres from kinsmen, others from the same provincial region, or higher status acquaintances in Lima. Some have chosen neighbors from the barriada, but it is not common.

It is somewhat difficult to predict the family cycle for the barriada migrants. Most of them were born into Cholo or Mestizo families in rural areas and small towns of the provinces. Some migrated with their parents to coastal farms or directly to Lima. Some migrated alone or with age peers during young adulthood. Most met their present mates in Lima, although many are from the same region as their mate. There is a strong tendency for relatives from the province to join the barriada families, particularly aged parents who abandon land in the provinces and can act as caretakers of grandchildren and property while both husband and wife work.[8]

There is considerable occupational variety in Benavides. Some individuals own property in the provinces but not one lives solely from rent. The highest-paid men in the community seem to be an owner of a small store and a white collar bank employee who is also a minor official of the militant bank worker's union. Both men have run for political office in the barriada. The men and some of the women work in many different parts of the city, although each tends to know only the part of the city traversed on regular routes such as to work or to a relative's house. Some women who have lived in Benavides for years, overlooking the city, have only been to the modern center once or twice. Unlike Vicos, where the father is apt to be working around home most of the time, Benavides is mainly a community of women, children and old people on weekdays. The jobs of the men range from the above-mentioned to policemen, soldiers, construction workers, factory workers, garbage men, salesmen, servants, waiters, drivers, and others. Benavides provides many more models for its children than Vicos, as does the general exposure to the urban milieu.

The Cholo segment of the population of Benavides compared to the stable Indian population of Vicos reflects one of the basic differences between subcultures in Peru. They represent essentially the same family pattern and cultural tradition, with a generation's lag and a rural-urban move between them. That is, some of the young children of Vicosinos who move out will have as much in common with the barriada migrants as with their own parents, even as most of the barriada children will have as much in common with urban participants in the national culture as with their own parents.

Anticipatory socialization to new patterns is more advanced in Benavides than in Vicos because of a greater desire for change for their children on the part of the barriada parents, and a greater knowledge of the national culture because of their knowledge of Spanish and their proximity to the chief disseminating center, Lima.

Benavides residents are increasingly aware of Peru as a country and are increasingly nationalistic and political, but not as much so as native urban residents or many of the young migrants to Lima, who become university students, union members, or government workers, and who reside in the center of the city. National political parties are active in barriada tenant's council elections.

In the barriada, parents are often naively optimistic about upward mobility for their children through education, and they indicate frequently that they think they are better off than they were in the provinces and that their children will be better off than they are. They also see their children leading different lives as professionals, teachers, white collar workers, etc., with more comforts and a more secure class position.

They see the solution to their problems in outside help. Out of fifty-six responses to a question about how the problems of the barriada should be solved, forty-six said that some agency, usually "the government", should help. Out of the remaining ten answering, only three suggested that the residents should help themselves.

For the Vicosino adult local interests are primary and aspirations are toward success in what Ralph Beals has termed an "internal prestige system" centering around local politico-religious office (Beals, 1953). There is a general lack of information about the outside world. Some individuals have been to Lima, some men have been in the army (not an especially broadening experience), many have been to coastal haciendas and more have been to Huaraz, the provincial capital, but at the same time few speak Spanish and few are particularly concerned with Peru as a nation. As yet, in spite of the ten years of the Cornell-Peru project, a large number of the Vicosinos, particularly the women, are ignorant of the national culture and only a handful of school-children and fewer than one hundred adults speak Spanish. The number of individuals who read Spanish in Vicos, in contrast to the high literacy rate of barriada residents,[9] cannot be more than twenty or twenty-five. In 1951 few recognized the national anthem, now the army veterans recognize it and the school children sing it rather badly. Many in 1951 did not recognize the name of Odria, then dictator of the country. President Prado is not well known in Vicos either, but many more people know that there is a president and a government.

The Indians are generally dissatisfied with their economic condition, but many of them are more or less satisfied with the hacienda system. They see the solution to their problems, much like the barriada people, in the coming of a "good *patrón.*"[10] They see their children having basically the same sort of life they themselves have but, hopefully, with more economic advantages. This hope has been stimulated by the Cornell-Peru Project's action to terminate the hacienda system and the up to now unsuccessful attempt to have the government expropriate the hacienda and sell it to the residents. One of the Indian leaders, an army veteran, speaking to a meeting of Indian delegates and U.S. and Peruvian government functionaries in Vicos, warned that if things did not change, Peru would go like China *nacionalista.* From a later conversation it was apparent that he meant China *comunista* and was thinking specifically of the fate of many Chinese landowners. This attitude is by no means typical, for, as I have said, most Vicosinos are still hazy about what Peru is, but such a speech would have been inconceivable in Vicos in 1952.

Despite the seeking for someone to depend on in problem-solving in both communities, the Cholos of Benavides and the Indians of Vicos show considerable initiative compared to other segments of the population. They both hold local elections which have seldom been held in the cities and towns of Peru, and national elections tend to be rare. The people of Benavides invaded state land in the face of police action and economic loss to establish their settlement. The Vicosinos have been actively trying to get hold of their property and had made two attempts to buy or rent it before the advent of the Cornell-Peru Project. They also share a tremendous common advantage over the traditional Mestizo and Criollo segments of Peruvian culture in that each community sets a high value on hard physical labor.[11] The lack of influence from Spanish colonial culture and the possession of the traits of hard work, thrift, sacrifice to educate children, and desire to own property will probably be of considerable assistance to both groups in the present rapidly changing Peruvian society.

Vicos and Benavides are not the only types of communities in Peru and one is not the polar opposite of the other. I am not suggesting that they illustrate the folk-urban continuum in any ideal sense. They are, however, two important types of social organization in Peru, both changing in different ways.

NOTES

1. This article is an expanded and revised version of a paper presented at the 1960 meetings of the American Anthropological Association. The field work in Vicos was done in 1951–53 and was supported by the SSRC and the Cornell-Peru Project. The field work in Benavides (a pseudonym) was done in 1957–59 and was supported by a grant from National Institute of Mental Health, U.S. Public Health Service.

2. For a discussion of some of the changes see Holmberg, 1960. For a discussion of kinship and other groupings in Vicos see Mangin, 1960b.

3. The census upon which these figures are based was taken by Mario Vasquez in 1952 and supplemented by Norman Pava and myself.

4. Murdock (1949) refers to this as ambil-anak marriage.

5. Zuidema (1964) sees Andean kinship as the product of a former bilineal system. My own observations in many Andean communities lead me to accept this view, although the bilineal answer did not occur to me. I have noted the presence of patrilineal and matrilineal institutions in Vicos (Mangin, 1960b) and Mario Vasquez (personal conversation) thinks the predominance of the patrilineal in the *castas* (lineages) is due to contact with the Spanish conquerors who dealt with males and recognized the land tenure system.

6. Stein (1961) has noted similar groupings in Hualcan.

7. The census upon which these figures are based was taken by the author Alberto Cheng with the assistance of students of ethnology from the University of San Marcos and students from the School of Social Work in Lima.

8. Cf. Hammel, 1961b for a similar situation in a city of the southern coast of Peru.

9. The statement about literacy in barriadas is based on the census of Benavides mentioned above and on unpublished census material collected by Dr. Jose Matos Mar of the University of San Marcos.

10. For a different view, see Fried, 1960.

11. For a perceptive comment on attitudes toward work among White and Mestizo Peruvians see Storm, 1948. For a dramatic example of the results of Cholo and Indian work patterns in a modern setting see Crooke and Doglio, 1960. See also Rotondo, 1959.

3 ....

Behind the Back of the City: "Provincial" Life in Lima, Peru

PAUL L. DOUGHTY[1]

This paper will examine the social life and character of highland migrant groups in Lima. It is my contention that the migrant regional associations serve a variety of important functions for the individual and the nation by helping to maintain key social institutions and relationships. These tend to slow down the stressful pace of social and cultural changes which often make demands on the individual new to the city. Through the use of the regionalist principle of allegiance to the homeland (*terruño*) migrants are led to contribute significantly to the rural modernization efforts. Because many migrants tend to enter the tertiary sector of the urban economy (working as vendors, domestic servants, and in various "services"), which is not especially productive in developmental terms vis-à-vis the provincial areas of the country, this is particularly important. Finally, the regional associations, despite their atomistic tendencies, contribute substantially towards the social and political integration of a nation which is fragmented not only by geographical barriers but by poor communications and deep social and cultural divisions as well.

Probably the most important social process in Peru at the present time is that of internal migration and the corresponding growth of the cities. The process places great stress on the traditional sociopolitical structure of the country by producing new social conditions, redistributing the human resources of the nation, creating enormous urban problems. That the difficulties of adjusting to the urban environment are felt by rural peoples almost everywhere is well known (Riis, 1957; Handlin, 1959). Indeed, it is usual to think of the impact of urbanization on the lower classes in terms of depersonalization, anomie, social and intergenerational conflict, and so on. If one reviews the growing literature on the "culture of poverty" in Lewis's terms, he might be led to see the people in the light of the "poverty of their culture" (Lewis, 1966a:lii). Lewis notes that:

> When we look at the culture of poverty on the local community level we find poor housing conditions, crowding, gregariousness, but above all a minimum of organization beyond the level of the nuclear and extended family. Occasionally there are informal, temporary groupings or voluntary associations within the slums (Lewis, 1966a:xlvi).

The people described in this literature have disordered, untidy lives, almost totally devoid of community and associational ties. Instead, their social relations are characterized by a spontaneity and capriciousness that places these people at the margin of society. This leads them to participate in that society only in limited and highly selective ways.

The process of adjusting to urban life can be seen as the constant struggle of people to maintain the integrity of family and personal life in a strange new setting. If this is difficult for the better educated and wealthier migrants, it becomes, in the case of the poor, uneducated, and ethnically differentiated *serranos* (highlanders) in Lima, a task akin to the labors of Hercules. Something of the nature of this stress is conveyed in the following lyrics of a popular *huayno* (native Andean music) heard in Lima. In it the singer chastises a female migrant for abandoning her highland cultural traditions and for "putting on airs." The singer, on the other hand, expresses pride in his origins. Thus this song brings into focus the cultural conflict involved in urban adjustment.

La Gringa

When you came from your homeland, you came as a country girl
Now that you are in Lima, you comb your hair in a mod way
You even say, wait "please," I'm going to dance the "twist"
Give me, oh give me Lola
Give me, oh give me your attention

Don't be pretentious, be less proud
Not because you are white do you color your hair
You came from your homeland being a real highland girl
Between your hair and my hair, there is no difference
You say that you are French, aren't you ashamed?
I'm an Indian boy but I have a white soul
I don't speak badly of anyone, my word is frank
I always speak of my homeland with much pride
With my woolen poncho I go where I please
If it deals with a fiesta, I am present there
If it deals with a fight, I leave
(Chorus)
I'm a highland boy, I'm a highland boy, I dance my little huayno
I'm a little cholo, I'm a little cholo, that I don't deny.[2]

Does one attempt to assimilate as quickly as possible, changing one's appearance and life style, or does one cling to his native culture? In Lima highland migrants have always been received at least with a certain amount of disdain if they are not overtly "put down" or discriminated against by native urbanites. Twenty-five years ago it was commonplace to find highlanders rejecting their traditions outright. Today, however, with the tremendous wave of migration to the city, highland culture has become more respectable, and the pressure for rapid assimilation has declined to some degree. In consequence the situation facing the individual migrant in Peru is complex, and one must be startled *not* by the fact that there is apparent social chaos and anomie at times, but that so many individuals and families are indeed able to retain their integrative structures or to reorganize their lives in meaningful ways. One of the mechanisms by which this is accomplished is through associations whose basic criterion for membership is the peoples' common place of origin. These associations or clubs sponsor activities which permit social continuity not only during the stressful initial period of adjustment to life in the metropolis but for a lifetime. In Lima, one is impressed by the institutional resiliency of the highland migrant; his family, circle of friends, means of recreation, and indeed his community are in varying degrees reconstituted and maintained in the city.

At other times and places we have seen similar reactions of migrant peoples in foreign environments.[3] The growth of unions, guilds, fraternal orders, religious societies, and other voluntary associations in the United States during the last two centuries has been a response to this situation. The appearance of such organizations with their "totemic" names and symbols mark the intimacy of these brotherhoods in which like-minded individuals can place their loyalty and trust, find support, recognition, and psychological sustenance. The basis of membership in these organizations often rests on identification with a place of origin (often specific provinces), common language and customs, or, religion. Sometimes a common economic position is the integrating factor.

Such phenomena are by no means unique to the United States' experience. Claude Meillassoux' discussion of the various types of voluntary associations in Mali reveals the similar efforts of African migrants to maintain their social life in the modern city of Bamako (Meillassoux, 1968). The pattern is similar to that described by Janet Abu-Lughod, who notes the emergence of migrant "benevolent associations" in Cairo, Egypt where a government agency listed 110 village-related groupings (Abu-Lughod in Potter, 1967:389). In his extensive work in West Africa, Kenneth Little traced similar developments in the cities there where he noted that:

> Nor in view of the strangeness of his surroundings is it surprising that the migrant often prefers to remain as far as possible in the company of previous associates. The result is that instead of weakening tribal consciousness, life in the new urban environment tends in some respects to make it stronger (Little, 1965:24).

The voluntary associations based upon tribal affiliations which Little and Meillassoux describe and which Abu-Lughod found in Cairo have their counterpart in Lima. Among the differences to be noted are that the Peruvian associations are more numerous and instead of tribal groupings, in Peru we find migrants forming "regional associations" which unofficially represent specific places of origin. These seem to resemble their Cairo counterparts more directly than others.

The organized "provincial" life in Lima is both intensive and extensive, involving a majority of highland migrants to the city at one time or another in their lives. Despite this fact, however, one can say quite accurately that it is a life that is carried on "behind the back" of the city as its older, more cosmopolitan inhabitants are, for the most part, indifferent to it or unaware of it.

It is difficult to calculate the number of clubs based on regional identification that exist in Lima, not only because their headquarters and membership may be hard to locate, but also, paradoxically, because they are so numerous. Utilizing a variety of resources — newspapers and other publications, radio announcements of club activities, interviews, and friends — an archive was compiled containing the exact identification of 1,050 associations. This paper is based on a sample of these, drawn from the highland departments of Ancash, Ayacucho, Junín and Apurimac which respectively rank second, third, fourth, and ninth in the number of migrants they send to Lima.

The size of the places represented by the associations varies enormously. There are clubs whose members come from hamlets with as few as fifty persons, while others purport to represent two or three hundred thousand people (departmental clubs, especially). Nevertheless, there are few clubs whose members' place of origin is less than one hundred persons — approximately four percent of the sample.

The size of club memberships varies greatly. Some associations have as few as five members and others, over 1,000. The great majority of clubs representing hamlets or districts have between fifty and seventy members — average being sixty-four (based on data from 130 clubs). Associations representative of larger areas such as provinces and departments have much larger memberships — 332 members is the average for the fifteen clubs for which data were available. In view of this, I estimate that approximately fifty-two percent of the censused migrant population in Lima for the four departments mentioned is affiliated with a regional association.[4]

It should also be mentioned that Lima is not the only city where the regional club phenomenon is found in Peru. Even though only on a seasonal basis, virtually every center that attracts migrants such as coastal plantations and mining centers has them.

SOCIAL STRUCTURE AND REGIONAL ASSOCIATIONS

To a great degree the regional associations tend to reflect the social structure which prevails in the place of origin, not only with respect to the personal social status of the members but also with regard to the relative social prestige and cultural condition of the place itself in the region in which it is located. This is explained as follows. In the highlands generally, the traditional sociocultural divisions of the population have been based upon cultural attributes and ascribed statuses related to the classic Indian-Mestizo social dichotomy. The Spanish-speaking (but bi-lingual), literate residents of the villages, towns, and cities who control the local social, economic, and political life think of themselves as Mestizo. This population has strong feelings of superiority toward those considered to be Indians. The Indians are, by and large, Quechua (or Aymara) speakers, primarily illiterate residents of rural hamlets and villages (*anexos, estancias*, and so forth) whose participation in the national society and whose share of wealth, power, and prestige is, at best, limited. Between these polar groups is a third, usually referred to as Cholo, which represents the socially mobile highlander of Indian origins who is in the process of integrating himself into the mainstream of national society. The Cholo and Mestizo sectors of the highland population are those which constitute the vast majority of urban immigrants.

Consequently, the regional associations, based as they are on place of residence, tend to manifest the social and cultural character of the home settlement. Clubs representing Departmental, Provincial, and District level units or the capital cities and towns are controlled primarily by those of Mestizo, local upper class backgrounds. The memberships of clubs from *Comunidades Campesinas, estancias* or *haciendas* are more apt to reflect the Cholo sector of the population. Also influencing the social status and memberships of clubs is the presence of social conflict and factionalism in the home community, apart from the mentioned stratification criterion. The associations show the lines of factionalism existent in the home localities — one of the principal reasons for the proliferation and creation of new clubs.[5] For our purposes here we can say that the clubs fall into socially ranked categories which are dependent upon the sociopolitical status of the place or origin.

The clubs (and their members) from the most rural, remote, and otherwise undistinguished places occupy positions of lowest esteem in Lima. Their members are most likely to be semi- or unskilled persons, whereas the members of departmental clubs are almost exclusively professional people — executives and bureaucrats, businessmen and teachers.

The regional clubs create a relationship between the urban social stratification system and that of the rural areas — a relationship that otherwise might not be apparent. Ironically, this "integration" of stratification systems at the urban-national level has the effect of confirming the lower social esteem of highlanders (who so identify themselves) generally, and particularly those of the hamlets. Thus for some joining a regional club involves the sacrifice of one of the older "advantages" of migration and urban life — that is, anonymity, which permits one to free himself from previous social stigma so as to achieve social mobility.

Nevertheless, the club is the scene of "social climbing" activity, often couched in terms which are dictated by provincial custom and context. For example, a member may rise to prominence in his club or even be a founder of one. His reference group and those who give him desired social esteem are his provincial compatriots. Thus this prestige is not recognized outside club circles.

On the other hand, clubs can be "used" by those with larger ambitions who experiment socially and politically (in the general sense) in the associational context to gain contacts and future advantage. This may be done by belonging at the same time or consecutively, to several clubs such as those from one's village, district, province, and department.

University students, for example, are active in the associations, particularly at or below the provincial level. Indeed, aggressive students from the small towns and hamlets may tend to dominate club organizations. In many cases, if there are a large number of students from a particular area, they may form a parallel regional student association which interacts with other clubs, both student and nonstudent alike.

CLUB FACILITIES

The places where association activities take place reflect the socio-economic status of the clubs and their memberships and, to some degree, the aspirations of the members. The clubs of departmental level for the most part have succeeded in securing relatively commodious headquarters, even on prestigious Jirón de la Unión (street) in the center of Lima.

For the most part, however, the associations of the districts and hamlets occupy borrowed or rented rooms and buildings of modest, old, and rustic condition. The Centro Social y Cultural Tauca, which is one of four clubs representing the remote, rural district of Tauca in the province of Pallasca (Ancash), unlike the majority, has club facilities of its own. The people of Tauca are typical Andean small farmers whose homeland is undeveloped and isolated. Located in the "barrios altos" sector of Lima, the club building occupies a narrow lot among the two and three story concrete residences of the working-class and lower-middle-class residents. Behind a brick facade (emblazoned with the name of the club) is a one-story structure of adobe and the ubiquitous, durable *esteras* (mats woven of flattened bamboo which are the basic building material of the poor). Its rooms contain a kitchen and bar area, a game section with a pinball machine and billiard table, a plain concrete dance floor, and simple toilets. A spigot in the patio supplies the water. At the far end of the walled lot is a two room adobe house in which the caretaker and his family live. The people who utilize this club are almost exclusively from the district of Tauca or its provincial neighbors, and it is doubtful that anyone of important social or political stature frequents the premises.

For those clubs which lack such facilities the alternatives are few — they must either rent from someone else or meet in the homes of members willing to host the customarily lengthy sessions. The latter is probably the case for the majority. Many utilize the quarters of unions or similar organizations such as the Asemblea de Sociedades Unidas, an organization which was formed in 1905 by several unions and regional clubs to provide a cooperative meeting place. Similarly, the locale of a chauffeur's union also customarily provides space for simultaneous club meetings — four or five each evening. Rooms are rented here by the hour for meetings which are scheduled regularly throughout the week, beginning about eight in the evening and lasting through midnight, in the fashion that Mangin has superbly described (1959).

We should emphasize that migrants are not prone to establish regional association headquarters in the squatter settlements (*barriadas*) except in such now well-established areas as San Martín de Porras where there are a growing number of club buildings. One of the reasons is that club members rarely reside in just one section of the city, but instead they are usually scattered throughout greater Lima. Consequently, the most inexpensive and central location is chosen.

ASSOCIATION ACTIVITIES

The clubs sponsor a great number of activities in accord with their organizational capabilities and purposes. These activities are notable on two accounts: (1) their frequency and (2) their uniformity of character. They are rites of intensification, par excellence. The most common events sponsored by the clubs in Lima are dances, sports events, meetings for business, religious festivals, Carnival celebrations, banquets, and "fiestas costumbristas," such as the *cortamonte* (tree cutting), *jalapato* ("duck pull"), *pachamanca* (barbecue), and performances of special dance groups — scissor dancers, *Negritos, pallas,* and others.

The remainder of this discussion refers only to district and hamlet level clubs unless otherwise indicated.

Events such as those listed above take place almost without exception within a period of twenty-four hours that begins at 11 on Saturday evenings. Social dances, which are by far the most popular events sponsored (perhaps because both men and women may participate equally), usually are held Saturday evenings. Sports activities come on the following day, beginning around 8 or 9 in the morning and ending around 6, when it becomes dark. Such a schedule also prevails on official holidays (*días feriados*). The "fiesta costumbrista," as mentioned above, often accompanies either a dance or a sports event but occasionally on Sunday afternoon "folkloric" exhibitions are held under the title of *"gran matinee danzant."*

The Sunday Soccer Match

The places chosen for the activities just described vary a great deal in size, quality, and location in the city. For sports, the favorite Sunday pastime of associations representative of districts and hamlets is soccer, and the question of the appropriate soccer field is crucial. In the course of my study, I was impressed by the great lack of public recreational facilities in Lima. To be sure, there are some, but for the most part the sports-minded citizen of Lima must be a member of an exclusive and relatively expensive private club (such as El Bosque, Regattas, or Revolver) or be associated with or employed by one of the more prosperous manufacturing concerns in order to enjoy relatively modern sports facilities. Soccer, of course, is the most important sports activity, and it requires a large playing area. Thus, all vacant lots are pressed into service. In some cases such places are given names which reflect the origins of the players who customarily use them. Although Limeños — particularly of middle- and upper-class status — are usually unaware of them, such places are well known to lower-class provincial immigrants (the urban majority). In fact it can be said that if one has not tread the dust of the Great Sara Sara Sportive Field, Camuco, Limatambo Sportive Field, Asnapuquio, or La Legua, he does not know the Lima of today.

Some associations, especially those organized into sports leagues of twenty to thirty teams, have the funds with which to rent the developed recreational areas which are run by the municipal governments of the districts of Lima or by schools, parishes, or army posts. Most associations, however, prefer to take advantage of vacant lots in and around public parks or in growing middle-class housing developments where lots have been graded. There on any Sunday afternoon one will find dozens of soccer tournaments in progress simultaneously. Such arrangements, however, are temporary, for once the houses are constructed the teams must look elsewhere. Such vicissitudes lead to logistics problems, and, as one player of an association team expressed it, "la cuestión de la cancha es una vaina" (the question of the field is a pain).

The demand for sports fields is such that the better fields are booked every weekend and for all holidays and are paid for ten months to a year in advance. The club which organizes the event, pays for the field rental. That club then charges the participating teams an amount which corresponds to their relative prestige as a team, the value of the trophy to be awarded, and the relative "prestige value" of the time they are scheduled to play.

The manner in which tournaments are organized (either in leagues or among "independents") bears much similarity to that of the traditional Andean systems of mutual aid, the *minga* and *ayni*.[6] These mutual aid institutions are based upon certain rules or themes of reciprocity which can be succinctly summed up as follows: if I work for you, you are obligated to work for me in a similar manner in the future. (Although there is some regional variation in usage, we should distinguish between *minga* and *ayni*. The former involves the participation of individuals as members of groups as in families, gossipreds, and so forth, whereas the latter is often simply a reciprocal arrangement between individuals as individuals).

This urban use of rural social mechanisms casts an interesting light upon the assumption that systems of labor exchange tend to lose ground in the face of increased economic rationality. The implication is that social needs as well as economic ones are key variables in understanding the exchange systems. In the heterogeneous and mobile urban context the importance of social rituals in the form of exchange systems such as those described here cannot be underestimated. Such rituals help us understand the maintenance of viable social networks for urban residents. That highland migrants use a traditional social form for this purpose is scarcely surprising for it is the essence of the syncretistic process which underlies human adjustment to new social conditions. Thus the question of the rationality of such events as the "soccer match" is overshadowed by the sociological importance of the ritual enacted. "Affective" and expressive human interaction are the items of exchange: the elaborateness of the social form maximizes opportunity for it.

Thus, the clubs that accept participation in a sports festival may anticipate that their act will be reciprocated by their host at some future date. Failure to fulfill such obligations not only produces a rupture in interclub relations but may result in the ostracism of the recalcitrant organization. Thus, as it was picturesquely put, a principal obligation of the clubs to one another was to "ayudarse deportivamente entre los clubes" or "prestar su colaboración" ("sportingly help each other's clubs" and "lend their collaboration"). By the same token it is customary to return the lesser trophies (silver plated cups and statuettes of soccer players) to competition when it becomes the winning team's turn to organize and sponsor a tournament.

To gain some perspective of the extent of these activities which I have outlined briefly, let us consider the following data collected over a six month period in Lima in 1967. Thirty-four percent (128 clubs) of the active associations in the sample organized sports events during the period from January to June, 1967. 1,917 clubs participated in these events — a total of 21,087 players. This, of course, represents only a part of the participants because Sunday events are customarily "family" outings. While the young men play their enthusiastic and usually very rough game of soccer, women, children and older men wearing their Sunday best observe from the sidelines, converse with each other, consume quantities of *anticuchos* (broiled beef heart), potatoes and *aji* (hot pepper) or *choclos* (maize on the cob), and *picante de cuy* (fried guinea pig in hot sauce). Young women organize impromptu volleyball games (extremely popular for girls in Peru), organize cheers for their favorite teams, and circulate among the spectators pinning *escarapelos* on them for which they collect "voluntary donations" to support the club in its activities. (*Escarapelos* are small, square or triangular bits of paper, stamped with the club seal.) In the afternoon, the men may leave the "family circle" to drink beer with their friends on the premises. Beer is one of the most important ingredients of such events, and the sponsoring club is responsible for supplying it for sale. All items are sold by the sponsoring association for more than the going commercial price since the object is to raise funds.

Saturday Night and the Grand Social Dance

The most popular activity for district and hamlet level clubs is the "Grand Social Dance." Almost every active club sponsors dances at least two or three times per year, and many do it more often. Of the active clubs in the archive, forty-three percent sponsored dances during the eight month period examined. As noted, dances usually take place on Saturday evenings. For special occasions, however, they may be on Sunday afternoons or holidays. The work involved in organizing a dance is similar to that described earlier for sports events.

The activities sponsored by the clubs are advertised in several ways: by "passing the word," through radio announcements, and by "flyers" (*volantes*). The latter are distributed at the soccer matches and dances of other clubs many weeks ahead of time.

The radio plays an important role in the diffusion of club information, and of the more than sixty-eight stations in Lima over half broadcast programs aimed at the highland migrant population of Lima. Although most stations devote only two or three hours daily to such broadcasts (one early in the morning, one or two in the evening), since 1964 one station has played fourteen hours of "highland" or "provincial" programs daily.

The dances begin at 11 p.m., usually an hour after the announced time. Club members and their families tend to arrive together; women are always escorted or chaperoned. The young people, particularly the women, dress in the very latest styles. The older people, especially if they come from poor families, may wear highland dress, though typical "Indian" clothing is rarely seen. The orchestras are inevitably composed of "eight professors" (suggesting that they are good enough to "teach" music, though they are not actually teachers). Lacking a band, music is provided by *"un potente picup"* (a potent record player).

Social interaction is subject to general highland standards of behavior. It is formal and reserved in the early stages. Friends and relatives greet each other with *abrazos*; men center their activities around the bar whose floor is soon awash with discarded beer. Drinking is always a social ritual involving two or more persons. Because there is usually a shortage of glasses it is considered a courtesy to empty the residue from the glass in a convenient place (most often, the floor) before giving it to the person one has toasted. Before drinking one must always toast another, and that person must do the same in turn.[7] Because of this inevitable circular pattern the only manner of avoiding heavy drinking is to dance. Women drink relatively little, and in several dozen such events I attended, few were observed to be inebriated. The same cannot be said for the men.

During the season observed the most popular dance by far was the Colombian *cumbia,* and it was danced and played in preference to the traditional Peruvian coastal music, the *vals criollo,* which I heard played not more than a half dozen times. Highland music — *Huaynos, mulizas, huaylas,* and so forth — are featured as special numbers during many dances, although on some occasions none of the traditional music was heard. Where possible it appears that clubs try to hire two bands: one for playing the modish popular music and another to play the traditional airs of the Andes. A quarter of the 274 dances of record featured this arrangement. In actual performance, the highland dances are reluctantly received at first — or so it would seem — gaining in popularity only as the evening wears on. Indeed, some dances end with *"puros huaynos"* (all *huaynos*). Often in conjunction with the dance, there is an election and crowning of a "queen and her court," the installation of officers of the club, a speech or two, several announcements, the enactment of some ceremonial events in the home town such as the exhibition of special dances like the *"Negritos"* or *"Pallas"* or an enactment of the irrigation ditch cleaning. If it is in celebration of the patronal fiesta of the home town, the club may actually own a statue of the saint which, arranged on its litter in a new robe, "benevolently observes" the proceedings.

MOTIVES AND ALLEGIANCE

The motives for organizing such events are expressly of two orders: first, for the benefit of the club members and their families and, second, to help the place of origin. The "pretext" for sponsoring a fiesta is more for the benefit of the club itself than the hometown. Recreation per se, of course, is a prime motive, but it is rarely presented as such.

Lobbying in government offices and congress on behalf of the hometowns is an important activity which is mentioned often. The amount of energy expended in this activity is incalculable. Congressmen and bureaucrats are wined and dined, invited to club fiestas, presented with awards, confronted with petitions, and invited to make pilgrimages to the remote provincial homeland. Many of these activities are coordinated by committees comprised not only of emigrants but also of the officials from the hometown itself, who make periodic trips to Lima to check upon the advances made by the club or to inform the club members about the progress in the *terruño* on some specific problem. Prominent here, particularly with the registered *Comunidades Campesinas,* are attempts to settle land disputes with haciendas, litigation in which emigrants often play major roles. Indeed, migrants and their organizations have played important if not key roles in achieving legal status and recognition for many of these communities.[8] It is not surprising in light of this to discover that many clubs think of themselves as "defenders" of their homelands and often include this word in the name of the club.

The club's identification with the place of origin is universal and does not disappear, even after several decades of existence. Thus, identification with the homeland is strong not only during the period of the migrants' initial adjustment to urban life but continues for club members no matter what their socioeconomic status becomes. For them, the "crisis" of identity in theory is never really a question. One's culture, family, religion, recreation, and friends are tied, ultimately, to a kind of totemic homeland. Even after thirty or forty years' residence in Lima, a man will be identified as a *co-distritano* ("co-districtman") of the homeland by the others.

The kinds of donations made or sought by the associations for their homelands reveal considerable variety on the one hand and rather focused concerns on the other. Fifty percent of all contributions in our sample were for the schools and included such things as notebooks, pencils, movie projectors, sports equipment, musical instruments, cement, scholarships, the purchase of land, and teachers' salaries. Other gifts to the hometowns included ornamental lamp posts, typewriters, public clocks, church roofs, floral arrangements for the patronal fiesta, cash gifts to the poor, land for public buildings, and toys for children at Christmas. In no sense does the data confirm the cynical urbanite stereotype that the *serranos* waste most of their money on fiestas.

Although the average yearly contribution of one hundred eighty dollars may seem small, it is, nevertheless, substantial when one considers that municipal expenditures for rural districts in Peru *averaged* about two hundred dollars a year until 1964 when the national government began to provide direct subsidies to municipalities (Austin, 1964:42). In this perspective one can say that the contributions of the regional associations in many cases were not only large, but in many instances they were the only outside assistance a community could expect. For this reason we can justifiably state that the associations have indeed played a significant material and psychological role in highland development and change.

PEASANT MIGRATION

The recent literature concerning peasant migration to the urban centers reflects two themes which are at once contradictory. The first, and perhaps most common, is that which identifies stress, breakdown, anomie, frustration, poverty, misery, and other similar problems among the migrant populations and their offspring in the cities (Lewis, 1959 and 1966a; Patch, 1967). The second theme, which is less often heard, emphasizes the opposite characteristics: family continuity, maintenance of community and community organizations, cooperative effort, and the general ability of the peasant to adjust to urban life despite the expected difficulties based upon urban history elsewhere (Mangin, 1967b). Thus, Oscar Lewis commented in an earlier work:

> We find that peasants in Mexico adapt to city life with far greater ease than do American farm families. There is little evidence of disorganization and breakdown, of culture conflict, or of irreconcilable differences between generations; many of the trends and characteristics are in direct opposition to those that occur among urbanized farm families in the U.S. (Lewis in Heath and Adams, 1965:434).

Since convincing cases for both positions can be presented, one concludes that this conflict is but two sides of the same coin. Some people, indeed, suffer greatly from sociocultural disorganization, others manage to surmount the difficulties and establish meaningful institutions and communities of interaction. The strengths and weaknesses which people bring to the city from their village cultures may well prove to be a key component in the adjustment process. Thus, one way to clarify the problem would be to examine the nature of the peasant communities from which most migrants come.

The nature of the peasant community — if we can speak of a unitary phenomenon at all — is also the subject of some debate. In their attempts to characterize the peoples who live and work primarily in the agrarian sectors of nations or regions which lack significant industrialization either in the city or on the farm, social scientists have now developed several conceptual models which suggest the nature of the social process. Following Lopreato, on the one hand we have the "consensus" model in which intracommunity harmony is seen to reign and, on the other, there is the "coercion" model wherein the peasant community is seen as riven with ill-feeling, mistrust, and a general unwillingness of people to collaborate or make sacrifices for the common good (Lopreato, 1967:97–102). In such a setting we do not expect, nor should we look for, good deeds or helping hands. Indeed, whatever change or progress take place occurs at the expense of a neighbor (Foster, 1965b). Thus, the peasant might say:

> Against my enemies, I'll guard myself;
> against my friends may God guard me (Lopreato, 1967).

This tough view of life, shorn of the bucolic neighborliness, perhaps can be seen by some as representing a kind of anticipation of the uncertainties of urban life. Yet, one questions this "anticommunity" position by asking how it is possible that such people can find the common thread which leads them to organize so broadly and effectively in an urban context such as Lima or other cities. It seems that the image of the peasant community completely rent with mistrust, misgivings, and misanthropy is too extreme and does not square completely with the now widely documented phenomenon of voluntary associations of peasant migrants in cities. It is doubtful if there have ever been totally harmonious communities, peasant or otherwise, whose members always got along perfectly together. Indeed, even "utopian" experiments are notorious for their in-fighting. But because gossip, "back-stabbing," and intrigues occur in Andean villages — indeed one often hears the phrase, *"pueblo chico, infierno grande"* (small town, big hell) — does not mean that the society is necessarily disintegrating. It is simply one of many aspects of community life: people argue and disagree, and there are means of resolving the more abrasive effects of such conflicts, and there are institutions which unite people with varying degrees of success.

The experience of large numbers of Peruvian peasants in the cities highlights important features of Andean life: the strong identification of the people to their homeland and their *paisanos,* common ceremonial life and belief, common occupations, and the tradition of collaboration and mutual aid systems. The ability to organize is notable. The weight of the evidence gives no credence to Foster's amazing statement that:

> An objective appraisal of a peasant village, however fond the ethnologist may be of his people, will in all likelihood reveal basic strains and tensions in interpersonal relations that make it difficult to understand how the community continues to function (Foster, 1960/1:175–176).

On the other hand, the Peruvian peasantry is also under great stress at the present time and has suffered vastly from abuse from time immemorial (Rowe, 1957; Holmberg, 1965). Nevertheless, the community structure of villages has managed to weather the vicissitudes of deprivation, economic stagnation, social abuse, political tyranny, and heavy emigration. They still constitute entities with which people are willing to identify themselves and for which they make sacrifices. This situation does not support Lopreato's statement that "disperazione" conditions are "endemic to peasants and other people" who suffer from a "precarious economy . . . and . . . recent and radical social change" (1967).

Although the cooperative image of Peruvian villages has suffered in the past from overly romanticized interpretations, it has, nevertheless, a basis in fact. In apparent contrast to the Italian peasant then, the Andean peoples, despite extreme deprivation and hardships, have always relied heavily upon various kinds and levels of interpersonal, interfamily and intracommunity collaboration — the *ayni,* the *minka* and *rantín,* and the *faena* or *república* — to get things done. These involve trust if they are to operate, a sense of community, and a positive view of the rules of reciprocity. As such, they appear to be useful attributes in the urban setting of Lima where the immigrants from the provinces struggle to reconstitute a new and meaningful social life. The regional clubs not only constitute important communities of social interaction for a large proportion of the migrants, but they also represent actual extensions of the rural society and culture of which the migrants voluntarily continue to be a part.

NOTES

1. The author is Associate Professor of Anthropology and Director of Latin American Studies at Indiana University. This research was undertaken between September, 1966 and August, 1967 with a grant given by the International Affairs Center of Indiana University. The author wishes to thank those who made this possible, James R. Scobie and Lynne L. Merritt, in the name of the University.

   Interest in the highland migrant groups in Lima, Peru was developed during 1961 and renewed in 1963–1964 when I was engaged in other activities. In the latter period I served as the Secretary of Culture of the Associación Distrital Huaylina, a regional association representative of the first place in Peru in which I worked. Thus, I owe a great deal to those of Huaylas District Association. I am grateful to them for their help and friendship. More recently, many other persons and associations have given me their assistance and to them, my thanks go just as warmly. Mr. Bartolomé Dextre of Radio Agricultura in Lima aided me in gathering publicity materials from clubs, and I am much indebted to him. Mr. Luís Negrón A. was of great assistance throughout the study as were José Sabogal W. and his students from the National Agrarian University at La Molina who aided with the many interviews conducted. I am also indebted to William Mangin for his many useful comments on this topic over several years and to my colleagues Richard T. Antoun and Shepard Forman for their suggestions.

2. Paulino Rebaza Rodriguez (composer), "La Gringa" (sung by El Trovador Andino) Sono Radio Company, No. 12043B (Lima) (author's translation). *La gringa* as the title is used here in a satirical manner can be interpreted as the white girl or the foreigner. *Alma blanca* or white soul, means being of "pure heart," that is, good. The frequent use of the diminutive form (*ito*) in Peruvian, particularly highland Spanish dialect, may have the effect as is the case here, of emphasizing the speaker's racial and ethnic background and his modesty and humbleness as valued qualities vis-à-vis the girl's pretentious social climbing behavior. The association of the qualities white and foreign with high status is also commonplace.

3. Handlin (1959, pp. 84–88) records that in Massachusetts there were mutual aid societies representing towns in Italy. Greeks, Swedes, Germans, Russians, Lithuanians, Poles, Finns, Belgians, and French, and others also are reported to have had clubs.

4. Although this calculation is speculative it suggests the degree of possible involvement of migrants in such organizations, for which estimates have been totally lacking in the past. It should be mentioned also, that urban researchers in Lima, at least, have rarely directed their attention to this phenomenon, Mangin's early article representing an exception (see Mangin, 1959). Since much of the urban data is gathered by survey techniques and formal questionnaires, "provincial" subtleties such as this are usually missed or given little due. Also affecting reporting on this subject is the fact that urban research in places such as Lima had tended to focus upon the famous *barriadas* (squatter settlements) *per se* and not on the larger city with the result that phenomena *which are not necessarily specific to the barriadas* escape notice. The regional associations fall into this category. They are not, contrary to what some may think, limited to *barriadas* but rather have constituencies throughout greater Lima, in all sectors of the city. Thus, when one questions the barriada resident about his organizational affiliations *in the barriada,* the regional association may not be mentioned since it is not specifically identified as pertaining to the squatter settlement itself.

5. For further discussion of Peruvian highland social stratification see: William Mangin (1967a), Gabriel Escobar (1967), Allan R. Holmberg et al. (1965), Paul L. Doughty (1968).

6. A definitive summary of exchange labor in the Peruvian Andes is found in Abner Montalvo (1967).

7. For further description of highland Peruvian drinking customs see Paul L. Doughty (1967).

8. Traditionally, the registered *Comunidad Campesina* (formerly known as Indigenous Community (*Comunidad Indígena*) was an organization with communal lands which established its existence back to colonial times when the Spanish crown granted its title. Since then many communities lost their titles and lands to usurpers or through illegal sales. Communities able to prove their colonial existence, however, are again given communal title. Because this required much legal paperwork and action, migrant clubs have played important roles in these procedures because of their access to government offices and resources. There are now over 2000 recognized communities in Peru, mostly in the highlands.

Urbanization Case
History in Peru

WILLIAM MANGIN

There have been big cities in Peru for at least five hundred years and they have grown largely through migration from the hinterland. The tremendous population growth in Peru, together with the centralization of social, political, economic and cultural rewards in Lima, the capital city, has led to recent intensified migration from the provinces to Lima. It is safe to say that at least a million of Lima's two million people were born outside the city. The increase in the numbers of migrants to the city and the subsequent dramatic resettlement of many of them in 'unaided self-help' squatter settlements, 'barriadas' on the banks of the Rimac River and on hillsides surrounding the city, have drawn considerable attention locally and abroad, and for the first time have made many Peruvians aware of the situation. The city has probably grown in the past in much the same way, but the magnitude and the visibility of the recent influx make

"Urbanization Case History in Peru" by William Mangin is reprinted from *Architectural Design*, 8:366–370, August, 1963, by permission of the author and publisher.

it seem to be a new phenomenon. The migrants come from practically all regions and all social classes and ethnic groupings in the country.

The composite case-history presented overleaf illustrates some of the human problems encountered in migration to the city and locating and housing a family in a squatter settlement. The couple referred to as Blas and Carmen do exist and their story of moving to the barriada is true.

Some of the details of slum life and house construction in the barriada were drawn from the experiences of other migrants in Lima.

Fortunato Quispe, a Quechua-speaking Indian from an hacienda in the mountains of Peru, contracted himself out to a coastal sugar plantation for a year's work in order to earn some cash for a religious festival.

After a year on the coast he took a wife and settled down on the plantation leaving his mountain home for good. He and his wife had seven children. When their oldest, Blas, was eighteen, he found himself with no job, no possibility of schooling, and under pressure from his father to leave and get a job. The small two-room adobe company house was hardly big enough for the parents and the seven children and the sugar company was mechanizing the plantation even as its resident population expanded rapidly. Blas, who had spoken mainly Quechua as a child, was, at eighteen, fully at home in Spanish. He had visited Lima, the capital city, twice, was an avid radio and movie fan and considered the life of the plantation town dull.

Six months after his eighteenth birthday he and his friend, Antonio, took a truck to the Lima valley and took a bus from the edge of the valley to the city. Having been there before, they knew how to get to the house of an uncle of Antonio's near the wholesale market district. The uncle had heard via the grapevine that they might come. He was renting a three-room house on a crowded alley for his own family of seven, and his maid and her child slept in the small kitchen. He was only able to put them up for one night. They moved into a cheap hotel and pension near the market, and through Antonio's uncle were recruited for a provincial club, Sons of Paucartambo, the native mountain district of Antonio's and Blas's father. Much of their social activity is still with members of the club, and their first orientation to life in Lima was from club members.

Antonio went to work for his uncle, and Blas, who had been robbed of all his clothing from the hotel, took a job as a waiter and clean-up man in a modest boarding house catering to medical and engineering students. He worked six-and-a-half days a week in the pension, taking Thursday nights and Sunday afternoons off. During his first year he saved a little money. He impregnated a maid from a neighbouring house, Carmen, and agreed to marry her sometime. Meanwhile, they rented a two-room, one-storey adobe house in a large lot not far from the boarding house. The lot was packed solidly with similar houses and the walks between them were about five feet wide. They had filthy, constantly clogged common baths and water taps for every ten houses and the rent was high. They paid extra for electricity and for practically nonexistent city services.

Through a relative of one of the students Blas got a better job as a waiter in a rather expensive restaurant. In spite of the distance and the extra money spent for transportation it paid to take the job. With the arrival of a second child plus a boost in their rent, they found themselves short of money even though Blas's job was quite a good one for a person of his background.

Carmen, Blas's common law wife, had come to Lima at the age of fourteen from the southern highland province of Ayacucho. She had been sent by her mother and stepfather to work as a servant in the house of a Lima dentist, who was also a landowner in Ayacucho, and Carmen was to receive no pay. The dentist promised to 'educate' her but, in fact, she was not only not allowed to go to school but was rarely allowed outside the house. During her third year with the dentist's family her mother, who had left her stepfather in Ayacucho, rescued her from the dentist's house after a terrible row. Her mother then found a maid's job for Carmen where she was paid. Carmen worked in several private houses in the next few years and loaned a large part of her earnings to her mother. Blas was her first serious suitor. Previously she had had little experience with men and when Blas asked her to come and live with him after she became pregnant, she was surprised and pleased.

In her own crowded house with Blas and their son she was happier than she had been since her early childhood with her grandmother. Although her work was hard, it was nothing like the work she had done in the houses in Lima. They were poor but Blas had steady work and they ate better than she had in any of her previous homes. Her infrequent arguments with Blas were usually over money. He had once hit her when she had loaned some of the rent money to her mother, but, on the whole, she considered herself well-treated and relatively lucky in comparison with many of her neighbours.

She did not have too much to do with her neighbours, mostly longer-time residents of Lima than she, and she was afraid of the Negroes in the area, having been frightened as a child in the mountains by stories of Negro monsters who ate children. She found herself being drawn into arguments over petty complaints about children trespassing, dogs barking and messing the sidewalk, husband's relative success or failure, mountain Indian traits as opposed to coastal Mestizo traits, etc. She was mainly occupied with her son and her new baby daughter, and the constant arguing annoyed Blas more than it did Carmen. Blas had also been disturbed by the crowded conditions. There was no place for the children to play and the petty bickering over jurisdiction of the small sidewalk was a constant irritant. Thievery was rampant, and he had even lost some of his clothes since they had to hang the washing outside above the alley. In Lima's damp climate, it often takes several days to dry clothes even partially.

He had been thinking of moving and, although Carmen was settled into a more or less satisfactory routine, she was interested as well. They carried on for another year and another child without taking any action. When their landlord told them that he was planning to clear the lot and build a cinema within six months, they decided to move. A colleague of Blas's in the restaurant had spoken to him about a group to which he belonged. The members were organizing an invasion of state land to build houses and they wanted fifty families. The group had been meeting irregularly for about a year and when Blas was invited they had forty of the fifty they sought.

The waiter's group came mainly from the same central highland region and their spokesman and leader was a bank employee who was also a functionary of the bank employees' union. The other major faction was a group of career army enlisted men, including several members of a band that plays at state functions, who were stationed near the proposed invasion site. About half of the group had been recruited as Blas was. Blas himself recruited a neighbour and another family from the Sons of Paucartambo, to which he still belonged.

They met a few times with never more than fifteen men present. They were encouraged by the fact that the government seemed to be tolerating squatter invasions. Several earlier invasion attempts had been blocked by the police and in many barriadas people had been beaten, some shot, and a few killed. The recent attitude, in 1954, seemed tolerant, but under a dictatorship, or under any government, the law is apt to be administered whimsically, and their planned invasion was illegal. Another factor pointing to haste was the loss of seven of their families who had found housing some other way. Blas was one of those suggesting that they move fast because his eviction date was not far off.

Many barriada invasions had been arranged for the eve of a religious or national holiday. Their invasion site was near the area used once a year, in June, for a grand popular folk-music festival, so they decided to wait until that was over. The next holiday was the Independence Day vacation, July 28th, 29th, 30th; so they picked the night of the 27th. It would give them a holiday to provide a patriotic aura as well as three days off from work to consolidate their position. They thought of naming their settlement after the dictator's popular wife, but, after taking into account the vicissitudes of current politics, they decided to write to her about their pitiful plight, but to name the place after a former general-dictator, long dead, who freed the slaves.

A letter was drawn up for mailing to the dictator's wife and for presentation to the press. The letter stressed equally their respect for the government and their abandonment by the government. They had no hesitation about wringing the most out of the clichés concerning their status as humble, abandoned, lost, helpless, and disillusioned but always patriotic servants of the fatherland.

During the last month word was passed from the active meeting-goers, still never more than 20 or 25, to the others and preparations were made. Each family bought its own straw mats and poles for the house, and small groups made arrangements for trucks and taxis. Each household was asked to get a Peruvian flag or make one of paper. No two remember the details of the invasion the same way, but about thirty of the expected forty-five families did invade during the night. A newspaper photographer was notified by the invaders and he arrived about the time the houses were being finished. The members had discussed previously what lots they would take, and how the streets were to be laid out and there was very little squabbling during the first day. By early morning when the police arrived there were at least thirty one-room straw houses flying Peruvian flags and the principal streets were outlined with stones.

The police told them they would have to leave. A picture and story appeared in two papers and by the 30th of July about twenty or thirty more families had come, including some of the old members. A few men, with the help of friends and relatives and, in at least one case, paid workers, had built brick walls around their lots. These families and a few other early arrivals, most of whom are still in the barriada in 1963, proudly refer to themselves as the original invaders and tend to exaggerate the opposition they faced. They were told to leave several times but no one forced them. A resident, not one of the original invaders, was killed by the police in 1960 during an attempt to build a school on government land. The unfavourable publicity caused the government to desist and the residents cut a lot out of the hillside and built a school.

Blas and Carmen picked a lot about fifteen by thirty metres on the gradual slope of the hill on the principal street. The lot was somewhat larger than most subsequent lots, an advantage of being an original invader.

Blas and some friends quickly expanded the simple invasion one-room house to a three-room straw mat house, and they outlined the lot with stones. He worked hard on Sundays and some nights, sometimes alone, sometimes with friends from the barriada or from outside. He soon managed to get a brick wall six-and-a-half feet high round his property.

Many of the residents of barriadas hurry to erect the walls around their lots and then take anywhere from one year to five or ten to finish the house. After about a year of working on the lot and making his 'plan,' Blas decided to contract a 'specialist' to help him put up walls for four rooms. He paid for the materials brought by the 'specialist' and helped out on the job. When the walls were done he roofed the rooms with cane, bricked up the windows and put in cement floors. With his first pay cheque, after finishing paying for the walls, Blas made a down payment on a large, elaborate cedar door costing about $45. With the installation of the door and wooden windows they finally felt like homeowners. They even talked of getting formally married.

About two years later, after a particularly damp winter during which his children were frequently sick, he decided to hire another 'specialist' to help him put on a concrete roof. He hired a neighbour who had put on other roofs and he found out that the first 'specialist' had sold him faulty cement and had also erected the walls in such a way that it would be difficult to put on a roof. It took considerable money, time, and energy to rectify the mistakes and put on the roof, but when it was done it was a good job and strong enough to support a second floor some day. Meanwhile a straw mat room has been erected on the roof and Blas helps out with the houses of friends and neighbours against the day he will ask them to help with his second floor.

Skilled bricklayers and concreters abound in barriadas and the bulk of the construction in these places is cheaper than on contracted houses. Much of it is done through informal mutual aid arrangements and when contractors are hired they are generally very closely supervised. There is considerable cheating by contractors on materials and many of the specialists hired for roofing and electrical and plumbing installations are not competent. Transport of materials is often expensive, but the personal concern of the builder often results in lower prices at purchase. Some barriadas have electricity from the central power plant and public water; the one in this story does not. The front room shop combination they have in their house is not only fairly common in barriadas but throughout the provincial area of Peru.

Their principal room fronts on the street and doubles as a shop which Carmen and the oldest children tend. Blas is still a waiter, and they now have five children. The saving on rent and the income from the shop make them considerably more prosperous than before, but, in spite of their spectacular view of the bright lights of the centre of Lima some twenty minutes away, Carmen has never seen the Plaza San Martin and has passed through the central business district on the bus only a few times. She has never been inside the restaurant where Blas works. She gets along with most of her neighbours and has the company and assistance of a fifteen-year-old half-sister deposited with her by her mother.

Blas and Carmen have a television set which runs on electricity bought from a private motor owner, and they are helping to pay for it by charging their neighbours a small amount to watch. It also brings some business to the store.

Carmen and Blas bemoan the lack of sewage disposal, running water, and regular electricity in the barriada, and they complain about the dust from the unpaved streets.

They are also critical of the ramshackle auxiliary bus which serves them, but, on the whole, they are not dissatisfied with their situation. They own a house which is adequate, Blas has steady work, their oldest children are in school, and Blas has been on the elected committee that runs barriada affairs and feels that he has some say in local government. Since local elections are unknown in Peru the barriadas' unofficial elections are unique. The committee passes judgment on requests from new applicants to settle in the barriada and cut new lots out of the hillside. They also decide on requests to sell or rent. Renting is against the rules of the association. Another important function is presenting petitions and requests to various government ministries for assistance. Until 1960 barriada residents had no legal basis for their ownership of lots. Any recognition by the government in the form of assistance or even taxation was an assuring sign. In 1960 the congress passed a law saying, in effect, that what could not be changed might as well be made legal, and residents of barriadas are to be given their lots. As of 1963 a few land titles had been given out by the government, but the people have been buying and selling for years with homemade titles.

The committees are also concerned with internal order. Barriadas are ordinarily quiet places composed mainly of hardworking family groups, but the public image is one of violence, immorality, sloth, crime, and revolutionary left-wing politics. Barriada residents are quite sensitive about this and the committees try to screen out potential trouble makers and control those present. They also try to get as much publicity as possible for the productive work done by barriada people.

The experience of this couple is probably happier than that of the average family but is certainly well within the 'typical' range. They feel, in comparison to people like themselves and in terms of their own aspirations, that they have done well. When asked what they would do if they acquired a large sum of money, they both answer in terms of improving their present property and educating their children. There is some resentment of the children, and Blas beats the oldest boy for not doing well in school, and all five children are bedwetters, but they give the impression of a happy family and, although Carmen cried during several interviews, they smile frequently and seem to be getting along. Carmen speaks some Quechua with her neighbours and her half-sister, and has actually improved her Quechua since coming to the barriada. Spanish is the principal language, however, and neither she nor Blas has any strong interest in their children learning Quechua.

The children themselves learn some Quechua, but they speak Spanish with their peers, and in a group of children it is difficult to distinguish those of recently arrived near-Indian migrants from those of the most *Criollo* coastal families. There is a certain amount of antagonism among the adult barriada dwellers over race, cultural difference, politics, and place of origin. The children, however, are strikingly similar in attitude and have very little of the mountain Indian about them.

The situation of Blas and Carmen is similar to that of many others. They have some friends, some relatives, and some income, but they could be ruined by a loss of job or any chronic illness of Blas, and they are aware of it. If there is a potentially disruptive factor in their lives, it is that the high aspirations they have for their children are vastly unrealistic. They are sacrificing and plan to sacrifice more for the education of the children, but they overrate the probable results. They say they want the children to be professionals, doctors, teachers, people with comfortable lives, and in this they are similar to most interviewed barriada families. But it is highly unlikely that they will be, unless there are monumental and rapid changes in Peru.

When the children come to this realization, they may fulfill the presently paranoid prophecy of many middle and upper class Peruvians who see the barriada population as rebellious and revolutionary.

5

Tales from the Barriadas

WILLIAM MANGIN

In Peru, as well as in most countries of Latin America, Africa, Asia, and parts of the Mediterranean and Near East, squatter settlements have grown up around large cities. The residents are mainly migrants from rural areas who have lived for several years in the city and who organized together to invade land, usually public, and usually against the armed opposition of the police. They have constructed their own houses and developed their own social organization. These settlements constitute a remarkable example of popular initiative and creativity, as well as courage and involvement. The opposition of the governments, although probably inevitable since the settlements are outside of the system, is misdirected, even in their own terms. That is, the squatters are not political revolutionaries except in their original seizure of the land and, for the most part, once the government gives up the opposition to the persistent invasion (usually after many beatings, much destruction of the meagre household goods of the squatters, and often the killing of some of them by the police) the residents generally become quite conservative and

"Tales from the Barriadas" by William Mangin is reprinted from the *Nickel Review*, Sept. 25–Oct. 8, 1968, by permission of the author and publisher.

identify themselves as property owners. This has been true in the favelas of Rio, the barriadas of Peru, the callampas of Chile, the bidonvilles of North Africa, the barongbarongs of the Phillipines, and the shantytowns of Puerto Rico, Hong Kong, Ankara, and Athens.

In Peru, around Lima, there are over 400,000 squatters out of a population of two and a half million. They come from all over the country, mostly from the mountan provinces, and although many of the adults are native speakers of Quechua, practically all of them speak Spanish and have had some schooling. They see some hope in the future for themselves and their children. Many of them think that their present, self-constructed, barriada housing has been a good investment of their time and money and constitutes more than they expected to get when they left the feudal mountain areas. Their aspirations for their children are probably unrealistically high, and this seems to be causing more political unrest in barriadas as the young people grow up and find that they are not going to be able to become the teachers, doctors, engineers, and businessmen that their parents expected them to, and that they would like to.

The early stereotype held by most middle and upper class Peruvians of the barriada dwellers as illiterate, nonproductive, lawless, recent communistic Indian migrants is still held by many — but is giving way among young architects, politicians, academics, and anthropologists to an equally false picture. Perhaps as an antidote to the first, it paints them as happy, contented, literate, productive, adjusted, politically conservative-forever, patriotic citizens. They are, in fact, about like the vast majority of Peruvians, moderately to desperately poor, cynical *and* trusting of politicians, bishops, outside agitators, and their own local leaders. They are alternately hopeful and despairing about the future of their children and themselves. They love and resent their children and their parents. They are, in short, human beings.

In the course of working in barriadas during three two-year stays and ten shorter visits since 1951, I have talked with hundreds of squatters and their children. In 1959 I had a chance to work for two weeks with a psychoanalyst, Walter Slote, during which time we administered the Rorschach test and the Thematic Apperception Test (TAT) to a number of people I had been working with for the previous two years. The TAT results of two men still strike me as the best and most concise illustration of the complexity, the pathos, and the ambivalence in the attitudes of many mountain migrants toward their families and their society. I saw both men in 1967 and 1968 and recalled the TAT stories to them and asked if they would mind having them published, maybe with their pictures. They both said they didn't mind. One joked about all the money I would get when the stories came out in *Life* magazine so I told him I would split with him if I made anything. I guess I can send him five *Nickel Reviews,* since I get ten.

In the TAT a person is shown pictures and asked to tell a story. The pictures are of white Americans and Europeans but no one in our sample group failed to identify the people in the pictures with themselves. In the course of showing the pictures a blank card is often inserted in the series. In the cases of the two men we used the blank card and I include the stories they told. The men are Lizandro and Julio. I won't use their last names but I guess you could find them if you wanted to. Lizandro was 29, Julio 30. Each was a native Quechua speaker but thoroughly fluent in Spanish. Each had migrated from the mountain in their late teens, worked and lived in slum areas of Lima, married, had children, and both joined the original invasion group of the barriada where they lived. They invaded in 1956 and had been living in the barriada about three years. Lizandro had five children, Julio had two.

Lizandro, a gregarious, talkative man, worked as a construction worker and was relatively prosperous. He also contracted work within the barriada, designing and supervising construction of houses. He was often referred to as the engineer of the barrio, and was well known and liked. Julio, an introspectve, quiet man, was unemployed at the time. He had worked in marginal office jobs and is presently employed as a messenger and receptionist for a lawyer. Both men are highly intelligent. Lizandro is more or less satisfied with his situation. Julio is anxious and depressed much of the time, and very worried about what will happen to his children.

The same cards were not used with every person and the order was not the same. Here I will present the last three stories of each of the two men, the last one in each case being to the blank card. Lizandro began the interview with great enthusiasm and told a folk tale about a king with three daughters that went on for about ten minutes. Then, to a picture of a young man and an old woman, both rather solemn, he said:

THE GRANDMOTHER

"This is a grandmother who is thinking and a grandchild who also is thinking. I think that what he is thinking might be favorable to him or something bad against him for there are thousands of thoughts that go through the brain. The grandmother says, 'Son, what have you done?' He hesitates and says, 'Keep quiet, grandmother, don't keep saying the same thing.' 'If you were not my grandchild I would throw you out and never love you again.' 'Grandmother, give me advice. Tell me what I can do.' 'Tomorow morning I will speak to your father, that he should send you away from here because grandchildren of this kind are not worthy of being loved.' He comes and kisses the grandmother and says, 'Grandmother, I won't wait until you throw me out. I'll go by myself because to remain here is to torment you day and night, also my parents.' The grandmother says, 'God bless you. Write to me from wherever you are and I'll see how things are.' 'Blessed be your name Grandmother. I'll also pray for you. Goodbye.' These are the type of words they use in popular literature. The boy was playing in a gambling house. There was a fight between friends. One fell and killed himself. He is being looked for by the police."

THE ORPHAN

To a picture of a figure slumped down against a bench Lizandro responded: "It looks like an orphan, a vagabound, no father and no mother, walking the streets. Finding himself alone in the silence of the night he rests his head on a granite bench. He's dreaming that he is well dressed, eating something good, and he is happy in his dream. When he wakes up, he finds himself facing a cold bench. His shoulders are cold. He gets up and starts wandering around the streets again. He stops at a corner and says how sad a poor man is without a father and without a mother. He starts thinking and walking and walking and says to himself, again tired, he sits down on a bench and says, 'God bless me and bless my parents.'"

HELEN AND JOHN

He was very subdued and depressed when he was handed the blank card. He said: "A tale of, let's ideate, a father has two sons and another mother has two daughters. Both love their children. The children grow up and come to love one another, they seek the love of one another, without knowing their parents hate one another. When the mother of one of these finds out that her daughter is in love with one of these sons, while the parents hated one another. The two children kept loving each other more and more, one because he had money and the other because he was poor. One was called Helen and one John. John says to Helen, 'You won't abandon me?' She says, 'No, I will not forget you and just because our parents hate each other we will not hate one another. Neither one of our families will separate us and for this reason we will leave this place.' Because of that they abandon their parents and go."

JULIO'S YOUNG MAN

Julio began with a story about poverty and Slote asked him a few times, "What happened then?" After the first two cards he was not asked any questions. To a picture of a silhouetted male figure he said: "This is in the night because of the figure that is black, observing from the door of his house. I suppose that someone from his family has gone out of his house and since it is night, he is at the door watching. A young boy has gone out. This *is* the young man and the family has gone out, his mother and his father, and he's standing there thinking. Both the mother and the father have gone out. He's thinking that something has happened to them. Since they haven't come back by this time he leaves and looks for them until he finds them and it ends."

THE POOR AND HUMBLE

To the figure slumped against the bench he said: "I observe a person alone, and having no place to be. He walks until he is tired and throws himself down to rest. After he sleeps he gets up and continues on the road. There are many things to say. We have many poor and humble people who don't have any place to eat or to go and they leave their houses looking for it. For example, an orphan without a mother or father, or a child who has behaved badly, punished by his mother or father, and he's gone someplace to avoid being punished. His father is going to look for him and bring him back. He has done something wrong, or it is their imagination. He could have done something bad such as taken some small change or not obeyed them. He wants to hide because of this. His father repents, looks for him, brings him home by his side, and doesn't punish him again."

Like Lizandro, he was very subdued and depressed after this card. To the blank card, Julio told a story that is a remarkable combination of Hansel and Gretel and a Quechua tale called The Achique, about a monster who pursues a boy and girl who encounter animals and obstacles in their flight. It also contains elements of his own invention. During the story he became agitated, almost elated, when describing the monster's death, but very subdued and pensive after his final statement about the echo.

THE MONSTER

"These are monsters, very ancient things. The monster had power because he was from God — against human beings. There was a married couple in a place where there was nothing to eat — a poor family. They had two children, a little girl and a little boy. The parents went far away to look for food. They found only one piece of bread for themselves at night. The children were waiting for their parents. When the parents arrived the children woke up asking them for bread. Not finding any food for themselves, the parents decided to throw the children off a precipice far away. The mother said it was better to kill them; the father said it was not better. They decided not to kill the children there but to put them in a bag and to take them to the precipice. They left them hanging in the air by a rope over the precipice. During the day the children cried for help. Hearing this, a condor came and took them, carrying them down to the ground. The children got out of the bag and started to walk. The condor flew away, scared. The children walked alone to an unknown place. The little girl was 10 and the boy only 5. The girl spoke perfectly and could walk.

"During that whole day they found only one kernel of corn, which somebody had thrown out; they divided it in two and ate. In that lonely place they cried in the night for their mother and father. A high voice answered their call. A little while later the monster presented himself to the children and took them to his cave. Then the monster spoke. He said, 'Who are you and from where did you come?' The children said they had lost their parents, and the monster said, 'I'll take care of you.' The monster put rocks in a pot and boiled them as though they were potatoes, but the children couldn't eat them because they were rocks. The monster began to eat the rocks as though they were stewed potatoes, trying to show them how to eat, but they couldn't eat them. He said, 'If you can't eat these potatoes, I'm going to eat you.'

"While the monster was asleep in his cave, the children escaped. The children, fleeing, found a wooden cross, and they said, 'Sir, save us from this danger, we've lost our parents.' They heard the monster coming. They went to hide under the cross, and when they hid under the cross there was no monster. They heard a voice from the sky that said, 'My children, come up.' Looking up they saw nothing but a rope ladder. They went up the ladder to the sky — into space. Then the monster came and asked the cross to put the ladder down so he could follow the children. The cross did, and he started up the ladder after the children. The monster said, 'Just as you have God, I also have God, and when I catch you I'll eat you.' But on the ladder the monster was climbing there were two rats and they were tearing the rope ladder. The monster said to them, 'Brothers, don't destroy my ladder, I have to destroy my prisoners.' The rats answered, 'For a bad person there is no ladder to God.' Then they tore through the ladder, and the monster fell to the ground, landing on the edge of a hill. His blood splashed all over one tremendous hill and on to others; the hill he landed on exploded like a bomb. The story ends now. Whenever anybody calls, the hills answer or, better said, they echo. When somebody calls, he thinks it is a person answering, but it is not a person."

Like the two children in the story, the barriada people, and mountain migrants generally, keep trying and looking. They trust their siblings, as a rule, but litigation and bitter fighting often ensue if inherited property is involved. Parents are trusted but show themselves to be unable and often unwilling to feed and take care of children. Fathers are seen as less rewarding and less punishing than mothers. The search for parents runs through all of Julio's and Lizandro's stories and the stories of our other respondents. In many cases an unconvincing happy end is supplied. Julio was the only one who managed to "kill the monster," and in his case it was through the action of two rats, after God had proven unreliable. The destruction of the monster makes all the more poignant his rapid retreat and classic statement of despair, "Whenever anybody calls, the hills answer or, better said, they echo. When somebody calls, he thinks it is a person answering, but it is not a person."

I have published that story in this country in another context, and recently some other works of mine about barriadas have been translated and published in a large circulation Sunday paper in Lima. Neither of the men had seen it, although many of the residents had. I had it with me and showed it, and the English translation of his story, to Julio. I asked him if he objected to my publishing such things and he said, "Put it in all the papers. The whole world should know how we exist here."

6

The Ritual Dimension of Rural-Urban Networks: The Fiesta System in the Northern Highlands of Bolivia[1]

HANS C. BUECHLER

Some generalizations can be made about the Latin American fiesta system which has received considerable attention during the past two decades. First, although large celebrations existed in pre-Columbian times, the basic elements of the fiesta system seem to have been a colonial introduction (Harris, 1964:27). Second, the fiesta system seems to be a rather flexible institution which has been adapted by various groups to different ends. This flexibility may be the reason for the institution's persistence in the face of change, and may explain why functional analyses have arrived at conclusions which are often diametrically opposed. Some authors (Cancian, 1965; Mangin, 1954) have stressed the fiestas' integrative functions; others see elements of discord (Martínez, 1963). The fiesta system has also been seen alternatively as an economic leveling device (Wolf, 1955) and as a lucrative enterprise for the entire community or for the sponsors (Harris, 1964:34–35). This paper will suggest that the adaptability of the fiesta system has furnished a large segment of the population, both Indian and Mestizo, with a language with which to express social relations.

Some researchers have been concerned recently with the symbolic aspect of the fiesta system (Carter, 1968; Crumrine, 1969; Moore, 1966; Nash, 1968). Having analyzed specific rituals, they conclude that fiesta symbolism frequently refers to social relations. Presenting a somewhat different approach to fiesta symbolism, this paper deals with fiestas as a complex means of communication in which messages about social relations are transmitted on at least two interconnected but distinct levels: one of ritual participation and one of ritual rules. These two levels are related in complementary ways: on the one hand they stand to each other as message and code, on the other as beginning and end result of the process by which rituals are created and transformed. Seen from the first point of view, ritual rules furnish a framework or arena within which the participants express social relations. The second viewpoint sees ritual rules as derived from ritual participation. Wallace's contention that ritual simplifies reality (1966:238) implies that ritual rules are messages as well as codes. Similarly, I contend that they stereotype salient social relationships and recurrent patterns of participation. For the outsider, local variations in ritual rules provide clues to parallel participation, for in contrast to the latter, which derives its meaning from social interaction, ritual rules often are assembled from heteroclite elements taken out of various contexts (e.g., from agricultural practices). This "processual" viewpoint also explains why ritual participation already constitutes a simplification of social interaction: for ritual participation contains embryonic ritual rules.

Because social interaction is simplified in the fiesta system, the latter provides a useful tool for analyzing complex or changing social relationships. Saint's-day fiestas — an important aspect of the lives of peasants, miners, townsmen, and a large proportion of city dwellers — assume a variety of forms even within a restricted area, though basic similarities allow an individual to participate in any of them when he is obliged to do so. This is important, for as we shall see, Aymaras and Mestizos have economic, social, and political connections with individuals in different ecological zones in rural communities, county or province capitals, and the city of La Paz.

Fiestas in the northern highlands of Bolivia are based on a variety of systems of sponsorship combined with a system of reciprocal prestations. Sponsors who agree to accept a specific commission,[2] or *cargo*, are aided by relatives, friends, community, or neighborhood members, and by persons who wish to "pass" a *cargo* at some later date. Most fiestas include two types of sponsors: the *prestes* and the dance-group leaders. The *prestes*, in charge of the church-related aspects of fiestas, pay for the Mass and for the saints' candles, and provide food and alcohol for their *ainis*, or retainers, and frequently for the dance groups as well. The *cabezas, cabecillas,* or *directorio* are dance-group sponsors who organize and partly or fully subsidize the brass band and the food and drink for all the dancers, musicians, and retainers who help back the fiesta. *Cabezas* must finance the entire cost of a brass band and all food and drink. They usually do not participate in the dances themselves but rather tend to their duties as hosts. *Cabecillas* defray a lesser share of the costs associated with dancing, and unlike the *cabezas,* they always dance at the head of their group. Finally the *directorio,* composed of a number of dance-group leaders has obligations intermediate between those of *cabezas* and *cabecillas.* The other dancers pay for the purchase or rental of their costumes and (except when their group is headed by a *cabeza*) for a share of the fiesta costs as well.

Sponsorship obligations often accompany political office. Previous to 1953, community leaders were obliged to sponsor a dance group to represent their community at the fiesta in the county capital; today market leaders in La Paz must sponsor fiestas. Other fiestas sponsored by the commisioners are part of an annual cycle, hierarchically ordered according to the importance of the saints and the amount of expense involved.

Because Aymaras and Mestizos are involved in wide networks of social relationships, they participate in fiestas at considerable distances from their homes. We shall analyze the relationships between the ritual and social dimensions of a small fraction of this network, namely the fiesta participation of Aymara peasants from Compi, a Lake Titicaca community. Such an analysis entails a step-by-step description of fiestas in Compi itself, followed by those in the county capital, and ending with the fiestas in the city of La Paz where many Compeños have migrated.

Like many Bolivian haciendas or landed estates, Compi originated during the nineteenth century as a result of the increasing encroachment (facilitated by republican decrees) of estate owners on communal lands of neighboring corporate communities. Hacienda and free community organization was based on similar leadership, fiesta, and land tenure patterns. Landowners simply adapted traditional patterns to an exploitative economy. Peasant families were allowed to cultivate variable allotments of land in return for twelve man-labor-days per week and other services. The *patrón* or his administator replaced the peasant leader as the supreme administrative and judicial authority. Compi was formed by a family whose landholdings constituted one section of the present community. Subsequently they purchased an adjacent hacienda and all but one section of a free community. The free section, Llamacachi, maintains marriage ties with the community of Compi. Historical variations in their origin and development differentiated the sections and gave some sections prerogatives such as the right to furnish work foremen. Major changes resulted from the social revolution and Agrarian Reform of 1952–1953 which gave peasants title to the lands they had formerly held in usufruct. Some of the land tilled for the *patrón* was divided among his former serfs, and eventually the rest was sold to them; the former landowner disappeared from the scene.

Just as the complex community structure and history of Compi present certain characteristics common to a large number of highland communities as well as some more specialized adaptations, so do the rules governing the fiesta system. But similarities in fiesta rules far outweigh the differences. As in other peasant communities, ritual rules are well established for each fiesta. Although the nature of sponsorship differs somewhat among the four Compi saints' fiestas, the obligations of the sponsors within each fiesta are precisely defined — even to the exact quantities of food to be proffered. Furthermore, the sponsorships are assumed in a fixed sequence by almost every married couple in the community. However, unlike many other haciendas and free communities, where an individual alternately assumes religious and political commissions, there is no strict linkage between political offices and community fiesta sponsorships in Compi; rather, each forms a parallel but separate prestige hierarchy. In hacienda times the *patrón* rather than the community named political authorities who remained in office for as long as the *patrón* desired.

This precluded the systematic interlinkages possible in communities where authorities changed annually. Llamacachi had a similar arrangement but for different reasons. There, the community leader's burdensome obligation of reporting to the distant county capital every Saturday made few persons willing to assume leadership positions voluntarily. As a result, the county officials forced extended families to furnish a leader in fixed turns.

The changing social relationships characteristic of Compi social organization are manifested in ritual participation to a far greater extent than in ritual rules. Sponsors and elders from Compi proper, the original section of the community, sit behind the only ritual stone table in the plaza where the main acts of the fiestas take place. In addition, Compi proper and Capilaya, the first section to be added, are the only sections required to furnish an additional sponsor for the major fiesta. While the other sections form their own dance groups in all fiestas, the nonassimilated section of the free community, Llamacachi, provides a dance group only for the major fiesta. Like the hacienda sections of Compi, it does not stage a fiesta of its own nor does it participate in the fiestas of neighboring communities. This reflects the marginality of Llamacachi in relation to the hacienda sections and its connections with the other sections through kin ties. Schisms within the sections are likewise mirrored in ritual participation.

Social structural change brought about by the Agrarian Reform is reflected in a decline in popularity of the fiesta of Our Virgin of Mercy, the patron saint of the hacienda chapel. Authorities from the various sections of Compi no longer gather at the ceremonial site of Compi proper, the section which, in the hacienda administration, used to furnish most of the candidates for the offices held by peasants.

Participation by Compeños in county fiestas reflects both continuity and change in jurisdiction on this higher political level. Before the Agrarian Reform, Llamacachi and other free communities were under the jurisdiction of a Mestizo residing in the nearest nucleated settlement. In contrast, the haciendas in the same area were only vaguely associated with the county, since most judicial matters which the peasant authorities could not treat were judged by the *patrón* himself or by his Mestizo administrator. The Agrarian Reform created many new counties which included free communities and former haciendas; in the northern highlands peasants began to head the counties. Simultaneously, in the new county capitals the number of rural markets grew to satisfy the needs of the peasants whose economic power was increasing. To qualify as a county capital, an Aymara community, with its dispersed settlement pattern, has had to replicate the nucleated Mestizo grid-town. Jank'o Amaya, the exhacienda neighboring Compi, founded a small, grid-plan settlement complete with stores, church, telegraph station, administrative building, and market (H. Buechler, 1968).

The new counties imitate traditional forms by patterning their fiesta rules and participation after the model of Mestizo towns. The major fiesta must include a bullfight which consists of tearing an *enjalme* (a cloth laden with small bills) from an enraged bull. All member communities and each group of vendors in the weekly fair pay for an *enjalme* or for one or more entries of a bull. New Year's Day marks the annual change of authorities, and each member community is expected to organize a band to honor its incoming and outgoing officials. The inherent instability of the new counties is reflected in the fact that only those communities which actually furnish county officials send musicians or even representatives to these celebrations.

Both community and county fiestas attract dance groups composed of migrants who return to their birthplace on these occasions. This reflects the continued ties between migrants and their home community. For example, they return often to help relatives in the harvest. Some migrants still have access to land through inheritance or purchase from the former *patrón;* others engage in commercial activities if their community has an established market.

Peasants also profit from kin ties with migrants. Compeños stay at the homes of their relatives when they market their onions in La Paz. Relatives in the city help in obtaining legal aid and employment for the peasant who wants to settle in the urban area.

Because every La Paz barrio commemorates its saint with a fiesta and participates in fiestas of neighboring barrios, migrants from Compi are involved in a complex fiesta system. In addition to this cycle of barrio fiestas, there are celebrations for personal and market guardian saints which may entail *prestes* or dance groups.

Sponsorships for barrio fiestas are more flexible than the fixed sponsorships of the Compi fiestas. In the city a *preste* is not obligated to invite all the dance groups to his home. Since the dance groups headed by *cabezas* are very expensive, those sponsored by *cabecillas* and *directorios* occur more frequently. Once a La Paz dance group is formed, it endures; though some changes occur from year to year, many Pazeños dance in the same group for three to seven consecutive years.

Participation in La Paz fiestas can best be analyzed by a dyachronic frame of reference because ritual rules depend on the history of each barrio. Much of the land around La Paz belonged to small agricultural haciendas and free communities which have maintained their original organization until quite recently.[3] The zone of San Pedro once consisted of a large free community governed by three local authorities and a Mestizo *alcalde* who resided in the city. It was subdivided into seven zones or *ayllunis* each with its own authorities. Relationships between the city and its periphery seems to echo those between communities and Mestizo towns. Like altiplano communities which provided personal services to the town's Mestizo authorities, the *ayllunis* served the national and departmental authorities. A generation ago the *aylluni* authorities gave personal service to the president himself and acted as messengers to Mestizo towns. As a recompense they were exempt from military service. Later personal services were restricted to include only departmental authorities.

The *alcalde* and the local city authorities nominated the *prestes* for the fiestas from among persons with large holdings. If no candidates could be found, the provincial prefect forced the *alcalde* himself to assume the sponsorship. Since the 1920s, however, when a liberal president ended forced sponsorships, dancers from a wide radius have formed groups voluntarily.

Strong kin ties linked the peripheral communities and barrios. Sometimes the fiestas themselves were formally affiliated. San Pedro furnished a *preste* in the fiesta of the barrio of Miraflores; reciprocally, the other *prestes* in Miraflores were invited to attend the San Pedro fiesta.

In the past generation, the city has grown at the expense of the free communities and haciendas. Free community members began to sell their lands to *señores* from the city and to resort increasingly to dairy farming, using the residues from beer breweries as fodder. Pressed by further encroachment from the city, they turned from dairying to trucking, mechanics, and other trades. The character of the communities has changed, but the original inhabitants still play a major role in fiestas. Only if none of the *originarios* volunteers as *preste* may a more recent barrio immigrant assume the sponsorship. These barrios also still have the most costly sponsorships.

The population of these areas has been augmented by migrants from the altiplano and elsewhere. One avenue of immigration to La Paz is commerce. Many Compi women who came into the city to sell their onions and other vegetables eventually took up residence in La Paz and established themselves as middlemen (J-M. Buechler, 1967). Other Compeños migrated to La Paz in the 1940's as the conditions on the hacienda became increasingly severe. Many began as bread distributors, a job which required no skills or knowledge of Spanish, and, with help from their relatives, worked themselves into other jobs ranging from carpenters to policemen. Others, from areas where there were no sudden pressures migrated gradually over generations, and developed skills which made their communities famous for certain trades.

It is therefore not surprising that some of the dance groups are based on occupational lines and place of origin. The costume-makers from Achacachi dance in the annual fiesta of their barrio. Analogous dance groups are present in the market fiestas of the *tambos*, or wholesale outlets for fruit, potatoes, and other staples. On the day of the patron saint of these markets the richer vendors volunteer to become *prestes*. Both stevedores and vendors organize dance groups, the latter grouping themselves according to the kind of produce they sell. A similar custom prevails in the subtropical Yungas valleys where vendors from the highlands are commissioned to become *cabezas* of dance groups. Since such sponsorships are costly, vendors without a strong commitment to a particular market stop selling there to avoid sponsorship. Sponsoring such a fiesta thus establishes a vendor's rights to sell in the *tambo* or market. La Paz retail markets also celebrate patron saints days but with only a *preste*.

Frequently, dance groups are associated with clubs whose members have immigrated from specific communities. The functions of the club usually are related to the socioeconomic development of their home community, i.e., aid in the construction of schools and administrative buildings or in attaining electric power. Political connections in the La Paz bureaucracy are sometimes exploited by the clubs whose members wish to obtain a higher political status (of county or province capital) for their home communities. Some clubs also help the migrant group by providing aid for medical expenses and transportation to home-town fiestas. Marketing and artisan unions whose membership includes a high proportion of migrants from a particular town also may be associated with these clubs.

Though most clubs function only intermittently and few can boast impressive accomplishments, their junior-level branches enjoy considerable vitality as associations of soccer clubs which compete against each other and against La Paz and home-town teams. Their Easter matches held in the home towns have become a permanent institution. Many migrant clubs, particularly the soccer clubs, also organize groups to dance in the home-town fiestas and in La Paz fiestas. Fiestas and the newer recreational activities are thus by no means incompatible, but may be interrelated forms of ritual expression.

The divergent histories of marginal barrios are paralleled by dissimilar fiestas. San Pedro, Sopocachi Alto, and Obrajes, for instance, with their peasant, dairy-farmer tradition have elaborate *presterios* to which dance groups are invited by *prestes*. Sopocachi Alto has the added distinction of two *prestes,* one representing *la indiada* and one *la cholada*. Although the overall cash outlay of both *prestes* is very similar, the *preste* of the *cholada* must rent more elaborately decorated taxis for religious procession than the *preste* of the *indiada*. In 1967 the house of the *cholada preste* was closer to a middle class neighborhood than that of the other *preste*. Similarly, dance-group sponsors whose families owned land are labeled *los ricos* (the rich ones), and those who did not, *los pobres* (poor ones), even though differences in wealth no longer distinguish them. In contrast, Alto Ch'ijini, a barrio built on terrain too steep for agriculture, has a poorly developed *preste* system and no religious procession whatsoever. Its fiesta consists of dance groups and two bullfights held by adjacent zones which celebrate the same fiesta. Villa Victoria, an old barrio of factory workers and artisans has another type of celebration with very large dance groups and a multitude of adjunct sponsors who serve food and drink.

Compeños and other migrants do not usually sponsor fiestas immediately upon permanent migration to the city. A study of two hundred market women in La Paz[4] revealed that city-born market women became sponsors on the average of five years earlier than first generation migrants. Of these, all but one had lived in La Paz for at least fifteen years before becoming a sponsor.

Folklore festivals add national dimension to the fiesta system. The first such festival mentioned in the literature took place in 1945 (Paredes, 1949:30–32). Increasing in popularity since the Bolivian revolution of 1952, they reflect the new national interest in the peasantry. Held on the altiplano, the Cochabamba valley, and in stadiums and open theaters in La Paz, some are sponsored by the municipal government, others by the tourist bureau, and still others are semi-commercial ventures organized by Aymara radio announcers who thereby gain a following on the altiplano and in La Paz. Compi, for example, became the site of one of the largest folklore festivals as a result of the efforts of Compeños who had lived in the city and a migrant employed by the national tourist agency. These festivals are a curious blend of *indigenismo* (e.g., they revive traditional dances), western style mass entertainment, and traditional dance-group organization. Although they differ sharply from traditional fiestas, they resemble other fiestas enough to remain intelligible to all potential participants.

CONCLUSION

An analysis of the fiesta system in the northern Bolivian highlands in terms of multiple levels presents an image of Bolivian society as a vast network of linkages in which it is meaningless to oppose smaller and larger human groupings as discrete types. An examination of the history of fiestas in some La Paz barrios, for instance, revealed that the relationship between the center and the periphery of old La Paz is very similar to that of counties and their surrounding free communities. Similarities in La Paz market fiestas and town fiestas demonstrate that La Paz constitutes merely one of a multitude of interconnected market sites, albeit a more complex one. Dance group formation in voluntary associations shows that La Paz is not a closed system, for these associations maintain intimate ties with the home towns of their members. Like its social systems, La Paz fiestas are not unique in kind. The city's fiesta system viewed as a whole is distinguished not so much by individual ritual patterns as by the concentration of such a large number of different patterns and the extent of their linkages outside the city's boundaries. Speaking of the *aini* relationships, one La Paz informant compared the fiesta system to a root growing in many directions at once. Our analysis of fiestas indicates that it is through such linkages and parallels with institutions in smaller settlements rather than by seeing cities, towns, and peasant communities as separate, bounded entities, that changing Andean social systems can best be studied.

NOTES

1. The fieldwork on which this paper is based was carried out intermittently from 1964 to 1967 and was supported by a Columbia Travelling Fellowship, The Research Institute for the Study of Man, The Peace Corps (Grant No. PC(W)-397), and The Canada Council. Some of the ideas and material were presented at the 66*th.* annual meeting of the American Anthropological Society (H. Buechler, 1967).

2. "Commission" is Van Zantwijk's (1967) translation of *cargo.*

3. The haciendas became urbanized through sales to individuals and factories as well as through expropriation by the municipal government after the Agrarian Reform. In the 1940's the owner of one hacienda parceled out the lower part which lies closer to the center of the city while the upper part was expropriated by the municipality in the 1950's as part of an urban reform program. We have not had the occasion to analyze the participation of hacienda syndicates in city fiestas.

4. This study was carried out by Judith-Maria Buechler in 1967.

7 ....

Rio's Favelas:
The Rural Slum
within the City

FRANK BONILLA

Until mid-June of this year when *Life* magazine's millions of readers saw Gordon Parks's photographic essay on poverty in Rio's hillside slums (*favelas*), the American image of the life of Rio's poor was based largely on Marcel Camus's moving film fantasy, *Black Orpheus*. Camus's movie fully exploits the magnificent scenic backdrop provided by the city as well as the exuberant sound and color of carnival. His *favelados* are a race of handsome blacks, who within the heart of a modern city manage to retain a natural, almost bucolic way of life. They are sleek and carefree, full of boundless energy and rhythm, with an unfettered zest for life. Parks's *favela* family is a proto-human band, weakened by chronic illness, callously indifferent to each other's suffering, living in a monotone degradation punctuated only by flashes of violence.

No one can quarrel with the artist's right to select and blend what he finds in reality to his purpose; both Camus and Parks catch essential

Rio's Favelas by Frank Bonilla, AUFS Reports, East Coast South America Series, Vol. VIII No. 3 © 1961 by American Universities Field Staff, Inc.

aspects of the meaning and feeling of life in the *favela*. If there is still magic and an authentic human quality in a Rio carnival, these spring directly from the infusion of vitality and joy in sound and movement that invades the city from the hills during the pre-Lenten festival. But the very intensity of that collective catharsis suggests the explosive potential that is built up day by day in the more than 100 *favelas* that scar the city's *morros* (hills).[1] Camus and Parks each fasten on separate phrases of the emotional cycle of the *favela*.

Recent estimates put as many as a third of Rio's three million inhabitants within these jerry-built, vertical islands of squalor. Children and adolescents make up a large part of that population. The median age among 169,305 *favelados* counted in the 1950 census was just over twenty years; about thirty-five percent were under fifteen years of age. By current calculations more than a half million youngsters under fifteen are living in Rio *favelas*.[2] The family chosen by *Life* photographer Parks to represent those many thousands had eight children who along with their parents were crowded into a six by ten foot shack.

The fact that Parks, himself a Negro, featured a white *favela* family in his pictures and that his essay makes no allusion to race provoked some comment in the local press. Statistically, his choice was not indefensible. Though Negroes are numerically slightly in the ascendancy within the *favela* (about thirty-eight percent), they are accompanied in their misery and hardship by sizable contingents of mixed bloods (twenty-nine percent) and whites (thirty-three percent). Brazilians, in fact, often point to the heterogeneity of the *favela* population as evidence of the country's racial democracy. When the asthmatic adolescent who was the central figure in Parks's *Life* report was taken to the United States for medical treatment, one Rio weekly proposed that *cariocas* counter by bringing a boy from Harlem to Rio, where he could live like a white man. The favored Harlemite, the story ran, would in Rio be able to study in any school, pray in any church, bathe at any beach, ride on any vehicle, bury his dog in any dog cemetery, and go to any movie. The writer neglected to note that the boy would also almost certainly be assured of a place to live in one of the city's *favelas*. For if the relative racial representation reported above has remained more or less stable and the *favela* population has grown in line with most estimates, Rio's Negroes may not be alone in the *favela, but they are almost all there.*[3]

THE GROWTH OF THE FAVELA

Structurally, the *favela* dwelling represents the intrusion into the city of a type of construction which still is the basic shelter for Brazil's majority rural population. The improvised shack of odd scraps of lumber, packing cases, tin sheeting, canvas, or rough tile is an incongruous anomaly when perched above the gleaming glass and concrete of modern Rio. In the Brazilian countryside the same crude habitation is the standard when not a remotely aspired-to luxury. When reformers and government officials talk about "urbanizing" the *favelas,* they raise the hope born of despair that a collection of rustic hovels can become a habitable city if provided with water, electricity, rudimentary sewerage, and streets. But even that degree of adaptation to city living has not accompanied the migration of the rural dwelling to the Rio hills. The *favelas* crawl in cancerous disorder up the steep *morros,* divided by labyrinthine paths and gullies that serve as precarious avenues of movement and natural sewers. The frequent rainfalls bring flash floods, landslides, and undermine the fragile hold of stilt foundations on the hills' flanks.

The inhumanity of Rio's *favelas* is matched in the *"villas miseria," "callampas,"* and *"colonias proletarias"* of other major Latin American cities. New York's single-room occupancy flats and rat-infested tenements belong to the same savage family. But in many of these cities the blight of the slum can be more easily ignored. The most unsightly housing clusters on the periphery of the city or is pushed into out-of-the-way pockets of undesirable land. Rio's *favelas* relentlessly meet the eye of anyone who walks the city's streets and lifts his gaze above eye level, no matter how elegant the neighborhood.

Not all of the housing in Rio that would be considered substandard by even very moderate criteria is in the *favelas.* But the *favela* is in part an outgrowth of the elimination of the city's more conventional central slums. The opening up of the Avenida Rio Branco, the leveling of the Morro Castelo, and the addition of a second main artery (Avenida Pres. Getulio Vargas) not only required the demolition of the crowded warrens (*cabecas de porco* and *corticos*) that housed Rio's poor but also dramatically increased land values in the central area. A substantial part of that population and of the constant flood of migrants from surrounding rural places put up their makeshift shelters on the city's outskirts and along the main rail lines running out of the city. The inadequacy of both rail and bus transport as the distances became longer and the population mushroomed has continued to feed the climb upward in search of space within the city (Goulart, 1957).

The growth of the *favela* is thus linked to the general flight from the countryside into the cities in Brazil, to a generally high rate of demographic growth, to the excessive concentration of industry and commerce in a few major cities, and finally to an almost absolute absence of serious concern with the process of urban expansion among city officials. The anarchic growth of the city marked by large-scale profiteering and speculation in real estate and construction simply took no account of the housing needs of the large number in the city automatically eliminated from the housing market by their low incomes.

MARGINALITY AND INTEGRATION

Living conditions in Rio *favelas* have been documented in exhaustive detail by a group of researchers under the guidance of Father Louis Joseph Lebret, an internationally known student of problems of economic and social development, and Jose Arthur Rios, an American-trained Brazilian sociologist.[4] In broad outline, that account of the life and problems of Rio's poor holds no surprises. The *favelado* is plagued by all the ills that beset his kind everywhere. As a group, the *favela* population is on the wrong side of every standard index of social disorganization, whether it be illiteracy, malnutrition, disease, job instability, irregular sexual unions, alcoholism, criminal violence, or almost any other on the familiar list. But these remain prevailing conditions not only in the *favela* but elsewhere in the city and throughout the vast rural spaces of Brazil. Thus the human waste and tragedy that the *favela* represents is only a small part of the problem, as is the health, police, and welfare burden the *favela* creates for a city lacking both capacity and practice in dispensing effective social services.

If the *favela* did not provide a framework for some working forms of human coexistence and social cohesion, the explosion of violence that some fear may some day descend on the city from the hills would have come long ago. From one point of view the *favela* can even be optimistically viewed as an integrative element — as a sort of staging area in which the recently arrived rural migrant is initiated into the mysteries of city life, learns new forms of solidarity, acquires new social and political skills. Though the number of *favela* children who achieve more than two or three years of primary schooling is extremely small, it is still higher than in the rural areas where often there is simply no school. The forced intimacy of the urban slum breeds conflict but also a variety of simple forms of organization to deal with common problems. Though the petty crime and violence of the favela fill the front pages of Rio's more sensational press day after day, a great many *favela* families are relatively stable, have fairly regular employment, and are even rigidly conventional by middle-class standards (Pearse, 1958; Gomes Consorte, 1959).

The core of the problem lies not within the *favela* itself but is national in scope. A nation that is embarked on a massive program of industrial expansion simply cannot leave half of its population behind without compromising its possibilities for future growth. A government that seeks to mobilize political support for economic policies that demand continued sacrifices and forbearance from those least able to give cannot expect that support to flow easily from those whose participation in national life is marginal in every way. The drama is not just one of the confrontation of what is old and what is new in Brazil — of the existence side by side of "developed" and backward sectors in the nation. The *favela* throws into focus long-standing inequalities that by and large continue being actively exploited or regarded with complacent indifference as much by "modern" as by traditionalist-minded Brazilians. It is the fragility of the social bonds, the lack of organic connections between the *favelado*, together with his rural counterpart, and the rest of the national community that threatens the hope for a peaceful social revolution in Brazil. Maria Carolina de Jesus, a Sao Paulo *favelada* whose diary created a literary sensation in 1960, made a memorable entry in her notes on a day in May of that year when she was too tired to do her daily foraging through the city's trash in search of something to eat or to sell. "When I am hungry," she wrote, "I want to kill Janio, I want to hang Adhemar and burn Juscelino. Hardship dims the affection of the people for politicians."[5]

No one can tell whether the *favela* can for long continue as an imperfect agent of integration or is bound to become an incubator of revolution. Certainly, more humane and efficient ways of incorporating the stream of rural migrants into city life must be conceived. In any case, some clues as to the sense of participation of *favelados* in national development, of how they perceive their links to other social groups in the city and nation, are available from a recent small survey among *favelados*. The study was carried out through the American Universities Field Staff in behalf of two United Nations agencies.[6] As part of a larger research effort, involving field work in four Latin American countries, only a fraction of the study was directly concerned with the problems under discussion here. Nevertheless, some of the preliminary results provide an interesting partial view of how *favelados* regard their own situation.

THE SAMPLE OF FAVELADOS

Two hundred favelados were interviewed; 150 men and 50 women. The disproportion between men and women ensured having a sufficient number of males to allow comparisons with samples of other male groups being studied in Brazil. In addition, *favela* women were expected to prove less fruitful respondents than males in such a survey. The women were included as a check on male responses and to allow estimates of over-all sentiment in the *favela* with respect to some items. The sample, though small, was carefully structured. Interviewers worked in five *favelas* selected at random from among twenty that had in turn been randomly selected from 132 *favelas* identified on a complete aerial map of Rio de Janeiro made in 1960. Thirty men and ten women were interviewed in each *favela*. Half of the respondents were over thirty and half below thirty years of age. In addition, interviewers divided their work so that half was done in the more populous and easily accessible lower flanks of the *favela* and the remainder in the middle and upper reaches of the hills.

The sample of men obtained in the *favelas* ranged from sixteen to sixty-nine years, with a median age close to thirty as had been pre-established. Three out of five male respondents had families (with an average of four children), the remainder claiming bachelorhood except for a handful of widowers and men separated from their mates. A majority are in unskilled occupations in industry, services, or construction; about a third have trades or industrial skills. A sprinkling of white collars and small proprietors rounds out the occupational distribution. Just over one in five claim to have completed primary school; a negligible number (less than ten percent) have had some schooling beyond that. About one in four earn less than the minimum wage in Guanabara state; another twelve percent have no regular paid work. Almost all the remainder earn something close to or slightly above the minimum wage (9,600 cruzeiros or $38.50 per month at current exchange rates).[7]

Fully two-thirds of the *favela* men interviewed were of rural or small town origin; about half lived in farm areas or small towns for ten or more years before coming to Rio. Their fathers were largely farmers or unskilled laborers. As a group, the respondents were only slightly above the fathers in years of schooling or occupational level.

The sample population thus did not differ in any important way from characterizations of the *favela* population that can be built up from other impressionistic or statistical studies. Though there is some variability in occupational level and earnings, the group in general clusters in the lowest rungs of the occupational scale, is receiving a subsistence wage, and has fairly recently emerged from the rural milieu.

INDICATORS OF PARTICIPATION AND INTEGRATION

There are a great many ways in which the *favelado's* sense of connection with the larger society and his active participation in national life might be measured. The research program of which the study described here is a part has as an important objective the empirical testing of a particular theoretical formulation of the nature of national identification. The complete analysis of the data will hopefully lead to the derivation of a number of indexes of relevant attitudinal and behavioral dimensions. This preliminary glance at the results will only examine singly a number of the items that seem most relevant for *favelados*.

Brazil is one of the Latin American countries with the most impressive records of economic growth in recent years. The average rate of growth from 1955 to 1959 in gross national product per capita with 4.2 percent, a rate exceeded only by Venezuela and Guatemala. In contrast with these countries and with Mexico, which also shows impressive growth, Brazil's advances have been constant during those years and outdistanced all of them in 1959 (Borges, 1961). One way of testing the *favelado's* sense of sharing in what goes on in the nation is to ascertain the extent to which he perceives national economic growth as producing real gains to himself. When asked in February of 1961 whether things had improved, had remained about the same, or had become worse for him during the last five years, nearly one out of two *favelados* replied that his present situation is worse. Another three out of ten found that their situation remained much the same.

TABLE 1   *"In the last five years did things improve, get worse, or remain about the same for you?"*

	Men	Women
Improved	21%	10%
Remained the same	30	24
Got worse	49	66
Total (percent)	100	100
Number of cases	150	50

As can be seen in Table 1, the response of the women is even more negative than that of the men. For the *favelado*, the gains shown in the economic indexes which he never sees are overshadowed by the constant pressure of rising prices. "It's the high cost of everything," says one. "What do I gain by earning 9,600 cruzeiros if I can't eat. When I earned 4,000, I was able to live better."

The general sensation that things have not improved noticeably for themselves has not created any great disillusion among *favelados* with the idea of industrialization as a road to prosperity. The *favelado* does not deny that the nation's industrial growth has produced benefits for people like himself; he only states that his own situation has not changed appreciably. Thus, when asked immediately after the above question whether the growth of industry had benefited people like themselves, most answered affirmatively. Their explanation, however, was almost entirely in terms of the expansion of job opportunities *for others* — friends, acquaintances, or simply other Brazilians.

Another way of testing the nature and strength of the social links between the *favela* population and important outside individuals, groups, and institutions was through a question that asked respondents whether they believed in the sincerity of the desire of various outsiders to help solve the problems of *favelados*. Again the results are not very heartening. *Favelados* harbor few illusions about the concern felt by important officials and other figures of power and influence in the nation with respect to the situation in the *favelas*. Strikingly, two of the groups that traditionally

TABLE 2 *"Brazil has been building many new industries. Do you think that has improved the life of people like yourself, or not?"*

	Men	Women
Yes	67%	42%
No	26	38
Don't Know	7	20
Total (percent)	100	100
Number of cases	150	50

have stood as champions of the poor in Latin America (labor unions and university students) are least regarded by *favelados* as helpful. The police, schoolteachers, and priests are most often cited as sources of real assistance though the most impressive finding is the apparent extent of the feeling that nobody outside the *favela* really cares about what is happening there.

The large proportion who approve the action of the police in the *favela*, despite frequent reports of arbitrariness and other abuses by individual police officers, reveals the genuine interest of most *favelados* in curbing the disorder and delinquency that disrupts life in their communities. Yet the police and teachers, though acknowledged as truly helping make life easier for *favelados*, are hardly ever credited with doing anything beyond what their assigned duties call for in behalf of the *favela*. The seventeen percent who credited priests with making an exceptional effort in behalf of *favelados* similarly referred to the fact that the Church or religious

TABLE 3 *"In your opinion do (insert name of group) give sincere help to people living in the favelas or not?"*

	Percent who say group does NOT help sincerely	
	Men	Women
University students	89%	96%
Labor unions	87	88
Journalists	81	94
The State Governor	75	80
The military	73	94
The President of Brazil	71	76
Priests	67	68
Schoolteachers	57	62
The police	45	46
Number of cases	150	50

orders sometimes permit *favelados* to occupy land without paying rent rather than to any direct pastoral activities by priests themselves.

Does the wholesale denial by *favelados* that outside groups have any real interest in the problems of people in the slums mean that the *favelado* feels entirely shut out from the larger society? A comparison of *favelado* responses with results from a similar study of skilled workers in Sao Paulo provides an opportunity to test still other aspects of integration and participation. The comparison is of interest because the sample of skilled workers is actually very similar in background and composition to the sample of men in the *favela*. The fathers of the skilled workers show much the same educational and occupational pattern as those of the *favelados;* the skilled workers are also predominantly of rural origin, only slightly older as a group, with somewhat smaller families and moderately higher schooling. They are in short, only a step ahead of the *favelados* in the transition from the rural to the industrial world; they differ from *favelados* primarily in that all have industrial skills, all work within a modern industrial organization, and their average earnings are between two and three times greater than those of *favelados*.[8]

Three questions are especially relevant for the present purpose — one testing the degree to which the respondents regard the society as "open" to upward movement, a second touching on sense of political efficacy, and a third composite question on political participation. The first of these items shows the most striking differences between the two groups. The workers who have moved into the nation's new industrial elite almost unanimously believe that high status occupations in almost every field are open to any capable person in Brazil.[9] Though considerably less sanguine than skilled workers in this respect, a majority of the *favelado* men still believe that the way up is not barred to their children, especially in busi-

TABLE 4 *"Do you believe that any person with the necessary capacity can become a _____?" (Question asked of skilled workers.) "Do you think a child from the favela here can become a _____?" (Question asked of favelados.)*

| | Proportion answering "YES" | | |
| | Skilled | Favelados | |
	Workers	Men	Women
High government official	93%	73%	50%
Owner of a large business	91	71	50
University professor	90	63	42
Lawyer	91	59	38
Deputy (Lower House of the National Legislature)	88	54	38
Number of cases	173	150	50

TABLE 5 *"In the last six months, did you _____?"*

	Proportion answering "YES"		
	Skilled	*Favelados*	
	Workers	*Men*	*Women*
Attend a party meeting	12%	17%	4%
Attend a union meeting	46	12	4
Discuss politics heatedly with a friend	19	19	6
Participate in a public manifestation or rally	17	24	8
Work intensively in politics*	6	14	6
Number of cases	173	150	50

* The phrasing for *favelados* was: *"did you work hard for a political party?"*

ness and government service. The *favela* mothers are notably more pessimistic than the men about the life chances of their children.

Thus the *favelado,* however unrealistically, does not feel hopelessly trapped in the *favela*. He sees the chances for escape of his children as good. But the apparent faith in the possibilities for economic and social advance is not matched by belief in the potential benefits to come through political action. Nearly half of the *favelados* said there is nothing to be gained by political activity, (*nao vale a pena tomar parte na política*); about the same proportion of skilled workers said they attach little or no importance to their political opinions and activities. Thus neither the skilled worker nor the *favelado* is highly politicized; the skilled worker differs politically from the *favelado* chiefly in his participation in an *organization* (his union) that is set up to defend his interests.

With all their limitations, these findings support the contention that the problem of the *favela* is not primarily one of social disorganization within the confines of the *favela* itself but rather one of the relationship between the *favela* and the rest of the society. As the final table below shows, the *favelado* to an amazing degree is conscious of receiving a fair amount of social support from those who surround him *within* the *favela*. Despite the conflict, frequent aggression, exploitativeness, and insecurity of personal relationships that according to the accounts of all observers are commonplace in the *favela*, the *favelado* himself feels that he is part of a fairly cohesive, solidary group. It is vis-à-vis the world outside the *favela* that he feels bypassed, forgotten, and excluded.

The indifference toward the *favelado* of the government and of private citizens is not as absolute as these findings suggest; a small number of dedicated people are working hard to ease the *favelado*'s situation. *Favelados* themselves have formed a few small associations that try to bring

TABLE 6   *"Do you think that the people who live in the favelas are very united, more or less united, only a little united, or disunited?"*

	Men	Women
Very united	35%	22%
More or less united	37	44
Only a little united	20	12
Disunited	7	20
Don't know	1	2
Total (percent)	100	100
Number of cases	150	50

some order and organization into *favela* life. But the groups at work simply do not have the money or the people to do more than give limited aid to a fraction of those in trouble or to improvise momentary stopgaps for situations that ran out of control long ago. The job of human and material rehabilitation that the city confronts grows relentlessly despite such efforts.

The *Fundacao Leao XIII*, basically an educational and social work agency, has been active longest of all (since 1947). The *Fundacao* was formerly financed by Rio's municipal government. After the national capital moved inland to Brasilia in 1960, the new Guanabara state government, which replaced the former federal district, has continued to support the *Fundacao*. In the most recent appropriation, the organization received about $200,000. *Fundacao* elementary schools currently reach some 1,400 children in seven *favelas*. These schools provide the regular primary-school curriculum with additional religious instruction. Social service centers function out of the schools, providing personal counseling, home economics, vocational training, and community organization services. Medical and dental care is also made available as well as a free prescription service and legal aid.

The *Cruzada Sao Sebastiao*, a lay group that functions through Rio's Archbishopric, began activity in 1956 with a fifty million cruzeiro grant from the Cafe Filho government. More importantly, the *Cruzada* was granted development rights over certain coastal lands in Guanabara state. The proceeds from the development of these lands have been applied in the construction of low-income apartments, the installation of water tanks, electrification, and other improvements in *favelas*. Funds have also been used for emergency aid in fires and floods for returning some migrants to rural areas. Ten large blocks of apartments have been built by the *Cruzada* on lands adjacent to the *Praia do Pinto favela*. The 900 apartments in those seven-story blocks will soon be totally occupied by former *fave-*

lados from the *Praia do Pinto*. After 15 years of paying a nominal rent (about ten percent of the minimum wage) the tenants will get legal title to the apartments. The buildings already occupied are maintained and administered by tenants' councils. A school, playground, and community center function on project grounds. Officials of the *Cruzada* report a ready adjustment to apartment living among the new tenants. Other experiments are being made with provisional housing that can be built cheaply from a simple blueprint on regularly plotted lots. But with great effort the *Cruzada* has managed to build no more than about 200 housing units per year, while many times that many families were pouring into the *favelas*.

In a recent regional meeting of state governors with President Quadros, the new Guanabara state government pressed strongly for federal assistance for the construction of low-cost housing and for the razing and "urbanization" of *favelas*. An impressive array of photographs was put together to point up the urgency of the situation on officials of the national government. So stark were the photographs that the exhibit was not opened to the public until legends had been added explaining what is being done or projected to solve the city's multiple problems. The State governor also asked President Quadros to support a State request for a $10,000,000 credit for housing construction from the Inter-American Development Bank. No immediate, substantial money has as yet been assured for this work.

In the meantime, the State government's Special Service for the Rehabilitation of *Favelas* and Anti-Hygienic Dwellings (SERFHA) has just announced a new self-help program for *favelados*, called *Operacao Mutirao*. The *mutirao* is a form of collective work common in Brazil's rural areas as in many agricultural regions. The present, urban *mutirao* is based on formal agreements between SERFHA and the local *favela* organizations. At a recent ceremony two *favela* organizations signed contracts agreeing to co-operate with SERFHA in a joint effort to improve and control construction, to better living conditions, and to enforce the law in their *favelas*. Another step announced by SERFHA's director, along with *Operacao Mutirao*, is the elimination of the word *favela* from the official lexicon; henceforth the *favelas* are to be known as *"vilas."*

Public officials facing overwhelming jobs with no resources can perhaps be forgiven for resorting to tricks of public relations to sustain the illusion of governmental action. Brazil's cities just do not have the capacity to absorb and regenerate the victims of its backward agriculture. The *favela* dramatizes what is wrong with the modern city everywhere, but it is also at last forcing into the national consciousness the plight of the mass of rural Brazilians. For the urban Brazilian, the *favela* is a most powerful argument in favor of agrarian reform.

NOTES

1. Researchers at UNESCO's Latin American Social Science Research Center in Rio identified 132 *favelas* on aerial maps of the city taken in 1960. A recent police report put the number at 194 and estimated the total *favela* population as close to a million (*Correio da Manha*, July 1, 1961).

2. *Correio da Manha*, June 30, 1961.

3. According to the 1950 census thirteen percent of Rio's population was Negro (*preto*). In a present estimated population of about three million, that would give about 400,000 *pretos*. If the present *favela* population is close to 900,000, as estimated by the police, and the proportion of *pretos* among *favelados* is still close to forty percent, practically all of Rio's Negroes must be in *favelas*. See "Aspectos Humanos da Favela Carioca," *O Estado de Sao Paulo*, Suplemento Especial, April 13, 1960, page 8. Part II of this report appeared in a second supplement on April 15, 1960.

4. "Aspectos Humanos da Favela Carioca," *op. cit.*, note three, especially Part II.

5. *"Eu quando estou com fome quero matar o Janio, quero enforcar o Adhemar e queimar o Juscelino. As dificuldades corta o afeto do povo pelos politicos."* The three men named were the present president, Janio Quadros, his predecessor, Juscelino Kubitschek, and Adhemar de Barros, a candidate for the presidency in 1960.

6. The United Nations Educational, Scientific, and Cultural Organization and the Economic Commission for Latin America.

7. *Desenvolvimento & Conjuntura (Journal of the National Industrial Confederation of Brazil)* in the February 1961 issue reports that the minimum wage in Guanabara state was forty times higher in 1960 than in 1940 while the cost of living only multiplied twenty-nine times in the same interval. However, another article in the same issue commenting on the various cost of living indexes in Brazil states: " . . . the results obtained are entirely divergent, since there is no uniformity in the methods of calculation, criteria for weighing, rationale, and what is more important, the data reported seem to obey no particular logic" (page 96).

8. One hundred seventy-three skilled operatives with a wide variety of occupational specialties were interviewed within a single large industrial plant in Sao Paulo. A random sample was taken from pay rosters covering all workers with skilled job ratings.

9. The major conclusions of the most intensive study of social mobility in Brazil are the following. "First, industrial development did not produce a dissolution of class barriers as had been anticipated. Second, the greater access to the educational system did not produce an increase in social mobility" (Hutchinson, 1960:229).

8

Urban Relocation and Family Adaptation in Puerto Rico: A Case Study in Urban Ethnography

ROY SIMÓN BRYCE-LAPORTE[1]

In the early 1960's I was employed as a resident field researcher in the study of the family life of working mothers in Puerto Rico. My assignment involved three months of residence (with my family) in a low-income public housing project in Metropolitan San Juan (to be known in this study as El Caserió). During that period I became interested in the way of life in the housing project and proceeded to carry out a hurried *exploratory* study which comprises the basis of this paper. It is not my intention, therefore, to make of this paper an erudite or conclusive document but rather to utilize it to describe social relations and events, to raise suggestions and criticisms, and to stimulate sensitivity to problems still hidden in urban studies and urban services.

El Caserío was a low-income housing project of about 2000 persons. About forty percent of its population had been transferred from a nearby shanty-town (to be known in this study as El Arrabal, and its occupants as *arrabaleños*). The remaining sixty percent represented a motley of people from various other slums and rural areas.

Until its destruction El Arrabal was populated by poor though not necessarily illiterate people. Some were old residents of the city; others were recent migrants from rural areas and other urban slums who had come to live with relatives or to find cheap housing. They lived in dilapidated block or wooden shacks which were located on contiguous lots of land called *solares*. Often owned by a member of an extended family, the *solar* contained many shacks which housed other members of the larger family network. As the number of residents increased or as new conjugal relationships developed, the family's shack was extended or additional shacks were built nearby. This created the congestion which was a prevalent characteristic of slum living.

Many *arrabaleños* were unemployed; some were employed irregularly in menial work of some kind; only a few were small-time or *ad hoc* shopkeepers and peddlers. Robbery, fighting, rape, dope-trafficking, prostitution, and illicit marital and sex affairs allegedly prevailed in El Arrabal. Repeated assaults on strangers and government workers contributed to the official decision to destroy the site and relocate its inhabitants. The people were encouraged to sign petitions for public housing and to permit their properties to be 'expropriated' by the government. Following this they were assigned and finally transferred by government trucks to one of three housing projects available for occupancy.

One of these, El Caserío, was comprised of twenty-three multifamily tenement structures and an administrative and service complex. Located on a main throughway about twenty-five minutes by bus or taxi from downtown and from the former site of El Arrabal, it stood adjacent to a slum which had stores, churches, schools, and other commercial and public agencies directed to lower-income clientele. On the other sides it was bounded by a range of newly built middle-income projects, one of which housed a few former *arrabaleños* and former residents of El Caserío.

Like other federal housing projects, El Caserío was operated under certain legislation and policies which were modified by the insular corporation and its administrators to "suit" the local situation. These policies and their modifications were aimed at correcting the social ills and "improving" the moral health and the socioeconomic standards of the residents. The ultimate execution of these regulations was in the hands of a local administrator and her staff who resided elsewhere; only the members of the maintenance crew lived in the project.

For the *arrabaleños* to become eligible for quarters in El Caserío, they had to be a pair of adults of opposite sex or an adult with children; they had to be proven to have a joint monthly income of less than a poverty-line standard established by local housing authorities; and they had to pass a screening test on their moral background. Once they were considered eligible, the housing administration located them in apartments according to the size of the "family." An effort was made to disperse them throughout the project amid the *nonarrabaleños*. According to a local official, this was done "in order to break up the cliques, immorality, and messy practices among them." Once located there, they were not to utilize the premises for any business or public services nor to house additional persons without the approval of the local office. They were expected to pay rent promptly in accordance with their total income, and they were to be ejected or transferred if they violated these housing regulations.

The point is that El Caserío represented a radical change in ecology and formal community organization for the *arrabaleños*. Furthermore, it constituted an arena for the confrontation of the melioristic sentiments of government welfare agencies with certain traditional social practices and values of the *arrabaleños*. One wonders what kind of social organization emerged among the *arrabaleños* after four to five years of subjection to the apparently incompatible conditions imposed by a new ecological setting, new structure, and new administrative regulations represented by El Caserío. In this paper the question is to be directed specifically to the case of the large extended family or kin network which was once located on the contiguous lot or *solar*.

A brief questionnaire was administered to a sample of thirty-six heads of dwelling units or *apartamentos* among the *arrabaleños;* a general census was conducted of the entire population of the housing project. Almost one hundred percent of the *arrabaleño* sample indicated that they were among the original set of tenants to have come to El Caserío when it was first opened for public use. Most of the *nonarrabaleños* came to El Caserío in individual family groupings later than the *arrabaleños,* or from isolated rural sites. Almost seventy-five percent of the *arrabaleño* units reported having other adults from El Arrabal aside from the recognized heads (male and female). Less than fifty percent of the units reported the loss of former adult members who had lived with them in El Arrabal or had come since to El Caserío. Almost every *arrabaleño* dwelling unit had at least one kin tie with at least one other *arrabaleño* unit in or around El Caserío.

It may be inferred from these observations that the regulations and ecological impositions of El Caserío resulted in (1) disruption of the original large kin network and the contiguous residential pattern under which such networks existed in El Arrabal, as well as in (2) relocation of parts of the networks into separate and dispersed dwellings in and outside of El Caserío. Information from the questionnaire indicated that these smaller units covered a wide variety of structures: some units consisted of a single resident, usually an older woman; other units had only one parent present, usually a woman; units in which both parents were present were apt to include children from previous unions or relations; other units contained more than two generations, in which case the additional generation tended to be represented by women or relatives of the women of the house.

It would seem that family organization among the relocated *arrabaleños* was neolocal in residence and matrifocal in structure. However, such a conclusion could be premature and misleading, inasmuch as the statistics showed that each unit was related by kinship to other units in the housing project. Furthermore, in response to a question on their preferences for residential patterns of married couples, the *arrabaleños* were overwhelmingly in favor of such people living "close to" rather than "far from" or "with" other relatives. Mutual assistance and freedom from inter- or intrafamilial problems were presented as the basic reasons for their choice. These two later observations seem to suggest that the prevalent forms of family organization among the *arrabaleños* were not separate households or nuclear families but rather modified forms of extended families, characterized by *propinquity* or *nearness of residence*.

Participant observation and elaborate, in-depth interviewing were carried out with specific households. The case of one such household headed by Doña Dada, our next-door neighbor, will help to explain the nature of family organization of the *arrabaleños*. Doña Dada was a seventy-year-old *arrabeleña* who occupied a one-bedroom apartment with her only son's two boys (one five years old and the other four). Doña Dada's daily schedule of activities, when limited to the apartment and its occupants, included marketing at a nearby shop, cleaning, making breakfast which she shared with the two boys, watching TV with them, disciplining and caring for them, and sleeping. During most of the day Doña was not at home; when she was at home, the persons present with her were not residents of the dwelling unit. Hence to locate Doña and her grandsons, or to observe their activities for the major part of the day, one had to know her relatives, their addresses, and their regularized activities in and outside El Caserío.

As a member of one of the most extensive kin networks in the project, Doña Dada was related consanguineously to four other domestic groups dispersed throughout El Caserío. Two of the four units were comprised of her two daughters, one of a sister's daughter, and one of a daughter's daughter. More indirectly, she was related conjugally to three other units or domestic groups: to her son's present wife's parents; to one of her son's child's mother's mother; and to one of the sisters of our laundress who "lived" with Doña's sister's daughter. In addition, she was related to at least three groups which dwelled outside El Caserío: her son's which was located downtown; that of another daughter which was located in the other project; and two others in the Virgin Islands by way of sons of two of her daughters.

The activities between Doña and the members of these domestic groups (each in its separate dwelling place) were intimate, frequent, and significant. They included exchange of visits, mutual assistance of an economic and defensive nature, disciplining and caring for children, and decision making.

Visiting occurs throughout the day between the relatives of Doña who live in El Caserío. Her daughter's husband rarely was seen at her home or at the home of her sisters-in-law. Doña's son visited her twice each week, rarely went to his sister's or cousins', but in passing shouted to them or joked with their children. Doña made a weekly visit to a daughter in the other *caserío* and made her rounds regularly to kinsmen in El Caserío. She ate at either daughter's home; often a daughter or another adult female affine would bring her food. Whenever her grandchildren from St. Croix were in town, they and their spouses would spend some time with her. On occasion, when there were emotional problems and illness in the larger network Doña was called or consulted, and visiting took place within the group. On one occasion when one granddaughter's husband left her, she came from St. Croix to live with Doña. When Doña's daughter in the other *caserío* became ill, it was Doña who stayed with her and Doña who dressed in black when she died.

Almost every one of the local domestic groups in Doña's network was on relief. The three exceptions were the domestic groups of a daughter, of the son's wife, and of the son's ex-mother-in-law. Many of the younger men and women were unemployed frequently. Doña was supported partially by her son; the other working men supported their own groups; and, in cases where the male spouse was unemployed, the wife, the son, or brother did "private" chores to supplement welfare. Foodstuffs were loaned within the network, and when facilities were lacking or in need of repair, the work was done by members of the network. When Doña's TV set was damaged, she and her daughters and their children went to the home of a niece. When her son was unable to repair the set, his former father-in-law came to complete the work. A daughter who made *tortillas* sent her sons about the neighborhood to take orders with the help of their cousins. Her husband sold some on the streets. The profits were shared in the home, and leftovers were distributed to other members of the kin network.

Doña seemed to be the central figure of the network. While her orders were not always obeyed, usually they were not openly rebuffed. Her daughters and niece complained to others about the inadequacy of her decisions, but unless they conflicted with their own group's problems, they rarely complained to her. The women and their children tended to scold younger members of the other related domestic groups freely and with marked effectiveness. The husbands disciplined their own wives and children with great effectiveness, but rarely did they try to discipline others. While the wives tended to be the more active disciplinarians and decision-makers, the husbands tended to have the last word, especially if such decisions and actions had to do with outsiders, irregular situations, or economic issues.

In Doña's network there were obvious differentiations of activities and interaction in terms of distance of kin, distance of residence, age, and of course sex. Even though matrifocality is not a principal concern of this paper, the point may be made that it seems even more pronounced on this level than on that of the neolocal domestic unit. Male spouses, especially if employed and present in the home tended to exercise great latent authority within their own domestic unit, and were particularly active on certain occasions. Their authority, however, was limited to their own domestic unit as opposed to the women, whose authority crossed domestic units. In contrast to Doña's central position, the few grandfathers tended to enjoy strong control only over their grandchildren (if they lived in the same domestic unit), but little rapport — much less control — over their sons or daughters-in-law (even if they lived in the same unit). Husbands tended to remain uninvolved in the affairs of their consanguineal relatives and to avoid the affairs of their married sisters.

Helen Icken Safa has advanced the notion that matrifocality is a prevailing characteristic of households in Puerto Rican public housing projects (1964:3–12; 1965:135–139). The observations made in this study do not challenge the high incidence and probability of such authority structures nor the reasons advanced, i.e., high male employment or underemployment. However, they do call for some qualifications inasmuch as strong, authoritative fathers did exist in large numbers in El Caserío, even among the *arrabaleños*. It was noticeable, however, that their authority was often latent, was executed at prescribed times, and was particularly operative on the level of individual, isolated, nuclear units. The scope of authority of male spouses within the larger extended family was relatively more limited than that of the women. Hence these observations raise questions regarding *levels* of matrifocality within modified extended family and multiple household situations. In fact, as Hazel Dubois (unpublished) has argued, one advantage of studying matrifocality from the level of the community, or of some higher form of social organization than the family or household, is that it provides the broad perspective necessary (1) to discern variation, complexity, and levels of operation of the phenomenon, and (2) to determine the extent to which it constitutes a shared pattern or a deviation within the larger cultural or subcultural context.

Some incidents and behavior patterns observed in El Caserío may help to shed light on the complex functioning of the principle of matrifocality among *arrabaleños* and *nonarrabaleños*. One set of questions was asked of each spouse of the larger population of El Caserío: "What person in the world do you respect most? . . . love most? . . . obey most?" Perhaps the single answer that we received most frequently was "Mi Mama." This answer usually was repeated for each of the questions, with an expression which said, "Isn't it natural? Could there be another answer?" This was true even in cases where the respondent's mother was deceased or living in continental U.S.A. The presence of the other spouse during the interview made little difference in most cases, even though the respondent would look at his spouse (somewhat apologetically) and say to me, "Well, that is a hard one, but I think I will have to say my mother." Verbal opposition to this response was never voiced in my presence by the spouse.

Despite this, it was my general experience that when interviewing women (especially of households *where men were away at work*) about financial or governmental matters, many would say, "Well, that you will have to ask of my husband. That is the man's business." In fact some would refuse to answer the questionnaire and ask that I return when their husbands were at home. One woman actually asked me to promise that I would cause her no trouble, because while she wanted to cooperate she did not want it to seem that she was taking her husband's place; she did not want to disobey him, nor give information that he would not like me to know, or that would cause him trouble. She did not want to infuriate her husband nor did she want to *lose* him.

One night there was a fight between two neighbors — a male homosexual and an older man. In the midst of the argument the mother of the homosexual (who, like her son, was a bit drunk) started to intervene in her son's behalf. Some of the men bystanders started to shout to the woman, "Why don't you stay out of it; this is men's business. Why don't you behave like a woman, a mother?" The older man tried to ignore and avoid the woman's intervention. She evaded one of the bystanders who was trying to prevent her from entering the brawl, and struck the older man who was fighting with her son. The older man responded by giving her two stiff slaps in the face. The bystander suddenly attacked the older man, hitting him ferociously and shouting hysterically, "Never hit a woman. She could be your mother or mine!"

These observations suggest that women (but more so mothers than wives, and wives more so than married sisters) do enjoy a preferred status in El Caserío. Yet, there are obvious limitations to what they can do (compared to their husbands, especially if the latter were employed), and what can or cannot be done to them (by men in general). Matrifocality in El Caserío, like any other form of role status or power principle, is complex. It must be understood relative to the various interacting parties and the situations or conditions under which it occurs. This broader perspective makes it possible to appreciate the principle involved, the various forms of its application, and the logic which relates them to each other.

During the period of our stay a few incidents were observed by us or related to us which indicated some other organizational-interactional consequences on the family life of the *arrabaleños*. These involved members of the network described above, and were directly related to their relocation in a new, different, structural-ecological milieu; in addition, they illustrate life in the larger caserío.

In El Arrabal Señor C. had been living in a shack with his wife and children, while his mother lived in another shack close by. To assure that his mother would obtain an *apartamento*, Señor C. declared himself to be living with her rather than with his wife and children. His mother was assigned an *apartamento* with him in a downtown housing project, and his wife and children were assigned quarters in El Caserío, the uptown project. At first Señor C. and his family visited frequently, and he supported them. Gradually, the visits between the units decreased, the wife had to ask the courts to withhold family support from his salary, and Señor C. became involved romantically with women who lived closer to his official residence. There was also a young woman who was in an advanced stage of pregnancy. She and the father, whom she said she had recently "married," lived with his parents in El Caserío. They claimed to be waiting in hopes that a vacant *apartamento* in El Caserío would be made available to them. *Urban relocation resulted in the destruction of a formerly stable, conjugal, coresidential family unit by eliminating contiguity or propinquity.*

Another incident occurred when a child who lived with Doña Dada, earlier described as the central figure of the network, could not be found anywhere in El Caserío. There was great anxiety among members of the network and among the neighbors. By afternoon the boy returned in the company of his father. He had hiked the long distance to town to visit his father's home. The grandmother and the others were relieved that he had returned, and he was not scolded. Gradually he began to do this more frequently, sometimes in the company of other boys of the network or neighborhood, without his grandmother's knowledge, and often on the spur of the moment. Whenever he was missing, the grandmother presumed that he was visiting his father, even though he may have wandered elsewhere. *Urban relocation not only has disrupted the normal propinquity between consanguinial or primary relatives, but also, in the absence of economic or transportational means, has introduced new and more extensive visiting patterns, has minimized opportunities for supervising children, and has complicated the traditional authority-responsibility structure.*

One of the daughters of Señor C. was ordered by the doctor to remain at "home" because she had the measles. As I moved around the project to interview residents I kept meeting the girl. Each time I would remind her of the doctor's orders, and she would respond, "Si, el doctor me dijo que me quedara en casa y que no fuera a la escuela. Doña Tal y Tal es mi familia, pues esta es mi casa." ("Yes, the doctor told me to stay home and not to go to school. But Mrs. So-and-So is my relative, so this is my home.") There may have been misunderstanding between the doctor's limited connotation of family and the girl's extended connotation. It is also possible that the girl may have understood the doctor very well, and that she was using the bicultural orientation so obvious among the adults to engage in some "ecstatic role playing," e.g., playing the fool, in order to rationalize her actions (Berger, 1963:152). Notwithstanding, *urban relocation has created problems of communication and control between middle class professionals and their target population by removing the common or traditional context of contiguous family organization.*

A close friend of this girl's mother and of the network was expelled from the project because she was "scandalous and a trouble-maker who couldn't get along with her neighbors." The woman, an *arrabaleña*, distributed her children for care between her sister (who lived in El Caserío) and a friend. During the days she worked as a laundress in the metropolitan area; at night she stole into the project to sleep with her sister or her friend. Doña Dada would be visited by a granddaughter from the Virgin Islands whenever she was having difficulties with her husband. This girl's aunt (a daughter of Doña Dada who lived in the downtown project) became seriously ill, and Doña Dada made frequent trips to help the dying woman. Each time she would complain that these two "girls" should have done what other *arrabaleños* did when they could not secure lodging in El Caserío: they should have moved close to the project and lived with her secretly as the laundress had done when she was evicted from El Caserío. *Urban relocation, because it separated relatives, created hardships on the arrabaleños and influenced them to maintain the tradition of the extended family by latent means and at irregular occasions.*

Adults were absent from many household units in El Caserío during the day. Few "families" could afford to hire a babysitter or nurse or to send their children to private nurseries. The housing project's day-care and nursery-kindergarten service, which included a teacher, a cook, and facilities for playing, sleeping, and eating, was attended regularly by only ten children. The *arrabaleños* did not use this service but were inclined to let their children roam in the yards. Sometimes children, unaccompanied by an adult, would be seen in the streets of the project coming home after midnight from a visit with relatives or friends. On a few occasions one little girl was seen playing on the balcony or in the courtyard of a relative's home after midnight, waiting for her mother who was late in coming home. The child probably felt safer in the courtyard or outdoors in night clothing (but within access of her relatives) than in the isolated and "dangerous" *apartamento* alone.

Even though these situations occurred in one housing project and in one network, students of Puerto Rican culture know that the generalizations are applicable to a much larger population of the island. In particular, the tradition of the extended family is maintained tenaciously by all classes of Puerto Rican society, though the role behavior differs among them. The upper classes manifest the extended family in political and economic coalitions and partnerships; the middle class in visiting patterns and mutual assistance; and the lower classes in residential patterns and mutual assistance. The lower class differs from other classes in its lack of the economic and educational tools with which to overcome geographical distance, e.g., money, vehicles, telephones, and so on. Thus, they tend to prefer common, contiguous, or propinquitous residence, and redevelopment rather than relocation; in this context, their latent, irregular patterns of organization and interaction are understandable.

Although rapid industrialization and urbanization have created more opportunities and demands for Puerto Rican women to work away from home, some Puerto Rican women always have worked away from home — usually women without dependent children or women with relatives who would serve as surrogate mothers to their children. Today upper and middle class women use nurseries or have maids, nurses, or babysitters when they must work away from home; lower class women rely on members of the extended family or neighbors, close friends, or fictive relatives in nearby *solares. Urban relocation not only imposed a different structural-ecological setting on its target population, but it also deprived them of many traditional adaptive means for overcoming the obstacles which the new environment presented. The family organization of the relocated continues to be different from traditions of other sectors of the society; the difference is not necessarily pathological or deviant, but rather adaptive to the conflict or disparity between valued ends and available means.* (Such adaptations Hyman Rodman calls the "lower class value stretch"; 1963:205–15.)

The housing project has been described as an arena of confrontation between melioristically inspired innovations or impositions and the tenacious traditions and aspirations of lower class peoples. Incidents have been recounted which demonstrate the consequences of this confrontation in the emergence of a new level of family organization among relocated slum dwellers. This form of organization — typified by Doña Dada and the *arrabaleños* of El Caserío — and known to social scientists as the *modified extended family* (Litwack, 1960a:178) is not confined to Puerto Rico but is increasing in incidence and complexity in other areas undergoing rural-urban development. In Black communities in Los Angeles we encountered active contiguous and noncontiguous extended families (Epling, unpublished). Such family forms are evident among both the established middle class and recently arriving Southern immigrants; in most cases these families still had relatives, "roots," or significant references in the rural South (see also Lewis, 1952:31–41; Marris, 1960:123–28). Urban social scientists and others in the applied sciences — social workers, planners, and demographers, even businessmen, public administrators, and technologists — give no more than lip-service to the new family forms (Sussman, 1962:231–40). The new family structures receive slight benefit from supportive planning or social action; experts often ignore them or categorize them among the pathos of the poor rather than as a by-product of prevailing inequalities (Mills, 1943:165–184). Their thrust then becomes rather to eliminate than to appreciate such family structure, and to challenge the afflicted population rather than the larger society.

In El Caserío there was a noticeable abundance of older adolescents and young people who seemed to be neither in school nor employed. The most common reason given by them for not working (or for not reporting their employment or source of income if they *were* working) was to prevent their families from being evicted from the housing project because they had surpassed the income level for residence in El Caserío. There were many other manifestations of this principle in El Caserío. There was the fireman who *secretly* owned and drove a pirate-taxi to earn money to put his son through private school. There was the carpenter foreman who could not accept a raise in salary since his salary would have been raised to a level beyond the income limitation for residence in El Caserío but would not have been great enough for him to afford a down payment on a private home in the middle income project. There were the persons who peddled goods or minor services for much needed extra income or to give some meaning to their lives. However, these same people had to hide their items or tools in the bedrooms and restrooms of their *apartamentos*. Hence, aside from its impact on family organization, *urban relocation promoted an unnecessary negative and subversive attitude toward activities that would normally be considered indices of the drive, ingenuity, and independence believed to be so necessary for socio-economic advancement and family autonomy in a society based on free enterprise.*

Most academicians, activists, and applied technologists continue to misinterpret the behavior of the lower class as *problems*. Sociologist Hyman

Rodman (1964:59–69) has urged that it be viewed instead as poor people's *solutions* to their problems. This study supports the view that, inasmuch as they are shared adjustments, the new behavior patterns are subcultural differences rather than indices of deviation or disorganization. However, to the extent that these solutions are adjustments, they are limiting and problematic inasmuch as poor and deprived minorities do not have the power, resources, or prestige to develop a supporting system or conducive setting for *their* solutions. Moreover, many of the new problems of the poor, including the limiting, adjustive subculture as well as the hostile or disparate conditions, can be attributed to melioristically inspired social scientists and their colleagues in the applied sciences. These new problems are often more complicated than the old because they are not anticipated, often not properly abstracted, and therefore not accompanied by any traditional or experimental effort to adjust or to solve them. Poor people often suffer not only from the merciless exploitation of their enemies but also from the naive exigencies of their "friends." They suffer *latent or secondary* problems which emanate from the misconceived and miscalculated solutions of such friends.

Still untried (to the best of my knowledge) are *schemes in urban planning and administration which begin with the primary and deliberate objective of maintaining the traditional extended family in a noncongested, modern environment, but, in contiguous or propinquitous space.* With respect to the traditional family such an orientation would lead to questions which are more specific than those which dominate the minds of urban experts and authorities today. What specific aspects of urban development can be implemented without necessarily disrupting the traditional family? What losses are sustained by the society when urban development destroys the traditional family? What measures can compensate for such losses? What would be the short-run and long-run consequences of an urban development scheme which took as its primary goal the maintenance of the extended family?

Such an orientation would lead social scientists, social engineers, and social workers to be less concerned with *correcting* deviant or distasteful behavioral patterns *per se,* and more concerned with *understanding* the adequacy or efficiency of these behaviors in terms of their context, consequences, and the conditions which produce them. They would be inclined toward a more humanistic, but nevertheless scientific, set of guidelines for their decision-making in urban development, renewal, or relocation. The framework is simple enough: decisions about retaining or removing the old context should be made in terms of (1) enhancing traditional forms which are adequate, (2) eliminating inadequate forms and undesired consequences, and (3) fostering desired objectives. Such guidelines should help experts to anticipate with precision the short- and long-run acceptance, adaptations, resistance, and rejection of their schemes and services by the target population (Bryce-Laporte, 1968:538–539; Litwack, 1960a:177–186; Seda-Bonilla, 1965:13–22). To follow these guidelines experts would need to research the intricacy and essence of the "everyday life" of their target population whose living conditions would have to be accepted as manifestations of conflict or disparity between valued ends and inadequate means. Experts who claim to be "friends" of the poor, but who serve as consultants to clients other than the poor, would learn that such clients may represent powerful, prestigious, and articulate interest groups which are unconcerned with the legitimate values and viable adaptations of the poor and "underdeveloped" to their conditions of life.

NOTES

1. This article is a revised version of a paper presented at 1967 meetings of the Society of Applied Anthropology in Washington, D.C. This study was supported under Grants MH-6445 and MH-05870 of NIMH and carried out under the aegis of the Social Science Program, Commonwealth Department of Public Health, Puerto Rico (then directed by Professor Howard Stanton).

9

A Study of the Urbanization Process among Mixtec Migrants from Tilantongo in Mexico City

DOUGLAS S. BUTTERWORTH

Since Ralph Beals called attention to the fact that sociologists have paid much more attention to urbanism than to urbanization, pointing out that the "primary sociological concern has been with the nature of the urban society rather than with the processes of urbanism or the adaptation of men to urban life" (Beals, 1951), sociologists and anthropologists have directed some attention to the processes of urbanization. In Latin America, the dozen or so years which have elapsed since Beals's call for interdisciplinary research in urbanization and migration processes have seen the appearance of a number of significant studies in those areas (Lewis, 1957; Mangin, 1960a; Fried, 1959; Whetten and Burnight, 1956; United Nations, 1957; Davis and Casis, 1946; Leonard, 1948; Caplow, 1949). Although such studies have only begun to scratch the surface of

"A Study of the Urbanization Process among Mixtec Migrants from Tilantongo in Mexico City" by Douglas S. Butterworth is reprinted from *America Indigena,* 22:257–274, 1962, by permission of the author and publisher.

urbanization and migration problems, they indicate that many traditional concepts concerning urbanization are not applicable to Latin America, or apply only with important reservations and modifications.

Oscar Lewis concluded from his study of Tepozteco migratory patterns that perhaps "some of the sociological generalizations concerning urbanization which have been accepted until now may be culturally limited and require a new examination in the light of comparative studies of urbanization in other areas" (Lewis, 1957).

Some of the sociological generalizations concerning the distinctive features of the urban way of life to which Lewis refers have been described by Wirth as consisting of "the substitution of secondary for primary contacts, the weakening of bonds of kinship, and the declining social significance of the family, the disappearance of the neighborhood, and the undermining of the traditional basis of social solidarity" (Wirth, 1938). The result of these urban processes is that the individual is reduced to impotency and thus joins organized groups in order to obtain his ends (Wirth, 1938).

"Whereas in the sacred, simple society the worst that occurs is a schism of values, allowing the person to take one side or the other, in the metropolis the individual is living in the presence of multiple definitions of proper conduct" (Ericksen, 1954). Disorganization and maladaptation are the presumed consequences of the kaleidoscopic series of changes which face the rural migrant in the city. The secular life of the city has also been thought to be an important negative influence on religious values. Personal relations become segmented and the urbane sophisticate, the "city slicker," develops.

It has been assumed *a priori* that persons migrating to the city will adopt the traits which are supposedly characteristic of the urban population. By virtue of his move to the city, the peasant becomes "emancipated from the control of ancestral custom, enjoying this new freedom, but at the same time suffering by the release from intimate group participation and responsibility" (Ericksen, 1954). The rather uneasy accommodation developing out of the urbanization process, we are told, results in the acquisition by the migrant of "an organ protecting him against the threatening currents and discrepancies of his external environment which would uproot him" (Simmel, 1957).

The investigation undertaken by this writer does not tend to support the great majority of the assumptions concerning the urbanization process among migrants.[1] During the past nine months the investigator has been studying Mixtec Indian migrant settlers in Mexico City from the Municipio of Tilantongo, State of Oaxaca.[2] The purpose of the study is to compare the differences in the lives of the migrants in Mexico City with the way of life followed in Tilantongo.

Interviews were conducted among thirty-one families from Tilantongo who have migrated to Mexico City. Life history materials were gathered in varying depth from the family heads. Participant observation was utilized to the maximum extent possible. Interviews and participant observation ranged from a minimum of one-half hour to a maximum of about 120 hours for each family. A two week ethnographic investigation (the first of a planned series) was made in Tilantongo in order to gather comparative data for the study.

The families studied by this investigator may not be typical of the migrants, Indian or otherwise, in urban centers in Latin America, Mexico, or, for that matter, Mexico City. Nevertheless, since we do not know what is "typical," the phenomena indicated in this study may have some useful bearing upon the problems of migration and urbanization. Basil Zimmer has pointed out that "important as migration is to the city, very little is known concerning the behavior of migrants in these centers" (Zimmer, 1955).

Tilantongo is a community in the Mixteca Alta. Within an area of 258.94 square kilometers live 3,701 people (Dirección General de Estadística, 1960), resulting in a population density of 14.29 persons per square kilometer. Although these figures do not indicate a serious overpopulation problem, such a problem does, in fact, exist. Tilantongo is an agricultural community, relying almost exclusively upon maize and wheat for subsistence. I estimate that less than ten percent of the land in Tilantongo is suitable for cultivation. If ninety percent of the total land area is nonarable, the population density takes on a new significance. A high natural birth rate combined with fragmentation of land, poverty of the soil, and frequent crop failures have caused many Tilantongueños to migrate to urban centers. The principal motive for migration is economic.

Between 1930 and 1940, a decade which saw little migration from Tilantongo, the population of the municipio grew from 2,782 to 3,463, a 25.4 percent increase (Direccíon General de Estadística, 1940). Emigration of the native-born population began in large numbers after World War II; nevertheless, the decade from 1940 to 1950 still saw a 13.8 percent increase in population, from 3,463 to 3,941 (Direccíon General de Estadística, 1950). Since 1950 migration to urban areas from Tilantongo has accelerated to the point where the population of the community is now declining. The 1960 census figure of 3,701 inhabitants for the municipio of Tilantongo denotes a population loss of slightly more than six percent since 1950 (Dirección General de Estadística, 1960). However, if we accept the 1930–40 increase of 24.5 percent as the "natural" growth of Tilantongo, it would appear that migration might be claiming as much as thirty percent of those born in the community. That figure is much too high, though, because those who migrate from Tilantongo are mostly in the eighteen to thirty-five age group, the most fertile part of the population. The population pyramid of Tilantongo has a peculiar hour-glass shape, bulging at the base, thinning to half the size in the middle, and widening again after the thirty to thirty-four age group is passed, only to become more slender than ever when we enter the forty age groups. The poor representation of the fifteen to thirty-four age groups in the pyramid indicates that the fertility rate cannot be nearly so high nowadays as the natural increase in the '20's showed it to be before large-scale migration began.

Migration from Tilantongo has not been in waves, but rather in a steadily increasing stream. Although some of the earlier migrants went first to smaller cities, such as Oaxaca, Veracruz, and Puebla, as indeed some still do today, the general pattern has not been one of step-wise migration from village to small city to capital city, which is characteristic of migration in other Latin American countries, and thought to be characteristic of Mexico as well (United Nations, 1957). Today the majority of migrants from Tilantongo go directly from their community to Mexico City.

The first emigrant from Tilantongo of whom the investigator has knowledge went first to Mexico City, then to Puebla, where he has resided for over thirty years. The first to settle permanently in Mexico City went directly there from Tilantongo fifteen years ago, after having previously spent three years in the capital city as a boy with his father. The informant made the move from Tilantongo principally for economic reasons. Upon arriving in Mexico City he worked as an unskilled laborer in various jobs for three years until he gained employment with a large firm in the city as an unskilled laborer. He advanced in the company until he attained the position of supervisor of general services. The history of this informant is gone into in some detail because he has become a significant influence on many of the migrants from Tilantongo who followed in his footsteps to Mexico City. Since he has risen to his present position, the man has found employment for twenty-one other migrants from Tilantongo with his firm, and has become the informal leader of a large segment of the Tilantongueños now residing in the capital city.

The term "informal leader" should not be interpreted to imply that there is an organization or cooperative alliance among the migrants from Tilantongo. Indeed one of the most striking aspects of the group of Tilantongueños now living in Mexico City is the complete absence of any formal or informal participation in organizations. Although Tilantongo has probably one of the largest migrant populations from the Mixteca in Mexico City, it is not an official member of the *Coalición de Pueblos Mixtecos Oaxaqueños*, an organization in Mexico City which protects the interests of its member communities of the Mixteca. Of the thirty-one family heads from Tilantongo known by the investigator, none is a member of a sodality of any sort, with the exception of the informal leader, who is a member of the *Instituto Nacional de la Juventud Mexicana*. Informal organization is limited to weekend get-togethers of relatives and compadres.

The writer found some support for the "fairly well-established dictum of urban studies that people tend to settle among their own kind" (Beals, 1951). Twenty-seven of the thirty-one informant families live in adjacent *colonias* near the airport on the eastern outskirts of Mexico City. There are many other Tilantongueños scattered throughout the rest of the city, but to the investigator's knowledge there is no other section of Mexico City which has a clustering of families from Tilantongo to the extent which have the *colonias* tangent to the Mexico-Puebla highway near the airport. Those *colonias* have many of the aspects of the "squatter settlement" typical of many large cities throughout the world.

As opposed to the declining industrial area slum, the "mushroom slum," of which the above section of Mexico City is an example, is characterized by rapid, haphazard settlement by rural migrants. There is at first no water or sewage, no electricity, no political organization nor recognition by the municipal government. Lots are purchased or merely claimed by the squatter, everyone being an "owner." Houses of adobe, brick, or cement are built by the landowners. The mushroom slum is typically located near a main highway on the outskirts of the city, allowing residents to take advantage of existing bus lines to reach the part of the city in which they have found employment (Lewis, 1959). As the area grows in size and population, recognition is granted by the metropolitan area and/or unofficially by provision of transported water, electricity, and bus service. Land speculators buy up tracts of nearby land to sell to the increasing stream of immigrants who wish to settle among their own kind.[3]

The majority of the migrants from Tilantongo arrive, usually without notice, at the doorstep of a relative or compadre already established in the mushroom slum of the city. The initial visit is generally looked upon by the migrants as a "trial." Many men come alone, leaving their wives and children in Tilantongo. The visitors come to stay for a few days, perhaps several months, during the dry season when there are no crops to tend. They come to the city with the intention of obtaining off-season employment, and plan to return to Tilantongo for the planting season. If employment is obtained, however, they generally stay in Mexico City, returning to Tilantongo only to fetch their family, although they later begin to make periodic visits to their *tierra*. Usually the visitors have been staying at the home of a relative or compadre. When employment is found and the men decide to settle permanently in the city, they rent a rudely constructed house in the *colonia* or in another section of the city until they can afford to buy their own land and build a home of their own.

Ownership of land, no matter how small nor how inconveniently located with respect to their place of employment, is a focal value in the lives of the migrants. When the decision has been made to settle permanently in the city, some migrants sell all or part of their land in Tilantongo to buy a parcel of land in a squatter *colonia*. Many others, however, prefer not to sell their land, or sell only part of it. The reason for this is that they may want to return to their village some day. This is a highly unlikely possibility. The writer knows only one migrant who returned permanently to Tilantongo after having experienced urban life for some time. The main reason the migrants hold onto a piece of land in Tilantongo is apparently that it provides them with a material tie to their *tierra*, otherwise only symbolically present in their blood ties. Unfortunately, the practice of retaining land titles by emigrants from Tilantongo tends to defeat the principal reason for migration: lack of productive land. Nevertheless, there are many migrants who have a relative or friend work their land, the profits being divided.

The continuance of strong ties with their "tierra" is a striking universal characteristic among the emigrants from Tilantongo, who are unanimously and vociferously linked in spirit to their village. Visits are made annually to Tilantongo, often coinciding with the religious fiestas, and great concern is manifested for the hardships endured by the villagers. When drinking in Mexico City, the migrants become almost maudlin in the expression of their emotions about their "tierra."

Drinking patterns have changed considerably among the Mexico City migrants. In Tilantongo, *pulque* is the most frequently consumed alcoholic beverage. *Pulque* is the fermented juice of the maguey plant (*Agave Americana*). It is drunk throughout much of the highland areas of Mexico. Those who have maguey plants drink *pulque* daily during the dry season, unless they are so poor that they have to sell it in the marketplace on Sunday. Those who do not own magueys drink *pulque* in the market once a week and occasionally at the homes of relatives and compadres. The advantage of owning maguey plants lies primarily in the utility of *pulques* as a thirst-slaker. There is a great scarcity of water in the municipio; *pulque* serves to supply most of the liquid requirements of the body. Those without magueys must make daily trips for water, which for many families means a journey of several hours.

Drunkenness is frequent in Tilantongo. *Pulque* acts as a lever or fuse in the process of intoxication. A certain degree of intoxication can be achieved through consumption of *pulque,* but it usually happens that the *pulque* is exhausted or the imbiber is bloated before severe intoxication has resulted. Rather than stopping at that point, the Indians switch to *aguardiente* or *mezcal,* distilled from sugar cane and maguey respectively. Contrary to the nondistilled *pulque,* both of these beverages have extremely high alcoholic content, the former being, in addition, well supplied with various impurities. The result of the change from *pulque* to *aguardiente* or *mezcal* is disastrous to the sobriety of the drinkers.

Market day is famous in Tilantongo for its drinking bouts, but only a small number of people attend the Sunday market because of long distances to be covered and lack of roads. The investigator visited a number of outlying ranches during his visit to Tilantongo and observed everywhere a drinking process similar to that described above.

Drinking sprees may begin at any time, day or night, any day of the week. They continue until all available liquor is exhausted, frequently including all liquor available within the radius of a day or night's walk. The fields may be left unattended for several days, but that is generally harmful only at harvest time, when it is said that there is less drinking. The "morning after" finds the Indian in the same psychological mood as when the spree started. Hangovers are common, but there are no guilt feelings observable, and no regrets about the drinking bout, except perhaps that it had to come to an end.

It is noteworthy that violence, physical or verbal, is absent during alcoholic binges, so the sober Indian is in no need to flay his conscience for having insulted a friend or compadre. Fiestas play an important part in the lives of the Indians in Tilantongo, and drunkenness is an integral part of them. The only difference between the drinking carried on during fiestas and that done during the rest of the year seems to be in degree rather than kind.

In Mexico City, the migrants become much more "regimented" drinkers. The frequency of drinking bouts as well as the quantity of alcoholic beverages consumed becomes greatly diminished. Drinking is not indulged in during the week, unless a relative or compadre appears from Tilantongo. The recent arrival always brings with him a *jarro* of *mezcal* from Oaxaca. The resultant party may last all night, and occasionally the host may not get to work the following day. Among the writer's informants, however, only one stays away from work with any frequency because of alcoholic binges, but that particular man does not need the excuse of a visitor to get drunk. The other informants are reliable workers and place a high value upon stability and dependability in their jobs.

Pulque is rarely consumed in Mexico City. The reason given by the drinkers for this phenomenon is that the *pulque* in the city is "adulterated with chemicals," and unfit to drink. The change in alcoholic beverages consumed is always from *pulque* to beer and *aguardiente* and *mezcal* to *tequila.* The *mezcal* available in Mexico City is also considered to be inferior to that obtainable in Tilantongo. The writer is led to believe that the underlying reason for the prejudice is probably an unconscious identification of beer and *tequila* with the "progressive" life of the city, and of *pulque* and *mezcal* with the primitive "Indian" way of life.

Many of the residents of Mexico City display an increased awareness of and identification with the Mexican nation. A slight correlation may be traced between length of residence and amount of identification with the national culture, but there are several variables which must be taken into consideration, the most important of which is whether the individual has been in the army. Military service inculcates in the migrants a sense of Mexican nationality which is not acquired by the most urbanized of the migrants who have not seen military duty. Nevertheless, the growth of national consciousness does not carry with it a corresponding decrease in identification with Tilantongo. Every migrant considers himself to be a Tilantongueño *and* a Mexican, many placing loyalty to their village first. Each migrant also considers himself an *Indio,* even those residents who have spent fifteen years in Mexico City. Migrants' children who are born in Mexico City are *Mexicanos;* children born in Tilantongo are *Indios.* Two explanations are offered by the migrants for the distinction between *Indio* and *Mexicano.* A person is an *Indio* if he was born or registered in Tilantongo. Thus a child born in Tilantongo, taken to Mexico City, and registered in the latter place, is a *Mexicano.* If the child is registered in Tilantongo, he is an *Indio.* More importantly, a linguistic distinction is made. Anyone who speaks Mixtec is an *Indio.* Children who speak only Spanish are *Mexicanos.* Offspring are discouraged from learning the Indian language in order that they may be *Mexicanos* rather than *Indios.*

Fried's conclusion from his study of migration in Peru among Andean Indians that "migration is a factor in the etiology of mental ill health, and very specifically of psychosomatic disorders" (Fried, 1959), is not supported by this investigation. Adjustment by the Indian migrants from Tilantongo to urban life appears to be highly satisfactory, most probably because of a combination of a psychological "set" to learn new skills and values, an earlier dissatisfaction with existing values, and a successful transplanting of kinship ties resulting in the continuance of secure emotional attachments.[4]

The substitution of secondary, contractual, *Gesellschaft* relationships for primary, status-based, *Gemeinschaft* relationships, considered to be the *sine qua non* of urbanization processes, is not characteristic of the migrants from Tilantongo. Except for necessary modifications in their jobs, all the migrants insist upon, and generally succeed in, maintaining primary face-to-face relationships. The "schizoid" character of urban personality produced by segmentation of human relationships described by Wirth (1938) is not a development which occurs in the first generation of Indian migrants from Tilantongo.

Family ties appear to remain as strong as they were in Tilantongo, and perhaps become even stronger. This finding directly contradicts the stereotyped concept of family bonds weakening with urbanization, but is consistent with the findings reported by Lewis in his study of urbanization process among Tepoztecos (Lewis, 1957).

Lewis found that the *compadrazgo* complex continues to function in the city, although it is often reduced to the rites of baptism and marriage. He reports that relatives are frequently chosen as compadres in the city, but not in Tepotzotlan (Lewis, 1957). The results of the present research differ in some respects from Lewis's findings concerning *compadrazgo*. *Compadrazgo* continues to flourish among the Tilantongueños in Mexico City and, in fact, takes on an added importance. Bonds of *compadrazgo* criss-cross throughout much of the Tilantongo group in Mexico City, insuring in-group solidarity and providing a strong feeling of security. Friendships are rarely formed outside the group, and only one informant has a wife who is not a native-born Tilantongueña. Compadres are, however, occasionally taken from outside the in-group. A step in that direction was taken initially by the informal leader. Other migrants have followed his lead hesitantly, but not to the extent that there is an immediate prospect of forming strong social bonds with non-Tilantongueños. Relatives are frequently taken as compadres, but it is not clear if the practice has increased through migration to the city.

The main motivations for migration to urban centers are economic and educational. They are economic in the dual sense that the subsistence level of the economy in Tilantongo exerts tremendous pressure on a portion of the population to emigrate; the attractions of urban life exert an equal attraction for the more enterprising young men. The lack of educational opportunities in Tilantongo and the availability of those facilities in large cities excites the enthusiasm of those family heads with ambition for themselves or their children.

Economically, the family heads are unanimously agreed that they are better off financially in Mexico City than in Tilantongo. They all hold steady jobs, with the exception of one semi-invalid and two men who are "retired," one living from an army pension, the other supported by his family. As is to be expected, the jobs are of various types, but it is noteworthy that none of the migrants is an ambulatory salesman, "peddler," or vendor of any kind. As mentioned previously, twenty-two migrants are employed by a large manufacturing firm in the city. Of those, one is in a supervisory capacity, two are warehouse guards, and eighteen are general service assistants. One informant is a doctor; one is a policeman; one is a laborer in a furniture factory; several are bricklayers or masons. The semi-invalid, who is employed part-time as a carpenter's apprentice, is the only man whose wife works. Salaries of the men employed full-time range from 400 to 1000 pesos per month. Although exact earnings for each one of the informants could not be ascertained, the mean monthly wage of those for whom precise earnings could be gathered (twenty-four individuals) is 550 pesos.

Rent paid by those who migrate from Tilantongo who have not yet bought their own land and built their own homes averages slightly more than fifty pesos per month. No reliable estimate could be made on the cost of constructing a house, since practices vary widely and many did not know in the first place how much they spent for their houses. Land values also fluctuate widely. Nevertheless, a typical case may be cited for illustrative purposes.

The informant in question came to Mexico City with his wife and child four years ago, having previously worked as a laborer in Mexico City for three years. After obtaining a job in a furniture factory, he rented a one-room house for fifty pesos a month. However, he objected to paying rent, so he and his brother requested money from their father in Tilantongo for a down-payment on a piece of land in a squatter settlement. The down-payment was 2000 pesos, which the father sent. The brothers then made monthly payments of 168 pesos until the land was fully owned. The total cost of the property was 6000 pesos. The informant built by himself on weekends a one-room adobe house on the lot of 400 square meters. He and his brother are now co-owners of the land and building. After completing the house, the informant returned to Tilantongo to fetch his two younger brothers, aged thirteen and fifteen, who now live with him and go to school. The informant supports the young brothers financially. In the house live the informant, his brother, his wife, his two children, his two younger brothers, a friend from Tilantongo, and the friend's common-law wife and child. In all, ten people live in the one-room house. The house faces on a small dirt patio which contains chickens and a pig. Contiguous to the patio is a small cornfield which supplies much of the food for the families. The cornfield is not typical of migrant families, who generally do not have enough land to raise anything more than a few domestic animals.

Insofar as possible, the patio complex typical of Tilantongo dwellings has been retained in the city. Where more than one structure is owned by the family, the buildings are placed around a patio. If the family, as is the usual case, has only one structure, it is so located as to form one side of a patio complex with other dwellings. Exceptions to this practice are the result of physical limitations of the property.

The number of rooms per family varies more or less proportionately to the economic status of the family. The informant with the highest salary (1000 pesos per month) has the largest number of dwelling areas. That man has a house consisting of a living room-dining room, two bedrooms, and a kitchen. In addition, there are three other dwellings constructed of cement blocks in the compound built around a patio. Those buildings house relatives and compadres. Only one of the inhabitants of those extra buildings pays rent.

The meanest home consists of one adobe brick windowless room, three by four meters, with a dirt floor. The majority of the homes contain two rooms furnished with beds, chairs, a bureau, radio, table, and cooking utensils.

Almost all informants own radios. Two families have television sets. Sunday afternoon visits to the homes of the TV owners are popular among Tilantongueños. At least two migrants own phonographs. Every family has an electric iron; many have sewing machines. All families sleep in beds, although frequently there is only one bed for the married couple and its children.

Sanitation is greatly improved over that practiced in Tilantongo; an outdoor privvy is owned individually or shared by a number of families.

Gas or kerosene stoves are found in every home. No one possesses a refrigerator.

The diet of migrants is without exception much improved over that of residents of Tilantongo. Food is generally cited as the material evidence of the improved standard of living of the migrants. Whereas in Tilantongo the normal diet is limited to tortillas and salt, beans being eaten only once or twice a week and meat weekly or semi-monthly, in Mexico City beans are eaten daily and meat is eaten at least once a week by even the poorest families. The better-off families in the city eat meat daily. Soups are served in the city as separate dishes or as part of the meat or bean dish. Tortillas of maize are eaten by all, even though wheat tortillas are more popular in Tilantongo. Wheat bread is not eaten by any family in Mexico City. In the city potatoes and squash have been added to the diet. *Guajes* are eaten in the city, as they are in Tilantongo. *Chiles,* a delicacy in Tilantongo, are commonplace on the tables of the migrants in Mexico City; they are served with all meals. Coffee is not taken regularly by any family, although every family drinks it occasionally. Beer and soda pop are the most popular beverages. Fruit is eaten now and then.

Desserts are never eaten, though the children enjoy sweets and are permitted to buy and eat them. One family serves popcorn on Sunday afternoons while guests are watching TV. Two families are known to use toothpicks.

In Tilantongo all eating is done with tortillas and fingers. Silverware is not employed, nor any other kind of tableware except small bowls in which beans or soup are served. The soup is sipped from the bowl or scooped in a tortilla. In Mexico City all food is served on plates at the table. However, eating utensils are limited to soup spoons. Paper napkins are provided for special occasions.

The men are served separately from the women and children. The men are served by the women; the latter then retire to the kitchen, if there is a separate kitchen, or to one side of the room with the children. This pattern is a survival from Tilantongo, where the men eat in one half the room, the women in the other half by the cooking fire.

Chicken or turkey *moles* are the most popular festive dishes in the city, ceding precedence only to the *barbacoas,* or barbecues. *Barbacoas* in the style of Tilantongo are big events in the lives of the migrants. *Barbacoas* and drinking parties are important sources of entertainment.

New entertainment media enter the lives of the migrants when they settle in the city, but are limited to the radio, TV, and phonograph. The only forms of entertainment in Tilantongo, where there is no electricity, are drinking, gossip, the annual fiestas, and, for the young men, basketball. In the city, drinking and visiting are combined with watching TV or listening to the radio. Three informants play basketball regularly; one of them also plays cards when he can find others with whom to play. No other forms of entertainment are sought, nor are they readily accepted. The migrants do not go to the movies, nor to so-called "cultural" activities, such as art galleries, museums, etc. The family circle of real and artificial kin apparently satisfies many or most of the entertainment needs of the ex-residents of Tilantongo.

One of the primary reasons for emigrating from Tilantongo is the desire to educate oneself and one's children. Illiteracy is widespread in Tilantongo. According to the 1950 census, 83 percent of the inhabitants are illiterate (Dirección General de Estadística, 1950). Almost all the migrants who settle in Mexico City enter school when they arrive, either taking a part-time job in order to attend school during the day, or going to night schools in the city. Over half the migrants finish the *primaria*. None of the migrants continues to the *secundaria,* although many express a desire to continue their education. Albeit the migrants do not keep on in school themselves past the *primaria,* they place a strong emphasis upon educating their children. It is common throughout some parts of Latin America for rural migrants to urban centers to send their children to live in a home in the city to work as servants without pay with the understanding that the family accepting the child will send him or her to school. That is not the practice among Tilantongo migrants. Sacrifices of some financial magnitude are frequently undergone by migrants in order to keep the children in the home and send them to school, even though the children are of an age when they could be making important economic contributions to the household.

Behind the economic and educational motivations of migration lies an ubiquitous psychological factor which operates to influence migration patterns. There is a deeply ingrained fear in the Indians of Tilantongo of extortion, political persecution, economic exploitation, banditry, and blood feuds. In addition to these "social" fears, there is an ever-present fear of the natural elements, which in one fell swoop can, and often do, wipe out a year's food supply. Thus the people of Tilantongo have a constant fear of losing what they possess, material and nonmaterial. This situation both foments and prevents migration.

In Mexico City, the migrants say that they have "lost the fear" which they had in Tilantongo. No longer are they servile creatures of the whims of the "bad elements" (*malos elementos*) in their community, human and natural. The rather obvious prosperity and newly acquired security which the migrants emanate when they return on visits to their *tierra* instill in many Tilantongueños a determination to emulate their envied cousins and join the stream of migrants.

On the other hand, the very thought of abandoning the things that they do have, material and nonmaterial, to set off for a distant place containing millions of unknown, potentially threatening, individuals, creates in many natives such strong anxiety that they form ingenious rationalizations at times for staying on their impoverished parcel of land. Certainly there are many logical reasons for staying in Tilantongo. For example, those who speak only Mixtec are obviously at a serious disadvantage for migrating to a city. Monolingual males, in fact, do not migrate. All the male informants of the investigator speak Spanish, and the wives have learned to speak it, even though they might have been monolingual when they came to the city with their husbands.

Migration of unmarried women is virtually unknown. This is another aspect in which the findings of the writer differ from those reported by other investigators. The only single women who migrate to Mexico City are the young daughters who accompany their parents.

A universal change which takes place in the lives of the migrants studied by this investigator is a remarkable reduction in the importance of religion, at least insofar as its outward manifestations are concerned. Nominally all the migrants are devout Catholics and all are, according to their own evaluation, sincere believers. However, none of the thirty-one family heads goes to church, except for *compadrazgo* ceremonies such as baptism and confirmation. The wives of the migrants do not attend church either. Most of the families, however, send their children to church, at least until confirmation has been achieved. After confirmation, practice varies widely. Some children continue to attend Mass regularly; others cease to attend church entirely. Only two of the homes visited by the investigator have shrines.

The ostensible reasons for the loss of religious activities among the migrants are that "one has to tell the priest everything if one goes to church," that "the priests are not to be trusted," and that "they are out for their own ends." Nevertheless, the same attitude is held by the residents of Tilantongo, and they do go to their local chapels — where there is no priest — or to the church in town every Sunday. The reason must lie in some aspect of the urbanization process. There are doubtless a number of factors which cause this rather sudden secularization of the migrants from Tilantongo, but one of the most important seems to be the "loss of fear" so often described by the investigator's informants. The meaning behind this loss of fear is that life is much more secure in Mexico City than in Tilantongo. Apparently the newly found security in the mundane world results in a corresponding diminution of reliance upon the church for spiritual guidance.

Changes in dress are part of the de-Indianization process undergone by migrants. Typical garb in Tilantongo is a white cotton shirt and white trousers worn by the men and a cotton dress and *rebozo* by the women. All men wear *huaraches;* most women go barefoot. All the men wear hats woven from palm leaves.

In Mexico City, many of the women change their attire, retaining the cotton dress, but replacing the *rebozo* with a sweater. Many women own shoes and sometimes socks, although around the house most women wear huaraches or go barefoot. The cotton dress is of better quality, and each woman has at least one good dress for special occasions.

The men discard all "Indian" dress that they wore in their village. The white cotton trousers and shirt are replaced by gabardine or good-quality cotton trousers of a dark color, and colored sports shirts or white dress shirts. Ties are worn for special events. Each man owns either a suit or a sports jacket. Shoes are worn by all men; the straw hat has been discarded.

Medical services are highly valued by the migrants. There is no evidence of an ill person returning to Tilantongo to be "cured," as Lewis observed among the migrant Tepoztecos (Lewis, 1957). Doctors are consulted by all migrants without regard to the length of residence of the migrants. The well-acculturated migrants aid the process of replacing folk medicine beliefs by actively discouraging folk beliefs and encouraging consultations with recognized medical practitioners in the city.

In summary, the outstanding characteristics of families studied by this investigator who have migrated from Tilantongo to Mexico City are the following.

(1) Steady employment is obtained and held by all men. (2) Land is purchased and homes are built in "squatter settlements." (3) Migrants enter school when they arrive in the city and place a high value upon education of their children. (4) There is a continuance of strong family ties with no evidence of family disorganization. (5) In-group solidarity with fellow Tilantongueños is very strong. (6) A high degree of mental

health is enjoyed by the migrants. (7) There is an extreme preference for and insistence upon primary face-to-face relationships. (8) There is an increase in identification with the Mexican nation without a corresponding decrease in identification with Tilantongo. (9) Strong emotional attachments are held to Tilantongo and annual visits are made to the community. (10) Migrants continue to call themselves *Indios*. Their children do not speak the Indian tongue and are considered *Mexicanos*. (11) Marriage is contracted almost exclusively with women from Tilantongo, even if that means returning to the village after years of absence to fetch a wife. (12) There is a diminution in drinking, a change in beverage drunk, and a change in occasions for drinking. (13) A marked loss occurs after migration in the outward forms of religious expression, including a nearly complete loss of churchgoing. (14) Unanimous agreement is expressed that life in Mexico City is better than that in Tilantongo.

In his study of migration of families from Tepoztlan to Mexico City, Lewis considered that the nature of the capital city is conducive to satisfactory adjustment of Tepoztecos (Lewis, 1957). There is, as Lewis realizes, a peculiar relationship between Tepoztlan and Mexico City, owing primarily to their proximity, which does not obtain between the capital city and other communities in Mexico. In any evaluation of rural-urban migration, the nature of the city in which migrants settle must be taken into consideration. In the case of Mexico City, the secular, impersonal vastness of the metropolis allows the maintenance and functioning of tight in-group solidarity and strong bonds of kinship within the framework of urban life. It is of great interest in this respect that migrants from Tilantongo who reside in Puebla, a smaller, less impersonal, religiously orthodox city, have adopted significantly different patterns of behavior from their kin in Mexico City. The emphasis in migration studies should not be limited to the nature of the city itself. Equal importance should be given to the nature of the individuals who migrate. The city and the individual form a continuously interacting phenomenon.

The explanation for the successful adaptation to city life by Tilantongo migrants probably lies in a well-balanced combination of maintenance of strong emotional ties within the family, with fellow migrants from Tilantongo, and with their *tierra*, and a plastic ability to learn new skills and values. The early-acquired value placed upon family and compadres and the newly acquired values of economic and educational advancement can be satisfied simultaneously in the new environment.

Migration is a prehispanic Mixtec pattern — including migration to Cholula, Tehuacan, Orizaba, Teotihuacan, Tetzcoco, etc. Tradition might favor and reinforce today's behavior.

In order to arrive at any valid generalizations concerning the urbanization process in rural-urban migrants, many more studies must be undertaken comparing the lives led by migrants before and after they left their village. Attention should be directed in these studies to the changes in values of the migrants.

NOTES

1. "Urbanization" in this paper refers to the "modification of human behavior imposed by the urban way of life" (Wirth, 1938).
2. The investigation was supported by a grant from the U.S. National Institute of Mental Health.
3. See Mangin, 1960a, for a description of the origin and direction of change of a typical *barriada* in Lima, Peru.
4. Both Lewis, "Urbanización sin desorganización," 1957, and Mangin, 1960a, in their studies of migration to large cities, found maladjustment and disorganization among the migrants to be minimal. Mangin states that his four-year study among Indian migrants in Peru does not support the expectation that "low-status migrants whose culture differs most from that of the dominant group will suffer stress and exhibit disorganized and maladaptive behavior. . . ."

10 ················

Morocco's Expanding Towns

HASSAN AWAD

Urbanization has been an essential and striking feature of Morocco's life since the end of the First World War. The proportion of urban to total population has increased steadily: it was ten percent in 1926. By 1936 the proportion had reached sixteen percent, and it rose to twenty-five percent in 1952 and 29.30 percent in 1960. Fifty years ago there was no single city in Morocco of more than 100,000 population. The 1960 census listed eight cities as having actually more than 100,000 inhabitants, with Casablanca in the lead with about one million.

RURAL MIGRATION

As a general rule the bulk of this rural emigration comes from districts with rapidly increasing pressure of population and meagre resources. This is the case in the arid and semi-arid lands of southern Morocco, where the limits of cultivation cannot be extended because of aridity. Some mountainous areas are no more favourable from a physiographic point of view.

"Morocco's Expanding Towns" by Hassan Awad is reprinted from *The Geographical Journal,* 130:49–64, March, 1964, by permission of the author and publisher.

In some of the rich Atlantic plains the problem is one of too little land and too many people.

Fifty percent of the urban migrants settle in Casablanca. The 1952 census stated that only eight percent of the population are of Casablanca birth, seventeen percent are immigrants from other cities, and seventy-five percent are rural immigrants.

The newcomers retain their country ways for some time. People of the same tribe keep together in the same quarter or even in the same street. But this temporary exodus often leads to a lasting migration, and as a result of gainful employment city life demands its dues. Nevertheless, certain groups, in spite of an urban past that is sometimes quite long, have maintained firm ties with the area of origin. According to R. le Tourneau (1952) this appears to be due to three reasons: first, these groups have kept in close touch with their country of origin, the members of one family going to the city in relays, so that although the family is always represented, it is by different individuals from one year to the next. Secondly, individuals comprising the same group often practise the same trade: the Berbers of the Upper Fuir are porters in Fez, the Jbala, who come from the mountains north of Fez on the Mediterranean coast, are Koranic schoolmasters and weapon manufacturers, the people from Sous are grocers. And thirdly, they hang closely together, meeting often after work and on feast days.

MOROCCAN CITIES

In this survey we will only examine cities with a population of more than 10,000 inhabitants. We can divide them into two large groups, one in which the rate of growth is less than the national rate, thus suggesting declining urban centres; and the other in which the rate is greater than the national rate. The urban centres that were found to be declining, as based upon the above criteria, include two traditional capital cities, Fez and Marrakesh, and one large port, Tangier.

TABLE 7 *Population of towns of more than 100,000 inhabitants*

	1960	1952	Percentage increase
Casablanca	965,277	682,388	41.4
Marrakesh	243,134	215,312	12.8
Rabat	227,445	156,209	44.
Fez	216,133	179,372	20.5
Meknès	175,943	140,380	25.3
Tangier	141,714	120,000	18.
Oujda	128,645	80,546	59.8
Tétouan	101,352	80,732	25.5

Declining Moroccan cities.   Until the twentieth century Fez was the most important city in Morocco, being at the same time both the political and spiritual capital. But the period of the French protectorate brought about a relative decline, a decline that was reflected most of all in a dwindling of its industrial, commercial, and agricultural functions.

The industrial activity in which a large part of the city's population was formerly engaged was of an artisan nature. At present this artisan class is in decline. Only leatherwork, shoemaking, and tanning are still fairly in demand, although Fez has lost its external markets in North Africa, the Middle East, and Senegal.

Trade, which was once the main activity, was dependent on the city's position on the great route from Tafilalt to Tangier, then the port for all connections in the north. At the present time trade is limited to that of barter with the countryside only, and wholesale and semi-wholesale trade has lost all its importance in favour of Casablanca, where the banks are also concentrated. In short, Casablanca is supplanting Fez, and many merchants are transferring their businesses to Casablanca from Fez. But the traditional, intellectual, religious, and historic capital does not wish to sink away into the glories of the past. For some years now, while keeping up its traditional activities, the city has been trying to develop modern industries, especially textiles.

Marrakesh, once the imperial capital and with memories of a sumptuous past in the Middle Ages, is now no more than a simple southern provincial capital. The city played much the same part in the south as Fez in the north. Both were in turn capital cities of Morocco and, up to the beginning of this century, eclipsed all other Moroccan towns. Nevertheless there is a broad distinction between the two cities. At certain periods the southern town almost ceased to exist. It would appear that the fate of Marrakesh is much more bound up with political circumstances than that of Fez (Deverdun, 1959). This is no doubt due to its geographical position, to the fact that it is in a region of which the economic output is much more irregular than in the north of the country. Unlike Fez, Marrakesh has not built up a solid business and shopkeeping class.

If the city still seems alive, it must be recognized that it is more lively than really active. Meanwhile, agriculture plays a great part; many people own gardens actually in the city, which were only made possible thanks to the introduction of the "Khetara" type Sahara technique (known as *foggara* in Algeria). It can be seen that the city takes little part in modern activities. Modern industry is almost nonexistent, while handicraft activities are passing through a period of growing crises. But the most promising industry for the future would seem to be tourism; in fact, an effort has been made in this field. The "Pearl of the South" draws tourists who come to enjoy its winter sun and sample its originality.

The last large city of which the rate of growth is below the national rate is *Tangier*. At the beginning of the twentieth century Tangier was only a fairly large village of 5000 inhabitants, but it started to grow rapidly. The city enjoyed a relative prosperity due to its barter trade with the hinterland, but above all because of its role as the diplomatic city and the "Gateway to Morocco." It was here that foreign diplomatic missions first landed on Moroccan soil. Moreover, Tangier was Morocco's main harbour. But the setting up of the Spanish protectorate over the extreme north (the Spanish Rif) and the French protectorate over the major part of the country, followed by the status of 1925 endowing Tangier and a narrow strip of surrounding country with an international government, completely upset the workings of the city, separating it temporarily from the remainder of the country. Thus Morocco was divided into three unequal zones: the French zone, by far the largest (200,000 square miles), the Spanish zone (8,000 square miles) and the International Zone of Tangier (225 square miles). The trade of the city has passed to some extent to Ceuta, which is still Spanish, but predominantly to the ports of the former French Zone which have grown rapidly (Landau, 1956).

From this time on Tangier developed its activities independently, or almost independently, of the Moroccan economy. Tangier became a centre of international trade, a refuge for foreign capital deposited in a number of banks, and the scene of financial speculation. The abolition of the international status brought about the decline of its trade and caused an important fraction of the population to leave.

In spite of its admirable maritime position and its exceptionally good geographical situation on one of the most navigated sea routes in the world, it must be said that its position in relation to Morocco, tucked away in the extreme north of the country, is much less favourable. Tangier is isolated from active Morocco and from historic Morocco by the Rif chain of mountains. Its economic isolation is underlined by the low port traffic which only represents two percent of the total trade of the country. The city has a hinterland of little importance.

To allow the free play of a certain amount of natural selection within the framework of economic liberalism is, in these conditions, to condemn to ruin a town with a population of about 150,000, still being swollen by immigration of peasants from the Rif, which has been heavy since unification of the kingdom. Does reintegration of Tangier into the country mean the eternal ruin of its former prosperity? The Government seems aware of this political aspect. In spite of these unfavourable conditions an effort is being made to find adequate activities for Tangier. The government choice is for installation of industries connected with a free zone which has just been re-created in the port. It has instituted too a policy of fiscal privileges in order to encourage the building up of some industrial plants connected with this free zone. But the changes of boosting the economy of Tangier are still very problematical (Mas, 1962, 1–2:153–155).

Slowly growing cities. Into this category fall two inland cities, Maknès and Tétouan, each of which has a long history.

In the centre of a rich region of intense agricultural activity rises the city of *Meknès.* A secondary town until the seventeenth century, Meknès knew a period of exceptional glory under Sultan Ismail (1672–1727), who made it his capital. During the period of the French protectorate the development of Meknès was intensified, thanks to various factors which included the presence of an important military base. The main factor was the European agricultural colonization of its rich country, and particularly, cultivation of the grape.

We must note the proximity of Fez, only sixty km away, which puts two large towns in the same regional context. It would be very interesting to see a total survey extending over the Meknès-Fez region which might enable one to understand the urban functions which these two regional capitals carry out.

Tétouan, once an imperial city like Meknès, is the regional capital of the Rif. Its very slow rate of growth is close to the national rate. Foreigners, who in 1952 represented thirty-eight percent of the population with 30,800 persons, represented no more than nineteen percent in 1960 with 19,685 persons.

Rapidly growing cities. These are Oujda, capital of eastern Morocco, Rabat, capital of the Kingdom, and Casablanca, economic capital.

Oujda's development is certainly part of an urbanizing movement that affects the whole country, but its tempo puts it in front of that of other built-up areas of Morocco. Coming into being in the tenth century at a crossroads of caravan routes, only since the beginning of the century has the town regained its position as a centre of communication after an obliteration due to the vicissitudes of a troubled history. Oujda is, in fact, situated at the intersection of the lines of communication between Casablanca and Tunis on the one hand, and the Mediterranean and the Sahara (Colomb-Bechar) on the other. But this role of turntable did not achieve its true importance until the rise in importance of eastern Morocco. This economic development has affected two different sectors, firstly mining and, more recently, agriculture.

Eastern Morocco is a region rich in mineral resources of which the most important are anthracite, iron ore, lead and zinc. Oujda contains the banking establishments and the head office of the mining companies. At the mouth of the Bou Regreg rise twin towns: on the right bank Salé, on the left bank *Rabat.* With 227,445 inhabitants at the 1960 census, Rabat

was the third largest city in Morocco. But at the present time all the indi-
catons are that it now occupies second place after Casablanca.

It was the choice of Rabat as capital in 1912 that was the cause of its
rise, since the town assumed above all a political and administrative function, containing all the ministries and large departments. There are certain
industrial activities and crafts to be found there but no present harbour
activity. The presence of Casablanca less than 100 kilometres to the south
end of Kenitra 40 kilometres only to the north has killed all competitive
spirit.

With its population of one million inhabitants, *Casablanca* appears as a
gigantic city for Morocco. Its growth has been spectacular. By its direct-
ing role, and by its importance in commercial and industrial activities, it
is the economic capital of the country (Ecochard, 1955; July, 1961).

FIGURE 1

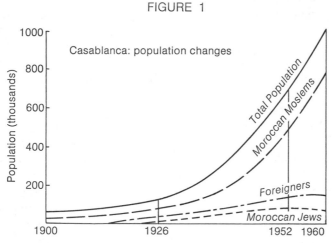

These activities rely first of all on the existence of a large harbour, which
handles more than 75 percent of Moroccan foreign trade. The volume
of its through-put, which does not cease to expand, is of the order of ten
million tons, being thus the highest in Africa. There is first of all the distribution within the whole country of products either imported or manufactured in the city, there is the collection of products bound for export.
There is further an important financial activity: in fact, more than half the
banking of the whole of Morocco is to be found there. The importance
of its trading function brought on an industrial one which soon became
the most important in Casablanca. More than half of the industrial enter-
prises of Morocco are concentrated there.

The demographic dynamism is much greater than the economic dynamism of the great city. The influx of country-folk goes on independently of the employment situation in the city, and occurred during the periods of depression in 1956 to 1960. An investigation made in 1958 showed that among the active population one man in four was out of work, and that one-fifth of the working population was heavily underemployed (less than a thirty-hour week). In addition, out of 100 people employed, 62 were employed in unproductive occupations (*secteur tertiaire*), and there was one shopkeeper to 20 inhabitants (Dubois, 1958). This proliferation of minor parasitical activities naturally hides the extent of unemployment.

CONCLUSION

The influx of population to cities poses some very important problems. On the one hand the original towns are overpopulated. In the two old centres of Fez, 172,000 human beings are concentrated in a town without sanitation, without mechanical means of communication, one might almost say without air (Degez, 1961). On the other hand, many of the new arrivals, for lack of lodging, have installed themselves on vacant lots where they have built precarious shelters made of waste timber or with walls of petrol cans arranged end to end, whence the name "bidonville" (tintown) that has been given to these miserable quarters. These tintowns are largest in the great coastal towns. Thus forty percent of the population of Kenitra lives in tintowns (Nespola, 1960). In Casablanca it is estimated that there are still 180,000 housed in tintowns, and this in spite of great efforts made with a view to the reabsorption of this sordid habitat by the building of workers' towns.

The problem goes deeper than that. The question is whether all these additional people in big cities cannot only be housed but employed as unskilled labour. In fact the problem of unemployment which is an inevitable consequence of the staggering extent of the migration of rural Morocco towards the towns, is one of the most fundamental problems that must be solved in this country.

The speedy development of industrialization, which is one of the authorities' objectives, could offer great possibilities to stem this type of unemployment. This industrialization is to be accompanied by decentralization. Although building of new works for private enterprise continues at Casablanca, the Government's preference lies elsewhere.

It is obvious, however, that the solution of this problem does not lie only in the towns, it involves the whole country, because it is not only a question of absorbing unemployment, which is already severe, but preventing great impoverished masses ceaselessly coming in to overflow the shanty towns of the large urban centres. The rational development of the agricultural potentialities of the country can play a large part in keeping men on the land more and more. But it is hard to see how this can be done without changing the technology and pattern of farming. Here and there, experiments in modernization and rationalization of methods of growing crops have been in progress for some time, but with varying results.

Most impressive, perhaps, among recent transformations on the land are the irrigation works that supply water to thousands of acres of fertile soil, where yields are higher and crops are grown throughout the year in fields that used to be fallow during the dry summer months. It is noteworthy that migration has not been so great from these places where the development of irrigation projects has, in some measure, enabled the number employed per acre to be increased.

11

Medan: The Role of Kinship in an Indonesian City

EDWARD M. BRUNER

Over a century ago Sir Henry Maine told us that kinship, the basis of primitive social organization, declines in importance in more advanced societies. The proposition has been widely accepted and has been restated in one form or another by many scholars during the last hundred years. Most recently, for example, Julian Steward (1960) writes that internal specialization, social classes, and state institutions come to supersede kinship groups, and Leslie White (1959:141) goes so far as to suggest that the transformation from primitive to civil society entails "the loss of kinship."

Criticisms have been made of Sir Henry's proposition on the grounds that not only kinship but also territorial groups and age-sex groupings are

"Medan: The Role of Kinship in an Indonesian City" by Edward M. Bruner is reprinted from *Pacific Port Towns and Cities*, edited by Alexander Spoehr, Honolulu, Bishop Museum Press, 1963:1–12, by permission of the author, editor, and publisher.

significant in the social life of many primitive peoples, and on the grounds that kinship often plays a crucial role in some urban social systems. These points are well taken; nevertheless if we take the long view, and especially if we compare carefully selected societies at extreme ends of the developmental continuum, Sir Henry's generalization appears to be essentially correct. It is perfectly clear that kinship was more prominent among Australian aborigines of the last century than it is today in urban centers of the Western nations.

The generalization is less clear, however, if we focus on intermediate level societies, those that are neither truly primitive nor fully urbanized, or if we focus on societies that have recently been exposed to modernizing influences and are currently undergoing rapid culture change. In many of these societies even a preliminary analysis of the role of kinship takes us far beyond the confines of Sir Henry's proposition. I agree with Oscar Lewis (1962) that the distinction between kinship-based versus nonkinship-based societies simply does not tell us enough for purposes of comparative analysis. We now have field studies of the processes of kinship change and of the details of the sequence in which change occurs, and on the basis of these data we must formulate theoretical distinctions finer than those proposed by Sir Henry. His generalization and other similar evolutionary propositions were and are important advances, but rather than repeat or defend them, we must aim for more sophisticated formulations which take account of the more complete data now being gathered by anthropologists from a wider range of societies.

This brief paper is more limited in scope. It explores the role of kinship among the Toba Batak located in the modern coastal city of Medan, Indonesia; demonstrates the inadequacy of broad statements to the effect that kinship declines in importance, is superseded, or even "lost" in urban societies; and presents some tentative conclusions which may be applicable in other similar situations.

HISTORICAL AND ETHNOGRAPHIC BACKGROUND

The Toba Batak are a Malayo-Polynesian speaking people whose traditional homeland is in the interior mountain region of North Sumatra. Wet-rice agriculture in terraced fields is the major economic activity. The society is patrilineal, patrilocal, and includes a segmentary lineage system and affinal alliances.

In the mid-nineteenth century the heaviest concentration of population was in the interior highlands. The coastal lowlands to the east were a dense tropical rain forest and hence sparsely settled, although Batak communities were located along the banks of the larger rivers. The rivers originated in the mountains and flowed through the lowlands into the

Malacca Strait. At the mouths of the navigable rivers were a series of small port towns. The language spoken in these towns was Malay, the religion was Islam, and the economy was based upon trade, fishing, and the collection of tribute. Batak traders came to the port towns for salt, cloth, dried fish, and manufactured goods in exchange for forest products and benzoin from the hinterland.

The situation began to change radically in the 1860s, with the arrival of Europeans. There were two major streams of contact; one was the penetration of German missionaries and Dutch administrators to the Batak highlands, and the other was the establishment of Western plantations in the lowlands. Almost the entire lowland region of North Sumatra was eventually cleared and transformed into a vast estate area in which tobacco, rubber, palm oil, tea, coconut, and other agricultural products were cultivated. These developments, however, did not extend into the Batak homeland; no plantations were established there, and the land remained under the control of village and kinship groups. It was not until 1907, in fact, that the interior was finally brought under the complete jurisdiction of the Dutch colonial government.

European contact brought about considerable cultural change, even for those Toba Batak who remained in their villages. Trade between the interior and the coast was increased through improved means of communication and transportation. A railroad extended to the edge of the highlands and roads were built throughout the Batak area. The missionaries succeeded in converting many hundreds of thousands to Christianity and, with financial help from the government, opened a series of village schools, some in rather remote areas. Many Toba Batak obtained at least the rudiments of a Western elementary school education and some went on to high school and even to universities in Java and Holland. Today there are Batak poets, artists, doctors, lawyers, engineers, and university professors, the majority of whom received their training since the end of World War II. Before the war, most Batak with the desire and opportunity for education and advancement could realistically aspire to positions no higher than that of teacher, clerk, or lower-level administrator.

By the 1900's, educated Batak, as individuals and as family groups, began migrating from the villages to seek their fortunes on the plantations and cities located in the coastal lowlands. From the migrant's point of view there had been both a push and a pull; on the one hand he wished to escape from poverty, overpopulation, and scarcity of terraced rice fields in the highlands, and on the other, he desired the opportunity to increase his standard of living and to enjoy the excitement, greater wealth, and higher social position offered by life in the city.

Many Batak migrants went to Medan, a city strategically located fourteen miles from the sea at the junction of an inland highway and the Deli

River. Medan was founded in the latter part of the nineteenth century as a commercial center to serve the interests of European planters, but it rapidly became the administrative, military, and cultural center of North Sumatra. Today, it is the primary regional metropolis in Sumatra and the second largest Indonesian city outside of Java (Withington, 1962).

Medan has increased in population from 14,000 in 1905, to 76,000 in 1930 and to 360,000 in 1959, according to official figures (*Statistical Pocketbook of Indonesia,* 1960). The most recent population figure is an estimate, since no accurate census was taken after 1930, and most authorities feel it is too conservative. There may well be as many as half a million people in the larger Medan area.

The city has been characterized by notable shifts in ethnic composition. In the late nineteenth century, Medan was populated primarily by indigenous Malay, European administrators and planters, and a few Chinese traders. The first wave of migration was a consequence of the need for agricultural laborers on the plantations. Rather than recruit labor locally, company agents located in Java, Singapore, and Hong Kong brought in Javanese and Chinese workers. After the expiration of their three-year contracts many of these laborers left the estate to settle permanently in the city. Thus in Medan in 1930, out of a total population of 76,000, there were 27,000 Chinese, 21,000 Javanese, 4,000 Europeans, and 4,000 others of foreign descent. The combined nonindigenous population was seventy-four percent of the total. Approximately three out of every four persons in the city were comparatively recent migrants, in that they or their parents had not been born in the area.

In the recent period the number of Europeans had decreased so drastically that today they may be counted in the hundreds rather than the thousands, and there has also been a decrease in the rate of Chinese population growth. The rapid increase in total population has been due to the migration of rural Sumatrans from many different ethnic groups in the highlands who have settled in the city. The Toba Batak are simply one group among many. Some are third-generation urbanites whose grandparents left their highland village, but most are recent arrivals.

The urban migrant finds himself in a radically different physical and social environment. The rural villages are approximately 3,000 feet above sea level and hence are considerably cooler than the coastal city. The villages lack electricity, running water, telephone service, and paved streets, while the city has all of these and more, including restaurants, hotels, hospitals, department stores, banks, theaters, publishing houses, daily newspapers, universities, a medical school, and other facilities normally associated with a busy metropolitan center and regional capital. The language spoken in the village is Toba Batak, while in the city it is Indonesian; the two are mutually unintelligible. Almost all village men, even those who are teachers or government employees, are at least part-time farmers, and village women regularly work in the fields along with their husbands. Most urban men work in an office and neither they nor their wives engage in any agricultural activity. But possibly the most significant difference is that in the village everyone is not only a Toba Batak but also a close relative, while in the city one's immediate neighbors are most likely to be strangers.

In sum, Medan is a relatively new city, characterized by a constant influx of migrants, by rapid growth, high population density, ethnic diversity, and cultural heterogeneity. The Batak migrant leaves his familiar village world or kinsmen to settle among strangers in an alien environment. It is in this context that we inquire into the role of kinship in the city.

THE ROLE OF KINSHIP

The Toba Batak residing in Medan are part of a single kinship community, in that every person is bound by multiple ties in a widely ramifying kinship network. The urban Batak are very aware of their relationships to kinsmen; they employ kinship terminology in daily life, and the kinship system is symbolized at all life-crisis rites and ceremonials.

Kinship ties are based on both descent and marriage. Let us consider each in turn. The Batak descent system is a patrilineal one which operates on many levels of segmentation. At the highest level the Toba Batak form a single super-patrilineage, since they consider themselves to be descendants of one man, Si Radja Batak, who existed, they say, about twenty-five generations ago. Below the super-patrilineage are groupings of clans, named exogamous clans, maximal and minimal lineages. Every Batak, living and dead, has a place on the tribal genealogy and persons in different descent lines are always able to determine their proper relationship to on ə another by tracing their social distance from a common male ancestor. In addition to the descent system, relationships are also reckoned through affinal ties, as every Batak marriage binds two or more lineages or clans. When a man is married, not only he, but every member of his descent group immediately becomes related to all members of the bride's lineage. These affinal bonds are always significant in social life as they involve a status relationship, ceremonial obligations, and the exchange of money, goods, and services. They may be further reinforced by additional marriages in subsequent generations, thus creating affinal alliances which have structural continuity over time. Every descent group, at any given time, has a series of affinal alliances or more transitory ties to those lineages to whom they have given wives and to those from whom they have received wives. Thus in Batak society there is a kind of kinship grid binding all individuals vertically through descent lines and horizontally through affinal bonds.

The system operates somewhat differently in village and city. In the village, kinship relationships are known from childhood, but in the city they have to be established, a consequence of the mobility and high rate of in-migration which characterizes the urban condition. Since there are approximately a million Toba Batak, and since migrants come to Medan from different rural areas, the urban Batak frequently find themselves in the position of meeting other Batak for the first time in the city. On these occasions the parties involved almost invariably determine their respective positions in the kinship grid before any extended interaction. There are, in fact, words in the Batak language for this procedure, *martarombo,* meaning literally "to genealogize," and *martutur,* to engage in the process of establishing a kinship connection. It is not always an easy or rapid procedure, because the correct kinship bond between any two individuals may not be readily apparent and there are often alternate possibilities. Then too, the Batak frequently prolong these preliminary discussions about kinship, since they find many satisfactions in the process. It is for them what the weather or baseball is for us — something to talk about — and it provides an opportunity to exchange gossip about mutual acquaintances, which most Batak thoroughly enjoy. Once established, the kinship relationship structures all subsequent interaction; the individuals involved relate to one another as kinsmen.

In order to establish a kinship connection to every other Batak whom he may meet, a man must possess fairly extensive genealogical knowledge and he must be aware of recent marriages in his own and related lineages. In the rural areas most men have acquired the necessary information by the time they become adults, but this is not so in the city, especially among the younger generation. There are, however, various short cuts for determining kinship connections. An urban youth who does not know how to relate to someone will simply ask his parents or possibly one of the genealogical specialists. The latter are older men who have distinguished themselves by their knowledge of Batak customs and genealogies; they are often consulted by the parents themselves as to the proper procedures for various ceremonies. Another short cut employed by the urban Batak is to reckon descent by reference to the number of generations a person is removed from a clan ancestor, without going through the intermediate descendants. A man will be told, for example, that he is sixteen generations removed from the founder of his clan; with this information, and a knowledge of how the system works, it is possible for him to determine his relationship to others with a minimum of consultation. Another procedure is for two persons to work out their kinship connection by reference to a known relationship to a third person. There are other procedures. The important point is not which particular procedure is utilized, but rather that all Batak have techniques enabling them to key into the system by one means or another.

The urban Batak form a kinship community, but the quality of interaction among kinsmen is different from that in the village. As we have pointed out, migrants come to the city from various highland areas, they represent many different descent lines, and there is a large number of Toba Batak in Medan than in any comparable rural area. The city man has more relatives distributed more widely in the kinship network than his village counterpart, but he interacts with them less frequently, in more restricted situations, and for shorter periods of time. Kinship sentiment decreases concomitantly. The affective component of kinship is dispersed; intimacy and depth of feeling are sacrificed for a wider and larger circle of relationships. In this sense, the range of the kinship system has been extended in the city, a situation notably unlike that in other areas of the world, where the kinship system has narrowed in range under modern conditions.

It will be instructive to examine the predicament of an urban man of wealth and power who finds himself in a subservient position in the kinship system to a distant relative of low status, since it is precisely this situation which is often seen as leading directly to the breakdown of kinship ties. Our wealthy Batak urbanite wants to preserve his capital and he must guard against excessive demands on his time, but he dares not offend his poor relative, particularly at public gatherings, because this would lead to widespread criticism from the entire urban community. It is not just criticism that he fears; he realizes that if his situation changes in the future he may need the support of his kin group. He is also aware that any flagrant violation of the Batak social and ceremonial system may lead to severe economic, political, or social sanctions. If he is a merchant, those who have been offended will not make purchases at his establishment; if he needs a political favor or a government loan, it might be denied; his wife may be ostracized by other women of the community; and it might be difficult to arrange a good marriage for his son. To ignore Batak tradition can hurt him economically and socially, so he naturally tries to avoid the application of these adverse sanctions.

My data indicate that the wealthy man plays the game according to the rules, but makes excuses when kinship demands become excessive. He attends the necessary rituals, contributes toward the cost of a clansman's ceremonial, and, in most situations, conforms to the requirements of his kinship role. If he behaves in this way, then his distant kinsmen will be less inclined to make demands upon him in situations in which it would be inappropriate — in the market place, a business office, or a government bureau. If, however, a request is made which exceeds the normal expectations of the kinship relationship, he will express great sympathy but claim that unfortunately he is not in a position to comply with the request; for example, he may say that he has suffered financial reverses, or that he has to repay a bank loan, or that he has to accumulate funds to pay for his son's marriage feast. His motives may be questioned by some, but no sanctions will be employed against him. The predicament of wealthy high-status urbanities is often a difficult, but not an impossible one; they generally handle conflicting sets of role expectations so as to minimize conflict, and some do so with considerable skill and finesse.

The attitude toward particularly close relatives is less calculating and impersonal. Those who are members of the minimal lineage, who trace their origin to the same highland village, and who are descendants of one grandfather or great-grandfather, do continue to constitute a corporate group and may cooperate economically. One wealthy urbanite contributed heavily toward university education of his brother's son; another permitted his father's brother's son to work his rice fields in the village without requesting a share of the harvest; and on the affinal side, still another paid the hospital expenses of his son's father-in-law who was recuperating from a long illness. Other examples of cooperation among lineage mates and close affinals could be cited from village or city. Most well-to-do urban families have had a succession of young people from their rural village reside in their homes. It is a reciprocal arrangement, in which the village youth assists in household tasks while the family provides room and board, and pays the cost of his attendance at one of the institutions of higher learning in Medan. The important consequence of this practice is that, in effect, the lineage invests in the education of its most promising young members; in Indonesia today this is an excellent capital investment.

The minimal lineage is a descent group, not a residence group. Some members of the lineage have remained in their village of origin, others have moved to new villages in the highlands, while still others have migrated to Medan; nevertheless they meet for all important ceremonies, assist one another in times of need, participate in the administration of lineage property, and visit each other fairly frequently. Residence in an urban environment does not necessarily mean that a man severs connections with his rural relatives or even that he becomes "urbanized." Some urbanites are, in fact, closer to their lineage mates in the highlands than to their next-door neighbors in the city.

Over a century ago the unity of the lineage was based upon common ownership of terraced rice fields — the key productive property in Batak society — and also upon the necessity for defense, since intervillage warfare, slavery, and cannibalism are reported to have been characteristic of the old culture. The lineage cooperated economically, fought together, and avenged insults to any fellow member. Today the rice fields are less important, particularly to urban businessmen; and warfare, slavery, and cannibalism were effectively stamped out by the Dutch colonial administration.

Why then does the lineage continue to constitute a meaningful corporate group? The lineage is a less closely knit group today than it was in the last century, and the functions it now performs are different from those performed in the past, but it still serves essential economic and defensive needs.

It would be beyond the scope of this paper to present a full analysis of the contemporary functions performed by the Batak lineage and the reasons why it has been maintained, but the bare outline of the argument will be presented (Cf. Bruner, 1961, for additional data). Indonesia is a new nation that lacks a strong central government, political stability, a rapidly developing economy, and a wide extension of welfare services. Without minimizing the tremendous strides made by Indonesia since its independence was gained, most observers and Indonesians alike would agree that the country still has a long way to go before achieving the degree of progress and modernization desired by all. In this context, kinship groups continue to serve important functions that in the established Western nation have been taken over by the state or other organizations. Further, there are a series of local conditions which have led to the maintenance of kinship ties in the city and which, to some extent, have strengthened them. The Toba Batak are a Christian minority in a predominantly Islamic society; their migrations to Medan have been comparatively recent and there is a constant influx of new migrants to the city; and Medan itself is populated by many different ethnic groups which compete with one another for economic and political power. Within recent times there have been knife fights between younger members of different ethnic groups, and the attitude of most Toba Batak toward other Indonesians in Medan, such as the Javanese, the Minangkabau, the Atjehnese, and the Karo, is one of suspicion and distrust. One response of the urban Batak to residence in an alien and sometimes hostile environment has been to solidify lineage and kinship ties.

Another response to the urban environment is the emergence of a new form of social organization in the city that has no exact counterpart in village society. The urban Batak form clan associations, *dongan samarga* (Bruner, 1959). Some associations have established scholarships and a revolving loan fund; all have officers and periodic meetings and serve as a corporate mutual aid and welfare society. Members assist one another in times of misfortune, but their primary function is to take responsibility for the organization of life-crisis rites that are performed on such occasions as a birth, a wedding, a house construction, or a funeral.

The clan association is simultaneously a residence group, a descent group, and a voluntary association. In order to join, a man must live in Medan, must be a descendant of the clan ancestor, and must choose to apply — membership is neither obligatory nor automatic. An additional criterion is that the applicant must pay the initiation fee and, to maintain membership, he must pay the nominal monthly dues.

The emergence of the clan association implies a need in the city for a social group intermediate in size between the minimal lineage and the larger community. In Medan there are, of course, occupational groups, restricted social clubs, labor unions, and political parties; but the clan association is a distinctly Toba Batak institution which crosscuts occupation, social class, and political affiliation. It is a product of the city, but it utilizes structural principles inherent in the traditional Batak descent system. In the village the clan is a descent category, whose members own no property in common, have no political headmen, and reside in noncontiguous areas; but in the city the clan association becomes a corporate social group.

Social affiliation is further extended because each nuclear family customarily joins both the clan association of the husband and that of the wife. The unmarried children become members of the two associations, and may participate in the affiliated youth groups. To put it another way, each urban clan association is open to both the male and the female members of the clan and their spouses, which doubles the membership and widens the scope of relationships.

In effect, it is the nuclear family rather than the individual, or even the minimal lineage, which joins an urban clan association. Husband and wife participate together. This is but one indication of the fact that the nuclear family, although important in the village, has become even more significant in the city. To a large extent this is a consequence of residence patterns.

In the rural areas today most households are occupied by a single nuclear family, but the family is located in a lineage context. A cluster of households forms a hamlet, and a series of hamlets, separated from one another by the rice fields, constitutes a village community. The core of each hamlet is a localized patrilineage, as patrilocal residence is followed in almost ninety percent of the cases. Thus a man's immediate neighbors in the hamlet will be his lineage mates; that is, his father, brothers, father's brothers, or father's brother's sons, with their spouses and children.

Residence in the city is neolocal, and there is no one section of Medan occupied exclusively by the Toba Batak. A newly married couple may select a home, which they either rent or buy, in any part of the city; their choice of location is dictated by such factors as personal preference, convenience, and cost. In most cases, the nuclear family will be physically isolated from lineage mates or other close relatives; a man's immediate neighbors are likely to be distantly related Batak or members of other Indonesian ethnic groups.

The physical isolation of the nuclear family in the city does not lead to the breakdown of unilineal descent groups, as indicated by the continued importance of the minimal lineage and the emergence of the urban clan association. All three social units, family, lineage, and clan, are meaningful corporate groups which serve somewhat different but significant functions for the urban Batak.

The aim of this paper has been to examine the extent to which kinship has declined in importance in an urban environment, and we are primarily interested in drawing conclusions about the direction of change. Thus we need a base line for purposes of comparison. Rather than compare the contemporary urban system with a reconstructed "aboriginal system" floating in a hypothetical "ethnographic present," the reference point for each statement about the changing role of kinship in the city will be the contemporary village system. My data support the following series of propositions:

(1) The urban Batak form a single kinship community, and the sense of ethnic identity is stronger among Toba Batak in the city than in the village.

(2) The range of the kinship system has been extended more widely in the city to encompass a larger number of more distantly related persons.

(3) Social relationships among urban kinsmen are generally less personal, intimate, and familial than in the village.

(4) The minimal lineage, which includes some members who reside in the village and others who live in the city, continues to be a meaningful, cooperative, corporate group.

(5) The urban Batak form clan associations, a corporate unit intermediate in size between the lineage and the community, which serve many social and ceremonial functions not performed by the village clan system.

(6) The nuclear family is more important in the city than in the village.

DISCUSSION

The major conclusion of this paper is that, for the Toba Batak, kinship has not been superseded or lost in an urban environment. Some authorities on the evolution of social organization apparently present us with a choice between a completely kinship-oriented society on the one hand and the absolute breakdown of all extended kinship ties, even the loss of kinship, on the other; and every system between is termed "transitional." The Batak data, in my opinion, do not support this position, with its implication that, as non-Western peoples become progressively modernized, they will eventually — and inevitably — develop a bilateral European type of family organization in which kinship plays a relatively minor role.

Clearly, the urban Batak kinship system has changed in comparison with the village, and it is highly probable that it will change even more in the future, in response to changing conditions in Medan and in Indonesia generally. There is an inherent conflict in the urban system between loyalty to the nuclear family and loyalty to the minimal lineage; most urban men prefer to pass on their property to their daughters rather than to their brother's sons. But the increasing importance of the nuclear family does not necessarily imply the complete dissolution of all extended kin groups beyond the personal kindred.

The emergence of the urban clan association among the city Batak supports my thesis. The clan association is a new and creative adaptation to the conditions of urban life, the reverse of breakdown and decline. It is not, strictly speaking, a unilineal descent group, since membership is not based exclusively upon birthright. I choose to call the clan association a "voluntary descent group," although it could also be regarded as a descent-based voluntary association. In any case it is a kinship group, in which all members are related to one another by consanguineal or affinal ties.

Indications of kinship breakdown should be more readily apparent among those segments of the urban community who occupy higher positions in the stratification system. Those who are wealthy, better educated, and who have lived in Medan the longest should have changed the most. A traditional, poorly educated, recent migrant is, in effect, a transplanted villager. The urban Batak community is stratified, but rather than study the differences between various groupings within the city, I was primarily concerned with a rural-urban comparison. In order to differentiate more clearly between village and city, I focused upon the wealthy elite and the upper classes of Medan; my aim was to contrast extremes. Thus the data on the urban system were gathered from among those who were the most modern and upwardly mobile in the city. If extended kin ties were in process of breakdown, I should have found it within this social segment; the fact that I did not lends further support to my position.

Nevertheless, the generalizations of the evolutionists may prove to be valid in the long run; possibly I have simply described one stage in the urbanization process. If this is so, then I am not entirely sure how long one has to wait for the process to complete itself: the customary one or two generations, or perhaps one or two centuries, or even longer. It is my feeling, however, that the creative adaptation to the city made by the Batak of Medan is neither unique nor transitory. The Batak clan groups bear some similarity to the clan associations of the overseas Chinese, to the turban tribal association of West Africa, and to the *zaibatsu* of industrial Japan. I suspect that future research on changing kinship systems among societies of the middle range now undergoing rapid cultural change, and among the newly urbanized peoples of Asia and Africa, will disclose not only the maintenance of existing kinship ties, but also the development of novel and stable recombinations based upon traditional structural principles.

12 ·················

Kishan Babu

JOSEPH LELYVELD

Mr. and Mrs. Kishan Babu and their two children live at a respectable address on Central Avenue in Calcutta, the site of a middle class apartment house. But thcy would not normally be considered either respectable or middle class, for they live outside — on the sidewalk.

There are about 100,000 such people in this teeming catastrophe of a city, presumably rootless and defeated. The assumption is correct in many cases, but not, surprisingly, in most of them.

At the age of twenty-two, Kishan Babu, for example, is neither rootless nor defeated. For orderliness and stability his life probably compares favorably with that of many of the apartment dwellers who live indoors at the same address.

He does not drift. Every night at about ten o'clock he and his family spread some matting on the same patch of sidewalk under the same portico. About forty persons are there — the same forty every night. They all say they are from Gujarat, a thousand miles away. But most of them, like Kishan Babu and his young wife, Lila, were born in Calcutta and grew up in its streets. They have never lived indoors.

The people under the next portico down the avenue are all from Bihar. And so it goes. On closer examination the clusters of sidewalk dwellers almost seem to be reproductions of Indian villages. The most striking difference is that the men greatly outnumber the women, and many of them send money home to their families.

Kishan Babu's cluster is more settled. Everyone in it pursues the same trade — one of the oldest, more marginal occupations known to this city in which productive work is even harder to find than a home. It is a three-stage operation, requiring plenty of enterprise. First they buy stainless steel pots from a wholesaler on credit. Then they go from door to door in middle class neighborhoods and exchange the pots for old clothes. Finally, they sell the old clothes, and pay the wholesaler. In this way, Kishan Babu and his wife clear four or five rupees a day (about sixty cents). They are always able to select their clothes from what they collect along the way, and their earnings are enough, barely, for their food.

Their only other major expense is the rent they pay for a locker, or stall, in a shanty on the other side of the avenue. It is five feet square, with a low metal roof that leaks and a damp dirt floor. It is here that they cook their evening meal over a wood fire. It was also here that Lila Babu gave birth to her two children, Dillip and Maya. To understand why the Babus choose to sleep on the sidewalk instead of indoors it is only necessary to visit the stall. The visitor regains the street with a deep sense of relief.

Most sidewalk dwellers, all but those who are completely down and out, have some tiny roofed space they can call their own, even if it is not inhabitable. It is this that gives them their legal existence: the address they need to qualify for a ration card, a vote, or a place in school for their children.

Kishan Babu is determined his children will go to school, as he himself did for a year. But he has little hope that he will be able to rescue his family from the sidewalk, something his own father never managed. "How can I?" he asks. "What is left after I pay the rent on that room you saw and buy the food for my family?"

This year the answer has been less than nothing. Food prices are higher in Calcutta now than ever before and Lila Babu's one gold earring — the family's most valued possession — is held by the pot wholesaler, to whom they owe eighty rupees, nearly eleven dollars. A good harvest, which could reduce food prices, would mean an opportunity to recover his wife's earring. Otherwise, Kishan Babu's life will go on as before.

13 ·················

Some Preliminary Observations Concerning the Anthropology of Industrialization

HAROLD A. GOULD

Because production is rooted in kinship structures in nonindustrial civilizations, occupational roles and the persons occupying them are ordinarily regarded as identical. The fact that most people are in addition residing in villages means that occupational role and status are easily discernible or, as Linton (1963) and those who have followed him (cf., Parsons, 1951, 1953) have put it, *ascribable*. The degree has varied somewhat historically but by and large stratification systems of nonindustrial civilizations have tended to be *ascription-oriented*, or caste-like. True caste has existed wherever the *ascription-oriented* stratification order has become *morally intrinsic*, by which I mean the development and ethical execution of the notion that the different occupational levels (some if not all) constitute different degrees of moral worth and purity and that,

"Some Preliminary Observations Concerning the Anthropology of Industrialization" by Harold A. Gould is reprinted from *Eastern Anthropologist*, 14 (No. 1):34–47, 1961, by permission of the author and publisher.

therefore, the people occupying these levels (because work role and persons are deemed one) are differentially morally pure. In such instances this has led to a concept of pariah or untouchable status where some are thought to be utterly morally impure because their occupations are contaminating. The final test of the degree of development of true caste is the degree of rigidity with which endogamy, anticommensalism, and other forms of social avoidance are maintained between functionally specialized groups that are mainly differentiated on the basis of occupation.

The nature of industrial technology works in strong opposition to the premises underlying ascription-oriented occupational stratification. Rural communities harbor an ever-dwindling minority of the total population while "feed back" from urban-centered productive and distributional systems converts even the rural remnant into an organizational- and value-satellite of the city. The need for efficiency in production, coupled with the increase in all forms of mobility, leads to a distinguishing between occupational role and role-occupant. *Achievement-orientation* becomes paramount in that one individual can theoretically occupy many occupational roles and thus statuses commensurate with his ability. In other words, stratification is in terms of *class* rather than *caste*.

In societies like India, nonindustrial civilization is still predominant although steadily yielding ground to emerging industrial civilization. Peasantries and preindustrial urban elements still abound even though demographic and economic factors are impelling more and more people to migrate into the city and get involved in the new pattern of life forming there. The villages themselves still manifest their dualistic character to a high degree — their admixture of centripetalness and contrifugalness, that is — and shall continue to do so for a long while even though the "feedback" process inherent in industrialization is very much in evidence (as, for example, in the N. E. S.). I have discussed and empirically illustrated this duality as it is currently operative in a previous paper (Gould, 1959) and have noted how its careful delineation might actually be made a basis for gauging change.

When peasants leave their kin groups in the villages and migrate to the cities, it may be for a number of reasons. But once they have done so, they are confronted with certain salient realities about their past and their present situation. They have come from rural communities where caste as a true system of ritually graded, functionally differentiated, endogamous, economically interdependent, localized social groups is operative; where fellow workers ordinarily are kinsmen or at worst fellow villagers; where places of work, socialization, procreation, and recreation are spatially coterminus; and where social relationships and obligations are founded upon personal ties, or what Parsons (after Weber) has called *particularism.* They have entered cities where work, play, procreation, socialization, and recreation are more often lodged in specialized groups that are not spatially coterminus in the sense that village activities are; where the personal relationship is rarer and far less dependable; where life's necessities and luxuries are obtained with money in a market that is bureaucratized and worldwide in its ramifications.

Thus, from an anthropological standpoint, what are the sociocultural environments into which the peasant enters when he comes to the city? What rearrangements must he make in the pattern of his social life and his personality? What are the most significant criteria for determining what he does and what positions he comes to occupy in the city? Why does he select this city rather than that one? And perhaps ultimately, at what point must we stop speaking of a person as peasant and begin regarding him as something else? What are the degrees by which a person is absorbed completely into the modern civilization?

At the other end of the process, we may ask what are the general and particular circumstances which lead to severance of an individual from his village community and kinship group and send him off into the city in search of his fortune? Within a given family, why is it, say, Son A rather than Son B who makes the break?

To begin with a very general observation, it seems accurate to say that when a person moves from the village to the city the determination of his social status shifts from its basis in a kin group to an occupational group. The effect of this is immediate, because the moment he arrives in the city, the person's job skills become determinant in the general location and level of his life there. It determines the former because the job obtained will be in some particular place and it determines the latter because the money income a skill commands dictates the general limits of amenities a person will be able to procure. In short, one's job is a major nexus of social interaction which in turn plays a profound and fundamental role in the delineation of all other patterns of interaction which a city-dwelling person will enter into.

Place of work and place of residence are spatially distinct in the city whereas they are normally coterminus in the village. A man or woman who holds a city job has a whole series of interactions during the hours of work with people whom they may rarely if ever see afterwards. This means that the variety of the backgrounds encountered in persons with whom one interacts in the natural course of one's life is infinitely greater than is true in a village. Take the matter of providing basic services to the families of "Sherupur" (pseudonym for a village in the Faizabad District). Eighty-one families in the village maintain service ties with specialists in washing clothes, barbering, blacksmithy, carpentry, etc., wherein a semi-annual payment of grain is made. Fifty-one specialists, or *purjans,* serve these eighty-one families and all of them reside in a total of only five villages which are inside a radius of two miles. In all instances it is a matter of a specialist *family* maintaining a perpetual service relationship with a patron *family* which, on both sides, is handed along from father to son as an aspect of the normal system of descent within the kinship units involved. Certainly such an arrangement crucially circumscribes the range of variety inherent in the interactions among villagers within a major section of the economic configuration upon which they rely. It is in marked contrast to Lucknow rickshawallas who reside in all portions of the city, on the one hand, and who, on the other hand, ply their trade over a very considerable area during the course of which they are in contact with a great variety (both occupationally and spatially) of persons. Furthermore, the rickshawalla sample indicated virtually no involvement in particularistic economic relationships of the kind which, in villages, fixes so rigidly the scope of interaction. In another sense, too, they reveal a heightened tendency toward freedom of movement: They tend to marry less frequently than villagers. Only forty-six percent of the rickshawallas were married whereas eighty-five percent of their comparable age group in the village (12–50) were. For them, occupational activity is not connected with maintenance of a corporate kin group through which *access to work* is determined.

Evidently, then, caste ceases to have much formalized relevance for occupational roles in the city. But this does not mean that it ceases to have relevance of another kind with respect to occupations, nor does it cease to have relevance for certain other systems of interaction which are of crucial significance to the city resident.

Among the fifty Lucknow rickshawallas interviewed, twelve Hindu castes plus Muslims are represented and these range from the purest Brahmans, to such deprecated groups as Kori and Luniya. All toil together in this single occupation and are daily rubbing shoulders with each other and with the great variety of humanity in addition. Groups or cliques of rickshawallas form at different strategic places in the city and at any given spot the clique may run the gamut of ritual purity. At one such place, the "regulars" include representatives of Brahman, Rajput, Jaiswara, Kahar, and Valmiki Hindu castes plus Muslims. They fraternise openly in gossiping groups, smoking groups, card games, jostling sessions, and the like. And they will at times join together to exclude from their station an "outsider" rickshawalla who seeks to operate from there.

Thus, as far as occupation and type and place of residence are concerned, rickshawallas form a category of the general class of *chhote-chhote kam karnewale.* As such, a Brahman or a Rajput in his day-to-day social intercourse is going to interact more frequently with a Luniya of comparable status that he is with a fellow Brahman who is college-educated and holds a job as an "executive" in a local business enterprise.

But it has been clearly shown by Srinivas (1957), Pocock (1957a), and many others that caste nevertheless occupies a place of importance in the modern urban environment. However, a distinction is made between caste as a system of functionally and ritually differentiated and interrelated groups and caste as a more general social category. The former is hardly possible to any meaningful degree under the *achievement-oriented* situation which prevails in the occupational sphere of the modern industrial civilization. Neither Lucknow rickshawallas nor business and professional elites could indicate any respects in which caste functioned for them in a sense comparable to the manner in which it functions in the village. They did not think of the obtaining or dispensing of goods and services as being in any respect formally connected with intercaste specialization.

Yet, both the socially high and the socially low knew their caste and unhesitatingly asserted that marriages are and should be caste-endogamous. I have so far recorded no case of a marriage which violates the *general* injunction against caste endogamy, although it seems possible that some of the narrower sub-groupings which would be a basis for endogamy in the rural areas cease to be in the city.

Where does the basis for this durability of the endogamous feature of caste lie? I would suggest it lies primarily in the kinship group where certain functions are still important which are reinforced by a concept of caste endogamy. What has been removed from the sphere of kinship control by movement from village to city are occupational and economic activities which are rooted in the urban division of labor. The bases of economic interaction in the latter are the impersonal market and the ability to take advantage of its opportunities for material gain through technical skill (part of which, perhaps the most important part of which, is obtainable through formal education in the broad sense that it includes both learning and training). Money is the predominant medium of exchange rather than grain (as in the rural, localized social system of the peasant farmer) and acquired abilities rather than "inborn" ones are the criteria of performance and reward. A morally intrinsic concept of occupational stratification fosters social and economic efficiencies in the nonindustrial civilization (given its technological base) but inhibits their attainment in the industrial civilization (with its very different technological base).

But clusters of kin groups ranked according to a morally intrinsic concept of valuation and kept endogamous on that account have a definite utility for the attainment of nepotic ends in Indian society as it exists today — in transition between the nonindustrial civilization and the emerging industrial order. They also continue to serve useful functions in the realm of the preservation of religious cohesion by keeping alive the concept of the patrilineal kinship group as a basic sacrificial structure through which the unity of past, present, and future is sustained. In many respects, that is, caste under contemporary conditions is a way of conserving and protecting interests and values in the face of the impersonalizing tendencies which are a fundamental consequence of the industrialization process.

In the job market, a caste tie is a kin tie at best and an extension of the logic of kinship ties to a wider circle at the least. And whereas, on the one side, the kin tie is restrictive it is, on the other side, obligational — which means that it can be the basis for circumventing purely technical criteria of entitlement to occupational mobility. In this sense it is akin to the "old school tie" and the "fraternity brother" or "lodge brother" so common in the West. Perhaps the added advantage of the caste tie is that it is invested with a great measure of sacred significance as well. As in the West, it is one answer to the impersonalization-bed "characterological" problems of 'alienation', 'loneliness', and 'authoritarianism' about which Fromm (1947), Adorno and his associates (1952), and Riesman (1950) have written so eloquently. Furthermore, in my studies of mobility so far, I have found that most peasants who migrate to the city do so along avenues laid out by kinship ties in the narrow sense and caste ties in the broader sense. One feature of this pattern which has struck me particularly is how almost any kin tie on the basis of which an obligational claim can be made is used for the purpose of establishing a personal (i.e., 'dependable') relationship which bridges the gulf between village of origin and city of destination. If none other is available, a wife's sister's husband's household may impel a young Kori in 'Sherupur' to make Ludhiana the city of his initial 'penetration' into the urban world of pecuniary opportunities. The quest for a personal tie overrides all the usual distinctions between affine and consanguine, lineal and collateral, relative once the peasant steps beyond his rural environment.

Caste, then, ceases to be a 'system' in the sense suggested by Bougle (1908), Pocock (1957b), Miller (1954), Leach (1960), Srinivas (1957), Majumdar (1959) and so many others — that is, a localized hierarchy of occupationally specialized and ritually differentiated groups oriented to local Brahmans — but comes to operate as a kind of social interlacing within the emerging industrial civilization.

At the same time, it would appear unnecessary to choose between caste and the caste system and say that one or the other is more permanent, more relevant, or more true. The nature of present Indian society makes it possible to affirm that *both* phenomena are vitally operative in their appropriate context. Not only this, which after all is fairly obvious, but I think that the peasants who have most recently migrated into the city and who still have ongoing kin groups in the village carry in their minds both aspects of caste and employ them interchangeably as they alternate from one environment to the other. At this stage of the transitionary process, in other words, it is not as much giving up one pattern of behavior and assuming another as it is a matter of adding a new structure to an already existing one and employing each where it has relevance.

Let me illustrate this by looking at urban-migrants' relationship to the division of labor in the village and the city respectively, both from the vantage of a village community which has given migrants to the city and from the vantage of an urban occupational category whose practitioners have roots in villages. These will, of course, once again be the people of Sherupur and the Lucknow rickshawallas.

In all the above cases we have represented individuals who have alternated or are now alternating between their characteristic village occupation and their urban calling. The two seem not to contradict each other in the sense that even though technically Sherupur families of Thakurs, Kayasthas, Muraus, and Ahirs have in common the (extra-village) occupation of railway employee, they do not claim equal ritual status within the village. Their extra-village job is one thing, part of one world, and their intravillage status and occupation are quite another, part of a different and distinct world. Just as the nature of the non-industrial civilization involves a symbiosis between distinct urban and village entities, so for the individual who straddles the modern imperfect repesentations of the worlds each of these entities represents must sustain a dual set of values and behavior patterns.

We can observe the same phenomenon in reverse order in the case of the sample of Lucknow rickshawallas.

Once again we can see illustrated the point that the relevance of occupational specialization to caste depends upon the setting. There is not a simple tendency for new castes to form in the urban area based upon its distinctive division of labor as some people have claimed. A caste of rickshawallas has not formed in Lucknow, nor a caste of chaprasis, nor mechanics, etc. Caste simply fails to be an operative factor for such occupations or indeed any occupations in the city (except for Dhobis and a few others whose services are still rendered on a familial basis).[1] Caste persists only in the respects in which status determinations can be made within the context of kinship structure. When ego is living in the city, his occupation is not embedded in his kin group; when he is living in the village it is. For in the latter, ego's kin group is an occupationally and ritually specialized unit which forms with other kin groups a component of the local caste system.

TABLE 8 *Occupational patterns of Sherupur migrants*

Caste	Traditional Occupation	Village Occupation	Extra-Village Occupation
Brahman	Priest	Agriculture	Land Manager Employee of Baniya
Thakur	Warrior-Ruler	Agriculture	RR Switchman Ekka driver Factory laborer Army Store clerk Gov't Farm laborer
Kayastha	Accountant	Agriculture	RR clerk Mason
Ahir	Dairyman	Agriculture Dairying	Gov't Dairy Railway coolie Store clerk Coal miner Dairyman Ekka driver
Kurmi	Agriculture	Agriculture	Gov't Farm laborer Yogi Cowherd Machine operator Weaver
Murau	Agriculture	Agriculture	Store clerk RR Signalman Apprent. mechanic Gov't Farm laborer
Sonar	Goldsmith	Goldsmith	
Lohar	Blacksmith	Blacksmith Agriculture	Gov't Farm laborer
Kahar	Water carrier	Roasting grams Menial labor	Coal miner
Kori	Weaver	Agriculture Farm labor Removing carcasses Midwifery	Farm laborer Rickshawalla Manual labor Ekka driver BA student

Chamar	Leatherwork	Agriculture Removing carcasses Midwifery Leather work Farm labor	Farm laborer
Gadariya	Goatherd	Agriculture	Gov't Farm laborer Ice-plant worker
Muslim	(No special)	Tailor Agriculture	Rickshawalla Tailor

The question arises as to who decides to straddle the two worlds. Who takes the first step toward potential alienation from the nonindustrial pattern of life and why?

I am not in a position to give any real answers at this juncture, but only to make some very tentative suggestions. It has been widely held that changed economic circumstances create the conditions which lead to peasant migrations. Bailey (1958) has shown how a point is reached in the partition or other forms of alienation of land where a family has to start selling land for the bare necessities like food and clothing. When this happens, Bailey believes that the days of a family as peasant proprietors are numbered and that other sources of income than land must be sought. Naturally, entering the urban job market is a major recourse under such circumstances.

There can be no doubt that the demographic, pecuniary, and other effects of industrialization produce such crises for peasants on a growing scale. But evidence from Sherupur suggests the need for a careful, detailed look at this process because the "point of no return" for a family with regard to commencement of the search by any of its members for urban employment may vary with caste status and other factors. For example, the socioeconomic level and ritual standing of a caste would seem to be of great importance in determining when a feeling arises that the "point of no return" has been reached which necessitates urban job-hunting by the members of a family. The evidence on which this statement is based, however, is as yet fragmentary and the whole notion may have to be changed or abandoned later on. But if two castes in Sherupur for which good data are available are any criterion, then the definition of the moment when fortunes have deteriorated sufficiently to induce urban migration must vary extremely widely. A comparison has been possible between families of the Kurmi and Kori castes who respectively did and did not have members who are or had been urban migrants. For each caste, two sets of factors were compiled: the average land-holding of families in each category and the average of their respective estimates of the number of months of food they derive from their lands.

TABLE 9 *Occupational patterns of some Lucknow rickshawallas*

Caste	Traditional Occupation	All Urban Occ's Given by Rw for Self or Kin	Village Occupation	Location of Village
Brahman	Priest	Food seller Cook	Agriculture	Gonda Sultanpur
Thakur	Warrior-Ruler	Laborer Hotel bearer Brick layer Servant Servant Pantry work Hotel bearer Army Chaprasi Clerk	Agriculture	Nepal Gonda Almora
Kurmi	Agriculture	Factory laborer Lohar Mechanic	Agriculture	Basti
Murau	Agriculture	Mali Chaprasi	Agriculture	Gonda
Jaiswara	Leather	Kitchen work Bearer Laborer	Agriculture Farm laborer	Azamgarh Faizabad
Kahar	Water carrier	Chaprasi	Agriculture	Faizabad
Kori	Weaver	———	Agriculture	Lucknow
Kumhar	Potter	Laborer	Potter Agriculture	Faizabad
Muslim	(No special)	Laborer Hotel chaprasi Tonga driver RR Fireman Truck driver Bicycle mechanic Cook Box maker Carpenter Hawker Tailor Kite maker	Carpenter Agriculture Darzi	Lucknow Gonda Garakhpur Etawah Allahabad Unnao Hardoi

In terms of land-attrition and food-security, the average Kurmi family seems to feel its standard of life and levels of aspiration cannot be satisfied within the village when land holdings sink beneath twenty *kachha bighas* and food expectations from land reach the vicinity of six months. Koris, on the other hand, are showing no strong tendencies to leave the village when in possession of no more than two-and-a-half *kachha bighas* with only two months or so food guaranteed them; but by the time losses have reduced their holdings below a *kachha-bigha*-and-a-half they are beginning to reach beyond the peasant community and into the pecuniary world of the city in search of supplementation. It must be remembered that in both cases we are dealing with kin groups who, in the case of migrants, have members working in the city while the preponderance of their relatives are remaining in the village. In this situation we appear to have something approximating the germinal economic condition which sets in motion, in India at least, the initial movement of peasants into the city.

TABLE 10   *Amount of land and food estimates of two castes in Sherupur*

Occupational Situation	Kurmi			Kori		
	Chulas N	Kachha Bighas	Months Food	Chulas N	Kachha Bighas	Months Food
Entirely in village	10	25.0	7.7	10	2.6	1.8
Members outside	12	16.6	6.4	6	1.4	1.0

Further research will be needed before deeper insights into the process are obtained, especially into the interpersonal component. For we eventually arrive at the problem of what psychological patterns within the kin group determine, once the wider socioeconomic conditions emerge, which individual or individuals are selected to make the break and go into the city. Obviously, patterns of interpersonal conflict are crucial factors in this, and I have data from both village and urban informants which suggest that very often he who departs is one who has fallen into conflict with his fellow kinsmen (especially the father or the brother). But this is a very general observation and to go deeper requires minute investigation of the psychic interactions of some families who have entered into the industrial civilization in the form of giving migrants to it and then comparing them with families who have as yet given no migrants.

We must remember also that it would be fallacious to assume that a dichotomy exists between "harmonious" fully peasant families and "disharmonious" migrant-giving families. All families are *personal communi-*

ties within which psychological dynamics are in constant operation, and under all conditions these include problems of frustration, displacement, neurosis, psychosis, etc., and mechanisms for dealing with them. The real questions are how and when does this inner psychological dynamic of the *personal community* incorporate into its structure the element of displacement of members outward into the industrial civilization as an aspect of attempting to deal with tensions.

Obviously, here is the connecting link between socioeconomic and psychological dimensions of the anthropology of industrialization. Future investigations must cast light on this issue. It is easily possible to demonstrate that no such simplistic social structural explanation, divorced from consideration of the role of the *personal community,* as Le Play's *famille souche* (that is, the elder son remains with the parents while younger sons migrate) is really adequate for our needs. Such a view is not actually an explanation at all but merely a component of one which speaks only of a general relationship between economic change and modifications in traditional social structure. Exceptions abound and prove as interesting as the rule, as the data from Sherupur and Lucknow rickshawallas indicates.

TABLE 11 *Kinship status of peasant migrants*

	Sherupur		Lucknow Rw	
	N	%	N	%
Where parents are alive				
Fathers only	7	18	2	7
Father and son	2	5	1	4
Only son	—	—	4	15
Elder son only	10	25	5	19
Junior son(s) only	2	9	2	7
Elder son and one or more junior sons	3	8	4	15
Where parents are deceased				
Elder brothers only	2	5	4	15
Junior brothers only	7	18	4	15
Elder brother and one or more junior brothers	6	15	2	7
Totals:	39	99.0	28	100.0

The foregoing shows that a great variety of combinations take place respecting urban migrations, combinations which can only be explained in part with economic and cultural generalizations. One sociological pattern which seems to be strongly manifest, however, is the preponderance of "senior" family members who are involved in migration — that is, persons who are in the category of fathers or elder siblings. Thirty of the thirty-nine *chulas* in Sherupur who have migrant members show this tendency as do twenty-two of the twenty-eight rickshawallas' *chulas*. And this pattern, incidentally, is diametrically opposed to the *famille souche* notion.

In psychological or interpersonal terms, it might by hypothesized that there is a level reached in the economic life of a peasant family where all of the labor at its disposal in the form of resident kin are no longer economically employable within the family's property domain. Before this occurs, the typical corporate unilineal family that is the productive base of the nonindustrial civilization, being relatively sufficient unto itself, is able to absorb the shocks and tensions generated by the interplay among its divergent personalities. The authority of the patriarch and his surrogates, the reinforcements supplied by the tightly knit village community, and the unfeasibility of "escape" from the local scheme of life combine with the economic vitality of the family to hold dissention down and to channelize it when it occurs into tradition-satisfying activities. But the economic changes brought about by industrialization upset this pattern. Conflicts can be acted out in entirely new terms. The city is a center of 'anti-tradition' where local authority in all its forms can be evaded. Internal family tensions get projected into an emerging setting which is yielding explosive population increases, ever more atomized concepts of property relations, and ramifying pecuniary standards of value and taste. Under these conditions, surplus members begin to be drained off into extra-familial, extra-village environments in accordance with the dictates of the opportunities newly presented, on the one hand, and the selective implications of familial interpersonal relations, on the other.

Thus, a major research problem for the anthropologist of industrialization is to see how and when the pendulum swings and at precisely what points the individual members of kin groups begin turning to these new pathways for solution of their interpersonal tensions. This inquiry is going to require much close observation of people in both the village environments and the various environments which the urban division of labor in the emerging industrial civilization creates for the migrant.

NOTES

1. And certain business castes like Khatris

14 . . . .

Urban Migration and
the Residence of Children
in Kampala

AIDAN SOUTHALL[1]

Some information about the extent to which women of different income and status levels in Kampala have their children living with them in the city or away from them in rural areas is here related to some of the main assumptions commonly made about migration and urbanization in Africa. These I take to be that most African cities are very new and growing very fast (Southall, 1961:6–11), fed by large-scale migration from rural populations which are also growing very fast, and that in these developing societies rapid economic growth is the top national priority, assuming political independence. It is also thought likely, as well as held to be desirable by public policy, that a more stable urban population should emerge as greater skill, education, higher wages, and fuller experience of urban living are acquired. At the same time, it is known that most independent African countries profess some form of socialism, often vaguely defined, together with the belief that the class differences of developed

150

capitalist countries are a foreign, Western phenomenon, which need not and should not be reproduced in African societies.

Like any general statements, these are subject to variation from country to country and person to person. Important qualifications may be noted without destroying their general validity. Where the evolving facts turn out contrary to the views held, the views still have considerable influence. Prevalent views actually may inhibit, delay, or modify a contrary outcome; they also may have unfortunate and unforeseen consequences, for they hide the facts of the situation from African elites and from foreign businessmen or agents of economic aid who would deal with them.

Many West African (and, of course, North African) cities have a much older urban and preindustrial tradition than those elsewhere (ibid.). Adequate data are not yet available, but it is already plain that the achievements of the Development Decade in bringing the desired improvement in the well being of the people have been disappointing for reasons both internal and external, political as well as economic. A more stable element in the urban population is emerging gradually (Vogel, 1968), but if population growth produces a rise in urban migration beyond the increase in available jobs, the unstable migrant element will be replenished constantly. The white minorities who rule the minerally rich and strongly industrialized countries of South Africa (especially the Republic of South Africa and Rhodesia) deliberately perpetuate a migrant element in the urban population through rigorous controls over movement and the failure to recognize some residents as legitimately employed. Countries like Kenya and the Ivory Coast warmly welcome foreign capitalist investment; others like Guinea and Tanzania restrict it while endeavouring to pursue more strictly socialist lines of development. Many others have been hampered in implementing a clear policy by changes of regime and internal disturbances. Meanwhile, in most countries marked differences in wealth and standards of living are becoming entrenched, so that it is difficult to see how traditional extended kinship obligations can prevent indefinitely the appearance of strong class feelings.

Uganda, with its capital city of Kampala-Mengo (Southall, 1966a), is representative of this general situation. With its present population of about 180,000, the city must be considered mainly a colonial creation, although it does have older roots of continuity and tradition in the capital of the Buganda Kingdom, whose presence on Mengo hill influenced the new colonial administrators to settle there. Since the Buganda capital had 10,000 inhabitants at the very most, it is apparent that growth has been rapid — especially since the Second World War.

Growth has occurred in the population of Uganda and in migration to urban areas and other centers of employment; yet the official figures of wage employment for the whole country and for Kampala Municipality have been rather stable over the last ten years or more. The number of employees in Uganda reached a peak of 244,539 in 1960, fell to 221,649 in 1963, then rose to 256,800 in 1967. In Kampala there were 30,900 employees in 1948, and 37,000 in 1966. Although the coverage of the labor census has improved, it still omits important categories of small-scale employment such as domestic service which accounts for several thousand in Kampala, and the more informal types of small-scale work for African employers. Furthermore, the figures refer only to Kampala Municipality and do not include Mengo and the whole growing urban fringe, even though the administrative boundary of Kampala was extended in 1968 (from 8¼ to 75 square miles) to include these areas. Great efforts in economic development have been necessary to keep pace with the rising population. The most recent figures gives an estimated real growth rate of 2.8 percent in gross domestic product for 1967, matched by an estimated population growth of 2.5 percent.

Sample figures indicate that for the poorest urban migrants the number of living children per woman is lower than it is for those who are better off, while the number of living children per woman is even higher for wealthy Ganda families long established in the capital. At the same time, more of the children of the poor than of the better-off are left behind or sent to reside in the country rather than in the town.

The primate city of Uganda has been described from many points of view (Southall, 1956; Southall and Gutkind, 1957; Southall, 1966a; Southall, 1967) as a duality, derived from the older component of Mengo, the precolonial *Kibuga* (capital) of Buganda (Gutkind, 1963) and the Municipality of Kampala, whose core, from 1890, was its European and Asian commercial and administrative settlement until the independent African government of Uganda assumed political power in 1962. Sociologically it is a single urban area. Hence, I have called it Greater Kampala, or Kampala-Mengo (Southall, 1966a; 1967), in affirmation of this compelling unity which finally was recognised officially when the Uganda Government made it a single urban corporation in 1968.

Since Mengo always has been the main area of African residence, the data for this study were drawn from two of its parishes. Traditionally regarded as the strict preserve of the Ganda royal family, the leading chiefs and their retainers, Mengo is now greatly altered. The pressure for accommodation by huge numbers of Africans of many ethnic groups, and by smaller numbers of Asians and Europeans, has brought great wealth to African property owners in the area, but has destroyed the former character of the capital. African workers have poured into all parts of the *Kibuga* to find living space. In the densest areas, such as Kisenyi and the parts of other parishes adjacent to the Kampala municipal boundary, the overcrowded conditions have driven out the old families. Some are still to be found in townhouses on their freehold estates in the less crowded parts of the *Kibuga* and are being joined constantly by *nouveaux riches* who succeed in acquiring the outward symbols of their status.

Wealthy Ganda families usually employ members of other ethnic groups who live on their property. Landowners divide their properties into smaller and smaller plots for leasing. Many houseowners rent rooms to migrant workers. Some absentees own 'long houses' (six or more rooms built in a row) in which they rent rooms to individuals or families — a system which inhibits the growth of concentrated ethnic settlements, since each tenant must accept whatever accommodation is available. Certain ethnic groups (Toro, Ankole, Karagwe, Acholi, and Luo) favour particular areas, although they cannot always be actual neighbours. One such cluster of thirty grass huts, occupied by about 120 persons, mainly Ankole, has been described.

> The fact that this is a settlement almost exclusively of one tribe, each individual having gained entry by introduction of his friends, has led to the development of a happy community, observing its own rules and customs for the benefit of all. This is a migratory community, with a marked pattern of movement which may be compared with that of a homing pigeon, in that they always return to the same colony. The main attraction appears to be the advantage of living among those who are known and trusted, and very low rental facilitating maximum savings. . . . This appears to be a successful tribal settlement. But while recognising the assistance given to developing a sense of community by such settlements, it might be unwise to encourage tribal groups larger than thirty persons, owing to the dangers of tribal disputes (African Housing Department, 1956, 60–61).

The settlement contained few women or children; its male population belonged to the lowest income group and earned about 65 shillings a month. Had a rent of more than five shillings been demanded, these people probably would have moved further out to avoid it. In fact, they were paying a rent of only one shilling per head.

> Temporary housing appears to be the most suitable for migratory labour. The migratory element in the population should be recognised, and frequent changes in tenants accepted by mutual consent . . . Improved standards of housing in town are neither expected nor desired.
>
> Clearly where large numbers of men are satisfied with insanitary accommodation which is not weather proof and whose almost sole desire is to save as quickly as possible a certain sum of money and then return home, such people are unlikely to be interested in the improvement of their conditions which will require greater outlay by them (African Housing Department, 1956).

Most migrants stayed for only six or seven months, housed in this way around the margins of the urban area. Most buildings in the denser areas were of mud and wattle with corrugated iron roofs. In 1953 such a room could be rented for about 15 shillings a month, but as much as 25 or 30 was demanded for a lodging of more permanent materials with cement floor. In the Government Housing Estates a bed-space cost five shillings a month and a house with one living room ranged from 10 to 16 shillings.

People of particular ethnic groups and income levels are associated to some extent with certain sectors of the urban area through the natural outcome of social and economic forces without any purposeful planning. For the most part, however, there is great variation of ethnic affiliation and income level in each locality, so that well-defined social relationships between close neighbours are often unlikely.

Both the upper and the extreme lower-income categories are insulated from the full impact of town life, which falls most forcibly upon the middle classes. The very lowest paid categories, like the Ankole described above, stay in town for the shortest period, tend to relie on their fellow tribesmen, and remain least affected by or committed to the urban environment. They contribute to the numerical preponderance of men over women in the urban population. No doubt they absorb urban attitudes from the talk they hear and the company they meet at beer parties in their leisure hours. The wealthy population receives less direct impact from urban life because their participation as an African élite in the professions, in local and central government, in business, in the religious missions, and in education, has prepared them to adjust to change.

The poor, short-term migrants form about 25 percent of the population employed in Kampala Municipality. The élite categories are approximately the upper 15 percent of income categories and more especially the top 10 percent. The middle range of earners, who become most involved in urban life with least preparation for it, form the remaining 65 percent of the total. Their situation will be illustrated by further data from Kisenyi. In 1953, the poorest short-term migrants earned less than 70 shillings a month, the middle range earned from 70 to 150 shillings a month, and the élite categories earned over 150 or even 200 shillings a month.

By 1963 monthly income had doubled. While in 1954 about 42 percent earned less than 50 shillings, and 77 percent less than 100 shillings, in 1963 only 25 percent earned 100 shillings or less per month. In 1953 only 8 percent earned over 200 shillings a month, but in 1963 this category had risen to 27 percent. In 1953 the category earning 150 shillings or less represented the poor (approximately 85 percent) including unskilled, lower-paid skilled, and clerical; in 1963 the comparable category would have been the 85 percent earning 300 shillings or less per month. This dividing line corresponds to earnings of $21.50 per month in 1953 and $43.00 in 1963.

Kisenyi is characterised by a high degree of independent economic activity in retail trade and petty professions (Southall and Gutkind, 1957). Most property-owners live elsewhere, others live off the rent of rooms, and some combine this with other occupations, especially brewing of beer. Another source of income is prostitution or rotating concubinage; of course, this is difficult to assess statistically.

Ganda are by far the largest ethnic group, but still a minority of the total population. At 41.3 percent of all adults, women form a higher proportion than in most parts of the urban area. Since many men prefer to leave their wives in their rural homes, most of the town women are actually single, in the sense that they are not living in permanent, stable unions. Their presence indicates the degree of emancipation of women, their freedom of movement, and the particular attraction which certain urban areas have for women of different ethnic groups.

In Kisenyi, Mulago, and some other inner suburbs, Ganda women considerably outnumber Ganda men; this is also true of Haya women in Kisenyi. Women form about 25 percent of all adults in the other main ethnic groups densely settled within two miles of the centre of the town. Further out in the two-to-four-mile belt where the poorest migrants live, Ganda numbers approximate those of a normal, nonmigrant, rural population, and the women are slightly outnumbered by the men.

Wealthy families, always a minority, have been displaced as certain areas increase in density. A court tradition from precolonial days motivates the chief Ganda families to maintain both town and country houses, and the new elite try to secure suitable land and residence near the town. For all these families, therefore, the townhouse in the capital is a very distinctive symbol. Interviews with the occupants of such houses in Namirembe parish revealed that most occupying families were the elite described above, but that some were relatives and caretakers.

The most striking demographic contrast is in the number of living children per woman in poor areas like Kisenyi or Mulago and in wealthy areas like Namirembe. The research design classified households with income less or more than 150 shillings per month, and women according to age — those under thirty, those between thirty and thirty-nine, and those forty years or over.

Kisenyi women of rich households have more children than those of poor households. The number of children per woman increases with age, except that in the poor households older women have fewer children than young women. (If older women had children on whom they could depend they would probably not be living in Kisenyi at all.) In Namirembe the average income and wealth of rich households is much greater than in Kisenyi and the number of children per woman is also much greater in all three age categories. Furthermore, older women form a far higher proportion of the total in Namirembe than in Kisenyi. The actual figures are given in the table below:

TABLE 12   *Number of Children*

Women Aged	Income of Household Head		
	Kisenyi		Namirembe
	Up to 150 Shillings	Over 150 Shillings	Over 150 Shillings
16–29	0.49	0.95	1.93
30–39	0.77	1.60	2.77
40 and over	0.43	2.42	4.88
	(n.288)	(n.143)	(n.189)

In the reckoning of biological fertility live births which do not survive must be included; such information is inordinately difficult to obtain. For the reckoning of social fertility it is the surviving children that count. This index is, of course, much cruder than a net reproduction rate. There can be no question that the largest families are the wealthiest and best-educated, with the highest standard of living and the greatest social mobility. Unfortunately, the factor of social class, so closely connected with wealth, education, and standard of living, has been grossly neglected in studies of biological and social fertility. We are fortunate to have data on the biological fertility of two of the ethnic groups, the Ganda and the Haya (Richards and Reining, 1954), but we have none which links this to the class referent.

To emphasize the significance of differential social fertility in the various categories of the town population we must consider the actual place of residence of children whose parents are in town. Because many men prefer to leave their wives in the country, this data is restricted to the numbers and place of residence of children whose mothers were in town. Women without children have also been included.

In the Kisenyi population, 288 children came from families with incomes less than 150 shillings a month and 143 children from those with 150 shillings or more. In the former category 163 children were actually living in the country and 125 were in town. In the latter category 59 were in the country and 89 were in town. Wealthy families have more children, and more of them live in the town. This is true for all the African population, though the emphasis varies, as the following figures show:

TABLE 13 *Residence of Children*

	Up to 149 Shillings		150 Shillings and Over	
	Rural	*Urban*	*Rural*	*Urban*
Income of Household Head in Kisenyi				
Women Aged Up to 29				
Ganda	14	16	12	14
Other Bantu	39	9	7	5
Non-Bantu	23	35	10	18
	76	60	29	37
30–39				
Ganda	24	17	11	14
Other Bantu	27	23	2	4
Non-Bantu	16	14	0	17
	67	54	13	35
40 and Over				
Ganda	4	8	3	8
Other Bantu	13	2	5	3
Non-Bantu	3	2	4	6
	20	12	12	17
All Ages				
Ganda	42	41	26	36
Other Bantu	79	34	14	12
Non-Bantu	42	50	14	41
	163	125	54	89

Income of Household Head in Namirembe

Ganda	Rural	Urban
Up to 29	3	53
30–39	2	46
40 and Over	35	50
	40	149

Even among the poor, the non-Bantu keep a far higher proportion of children in town than the Ganda and other Bantu. The non-Bantu in Kisenyi are largely nilotic Luo from Kenya who constitute an ethnic group second in size to the Ganda themselves, whose home area it is. Traditionally organized in localised, segmentary lineages and contracting marriage with a high bridewealth payment in cattle, Luo marriage is much more stable than that of most Bantu peoples of Uganda. The collective authority and control of Luo kinfolk remains quite effective even in town and is expressed in the organization of ethnic associations (Southall 1966b). Within this framework more Luo feel capable of rearing children in the urban environment; whereas, many others find the urban environment so unfavorable to stable family life that they leave their children with rural-based relatives.

Assuming that the present demographic situation of the urban area is maintained over time, a continuous migration from the countryside would be required to replenish those males and females who do not reproduce themselves. It would also require redistribution in the countryside of surplus men and women from the wealthier urban families, or their absorption into the urban population. This estimate also assumes the regular turnover of short-term migrant labourers and their families. It is somewhat paradoxical that, among the poor, those who spend least time in town have the highest social fertility, but in the country and not in the town, while those who stay longest fail to reproduce themselves and have to be replaced from the countryside. It is not only the fact that many men leave their families behind when they come to town, but that men who remain in town seem to be socially infertile in both the urban and the rural axes of their existence. It is impossible to say whether town life causes low social fertility among the poor or whether it attracts those who already display it.

If we reject the unreal assumption that the urban demographic situation is unchanging, the most acceptable alternate assumption is that, in absolute terms, all categories of the population are increasing, and that the average length of time spent in town by each category is also increasing. This means that the socially infertile category, which has to be replaced from elsewhere, will require a larger replacement than before, while the socially fertile wealthy group will produce an increasing surplus.

It is vitally important to secure adequate demographic data which takes proper account of income and status differences, as well as ethnic factors. Meanwhile, it should be noted that the correlation demonstrated of larger numbers of children with high-status families and smaller number of children with low-status families is contrary to contemporary demographic assumptions in advanced countries. The number of surviving children is a cruder measure than the net reproduction rate, but undoubtedly on either basis higher-status, residential families are associated with the more fertile categories. The association of larger families with higher status in Kampala (instead of lower status, as in the West) may bear formal comparison with the early phase of the industrial revolution in Europe, and may be a passing phenomenon in Kampala if policies of population control gain strength. Because this seems unlikely in the near future, the situation holds important implications for policy and planning in education, housing, and urban development. It also could influence social stratification, since, if more children grow up in high-status than in low-status families, the experience of downward mobility will be more frequent than that of upward mobility in African economies where real output and income per head are only growing slowly.

NOTES

1. I gratefully acknowledge the support of the East African Institute of Social Research (now Makerere Institute of Social Research), Kampala, Uganda, and of the Uganda Government, which enabled me to carry out this research.

15

Africans in Industrial
Towns in Northern Rhodesia

J. CLYDE MITCHELL

The rapidly developing towns in Africa are presenting some difficult problems to those who are interested in human affairs. One of these problems, which is likely to have considerable bearing on the future of African territories, is the emergent pattern of social relationships. When we are faced with this problem we are tempted to compare the course of events in Africa with that in England following the Industrial Revolution. There are, to be sure, a number of interesting parallels, possibly because an industrial system imposes its pattern on any society; but this should not obscure the important fact that there are also some significant differences.

These differences must be related, I think, to the social backgrounds of the people from whom the towns in England and Africa drew their num-

J. Clyde Mitchell: *Africans In Industrial Towns In Northern Rhodesia* from His Royal Highness the Duke of Edinburgh's Study Conference on the Human Problems of Industrial Communities within the Commonwealth and Empire published by Oxford University Press.

bers. The salient feature of African rural societies is that kinship dominates all social relationships. A man's status in a tribal society is largely determined by his position in a kinship group. He lives in a village area almost invariably because he is a kinsman of the village headman; he cultivates his gardens with the aid of his kinsmen; he rises to positions of authority through succession within a kin-group. His relationship with his chief tend to be cast in terms of kinship and even prolonged commercial relationships tend eventually to be transformed into fictional kinship relationships. For African tribesmen, therefore, the kinship system tends to reduce all types of social relationships to a few categories, and there are customarily defined ways of proper behaviour towards persons in these categories. A man knows that if by some devious reasoning he must call another 'my mother's brother,' then he should behave towards him in a particular way and that that person should reciprocate in another. Kinship thus imparts a structure to social relationships, thereby providing African tribesmen with a certain order and stability in their dealings with their fellows.

In England the social structure in the rural areas has developed from the feudal system in which a man's position in society was determined not by kinship but by his relationship to the lord of the manor. Land rights were an essential element of this relationship. The feudal system gave way to a society in which social relationships were determined particularly by the position men held in a system of social classes between which standards of living increasingly became the main distinguishing feature. The English labourers who were drawn into the rapidly growing industrial towns at the end of the eighteenth century, while they may have missed the neighbourly help and intimate life of the village or farm, were at least accustomed to a life in which social relationships were determined not by kinship but primarily by the part played in the productive process. When we come to consider the system of social relationships which is developing in the towns of Africa we must take into account the fact that the majority of those being attracted to them have had no experience of social relationships outside the closely knit and essentially personal kinship system.

Before we consider the pattern of social relationships among urban Africans we should appreciate certain essential demographic features. I confine myself from now on to the towns in Northern Rhodesia in which, under the auspices of the Rhodes-Livingstone Institute, I conducted social surveys during 1951 to 1954.

It is common knowledge that industry in Southern Africa has been developed on the basis of migrant labour. A man leaves his tribal area, works in town for a relatively short period, and then returns home triumphantly to his rural relatives with the spoils of his trip to town. The skilled component in the labour force has been provided by Europeans, while the

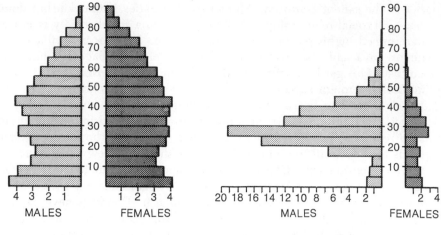

FIGURE 2
*Towns 50,000–100,000,
Great Britain, 1951*

FIGURE 3
Witwatersrand, Africans, 1936

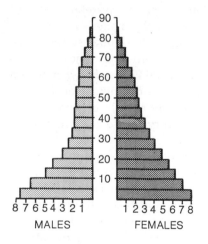

FIGURE 4
N. Rhodesian Rural Africans
(Estimated) 1951

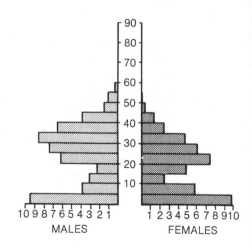

FIGURE 5
N. Rhodesian Copperbelt,
Africans, 1951

relatively unskilled Africans perform those tasks which as a rule require physically fit and energetic men. The tendency, therefore, is for Africans in the towns to be predominantly in the working age-groups. The diagrams opposite show the relative proportions of men and women in different age-groups in four different populations. The first is in English towns of medium size, the second is the African population in the gold-mining areas of the Witwatersrand, the third is on the Copperbelt of Northern Rhodesia, and the fourth is what I estimate the rural population of Northern Rhodesia to be.

If we compare the Copperbelt diagram with the one for the rural areas we see immediately the extent to which the urban population is drawn very largely from people between the ages twenty to forty-five. In other words, there are relatively few older children aged from ten to twenty, and relatively few mature and old people on the Copperbelt. Another feature of the Copperbelt population emerges if we examine the diagram for the Witwatersrand. The striking feature of the population on the Witwatersrand is the relative lack of women. On the Witwatersrand there are 596 men to every 100 women between the ages of fifteen to forty-five. On the Copperbelt this figure is 142. In other words there is a large pro-portion of married couples on the Copperbelt. The following table shows this:

TABLE 14

	Adult males percent	Adult females percent
Single	20.3	2.3
Married, spouse in rural area	14.3	0.9
Divorced	2.8	1.1
Widowed	0.3	0.3
Married	62.2	95.4

From Table V, *African Urbanization in Luanshya and Ndola.*

In short, a striking feature of the Copperbelt African population is that it is composed very largely of young married couples and their young children. The particular significance of this emerges when we have con-sidered some other demographic characteristics of the population.

The African labour in the mines is, as I have said, principally migratory. In our consideration of the system of social relationships developing in the towns we are interested in two different aspects of the migratory be-haviour of labour. Finally, we are interested in the degree to which they have been out of contact with their rural kinsmen. Those who have been away for a long time may be presumed to have forfeited their claims to land in the reserves and to have chosen to live permanently in the in-dustrial areas. Secondly, we are interested in the mobility of Africans within the industrial areas, whether from town to town or from one resi-dential area in the town to another.

It is not easy to assess the amount of contact of an African townsman with his rural home. The contact may be maintained either by relatively short visits home, by the visits of his rural kinsmen while he is in town, or indirectly by his sending gifts and letters home. As a rough rule-of-thumb we may look upon those who have spent more than two-thrids of their time in town since they turned fifteen years of age as being predominantly town-dwellers. On this basis between 40 and 45 percent of the adult men in the two Copperbelt towns and Broken Hill fall into this category (Mitchell, 1954b). In Livingstone the figure is 33 percent (McCulloch, 1956).

These men, however, must not be thought of as forming a settled population in any particular town. There is a good deal of movement between towns. In a survey in the non-mining residential area in Luanshya, for example, 47.5 percent of the adult men and women had been in Luanshya for less than five years (Mitchell, 1951). In Livingstone the proportion was 68 percent (McCulloch, 1956), and in Lusaka 56.2 percent. (Thomson, 1954). If we had the data on the movement of the population from one residential area to another within these towns we would find that the instability is even greater, and that on the average a family stays in any one particular area for only a very short time. This extreme mobility of the African populations in towns is related to many social factors which I do not wish to describe here. For my purposes at the moment I merely wish to indicate that in addition to the youth of the population, its high mobility is another outstanding characteristic.

A third feature of the African population in the towns of Northern Rhodesia is its diversity of origin. Each town has a hinterland from which it draws its labour. The labour hinterland of the Copperbelt is very wide indeed, extending as it does from Angola in the west, Tanganyika in the north, and Nyasaland in the east. (Towards the south the labour is attracted to Southern Rhodesia rather than to the Copperbelt [Mitchell, 1954a; Niddrie, 1954].) The labour in the towns is therefore drawn from many tribes: in the social surveys on the Copperbelt we have encountered over 100 different tribes. The proportion of men from these tribes on each of the mines and in each of the towns on the Copperbelt differs, but in general the most numerous single tribe accounts for no more than about one-tenth of the total population.

There is a tendency for men from the same tribe to live together in single quarters, but the men with families are usually on a waiting list for married accommodation and must take the first house that falls vacant. The result is that the tribes are not congregated in particular parts of the residential area, but are mixed throughout. It is as likely as not for a man in a house in the married area to find his next-door neighbour to be a man from a tribe whose customs are unfamiliar and indeed whose language he cannot speak.

The picture of the urban population that emerges from these basic facts contrasts directly with that of the rural areas. Instead of a population long familiar with each other through having been brought up in small village communities, the urban population is one in which contacts must of necessity be mainly with strangers and be fleeting and transitory. Instead of having their senior kinsmen as village elders to impart authority and stability to the community, they have compound managers, location superintendents, district officers and their African employees.

We could not expect that kinship would operate in towns as it does in rural areas. In industrial areas European supervisors draft men to their work gangs as they present themselves for employment. It is extremely unlikely that two kinsmen will land up in the same gang. The clock and the production schedule dominate the days' activities and there are few opportunities, except at weekends, for kinsmen to gather and participate in the joint activities that encourage and express their unity. More important than this is the fact that in any one town there are likely to be few kinsmen of the appropriate degree necessary for joint activities and these are likely to be scattered in distant houses. In the towns, therefore, the kinship system changes to meet the demands of the new situation. In rural areas kinsmen of a particular degree support each other and operate jointly in the daily tasks of living. In towns kinsmen of any degree whatsoever may be called upon to perform tasks which normally they would not do in rural areas. For example, when a Bemba couple decide to marry in a rural area the wife's sponsor, who is the kinsman chosen to represent the wife's people in all transactions concerning the marriage, is almost invariably either her own brother or her mother's brother. In a sample of 183 marriages contracted in Luanshya I found that only one-third of the sponsors were brothers or mothers' brothers of the wife. The others were a wide variety of kinsfolk: only two were nonkinsmen. The rights and duties associated with only particular categories of kinsmen in rural areas are spread in towns over kinsfolk of all degrees. In this way the kinship system is widened to accommodate the changed conditions of urban life.

But because of the great diversity of the urban populations, a man or woman in everyday casual contacts with his or her neighbours and fellow townsmen is likely to deal not with kinsmen but with strangers. The stranger may in fact come from the same tribe but be unknown, but it is more probable that he will come from a different tribe. People in rural areas are apt to take their tribe for granted, but when they come to town their tribal membership assumes new importance. Where there is such ethnic diversity, fellow tribesmen feel they have sufficient in common to stand together in the face of other tribes in spite of their possible previous lack of association. There is therefore an active manifestation of tribalism in urban areas. Men who were possibly opposed to each other in their rural homes now combine in a faction fight against some other tribal group or cooperate to form a friendly society or a dancing-group. Because tribal characteristics are so easily displayed in dress, behaviour, and, in particular, in speech, tribalism becomes the most important means whereby day-to-day relationships on the Copperbelt are organized. Certain groups of tribes either through historical connections or cultural and linguistic similarities have affinities. Others are linked through special joking relationships which prescribe performing certain burial rites on the one hand and ribald joking on the other, but in general, from the point of view of any one tribe, the others can be arranged in an order which reflects the social distance between them. The network of tribal relationships thus provides a framework by means of which any African is able to fix his relationship with any other.

It should be emphasized that this tribalism is something new which has grown up in the industrial areas to meet the new situations in which the Africans find themselves. It is something quite different from tribalism in the rural areas, where we imply the whole structure of the tribe, based as it is largely on land-rights and kinship. Tribalism in towns provides categories into which people may arrange themselves in day-to-day interaction. It follows that the system of social control appropriate in a rural area will not necessarily operate in a town; indeed it is difficult to see how it can, since in the tribe much of the social control is exercised through the ancestor cult by senior kinsmen.

From the point of view of the developing social structure on the Copperbelt the history of the Tribal Elder system is particularly instructive. Early compound managers appreciated the significance of tribalism to Africans in towns and appointed a representative from each of the more important as a member of a council. This council was to provide a means of expressing the Africans' opinion to the Compound Manager and also as a channel through which the instructions of management could be conveyed to the people. These tribal representatives also undertook the duty of settling all the minor domestic disputes which formerly had been brought to the Compound Manager. The tribal representatives had only been in operation for four years when they were put to test in an industrial dispute. In 1935 the African workers on some of the mines withdrew their labour, following an announcement by the Government of increased taxation. From the point of view of the mine managements the tribal elders were the representatives of the African workers. Far from being a go-between between the workers and the managers, however, the elders either became the militant leaders of the riots that ensued or they were completely rejected by the workers and had to seek the protection of the Europeans. Again in 1940 at Mufulira, when African workers struck for higher wages they rejected the tribal elders as their organ of negotiation with management and instead elected their own 'committee of seventeen' for this purpose. In 1948 the African Mineworkers' Union came into being and for some time the Tribal Representatives system operated concurrently with the union as a means of approach to management. But this competitive situation did not last long. The management issued all tribal representatives with gowns presumably as some sort of badge of office. This precipitated an acrimonious dispute between the African Mineworkers' Union and the tribal representatives during which a union official assaulted a tribal representative and was consequently charged, convicted, and jailed. Shortly after this, in 1953, the union held a ballot among its members on the future of the tribal system. They voted overwhelmingly for its dissolution and it ceased to have any further official existence (Epstein, 1956).

The lesson we must draw from the history of the tribal elders is that while tribalism is significant to Africans when they are interacting with each other, it loses its significance when they interact with Europeans. The total social structure of Northern Rhodesia (and any Southern African community in fact) is dominated by the colour cleavage. Those on one side of the cleavage tend to appear to those on the other as an undifferentiated mass. Hence as far as Africans are concerned, Government, mine managements, commercial concerns, and all other organizations in which Europeans hold dominant positions appear as one category — 'the Europeans.'

In a situation where Africans as a whole are placed in opposition to the Europeans the Africans tend to overlook the internal differences within their community. During the strike in 1955, for example, some authorities confidently expected that the Nyakyusa would not come out on strike. The Nyakyusa represent a substantial proportion of labour on the mines and are noted for their essentially 'labour migrant' attitude to work on the mines. In fact almost all labour outside clerical and professional positions came out. On the other hand it is extremely significant that a struggle for power *within* the union was phrased in tribal terms, so that we must conclude that while tribalism is a significant factor in determining social relationships among Africans themselves it disappears when they interact with Europeans.

Tribalism is not the only factor which determines social relationships of Africans outside their own circle of intimate acquaintances. Position in the civic structure is also important. Certain Africans are employed in positions of influence, such as clerks, supervisors, and to some extent policemen, by the mines, central government, and local government. The prestige of men in these positions is derived from two main sources. First by virtue of their position in the line of authority they are seen to be men of power and are respected accordingly. A large proportion of the leaders in various types of quasi-political urban associations have been recruited from men in these positions.

But a second source of prestige is equally important. Tarde, a French philosopher writing sixty years ago, pointed out that imitation proceeds from the socially superior to the socially inferior. An acute observer wrote of Africans in Broken Hill in 1940: 'The African cannot but wish to gain the respect and to share the civilized status and the new wealth of the Europeans, whose general social superiority is always before them' (Wilson, 1942, p. 15). The way of life of the dominant Europeans has thus become the scale by means of which urban Africans measure prestige. Most Africans in town, particularly those in semi-professional white-collar and supervisory positions, strive to attain what they consider to be 'a civilized way of life'. They aim to be meticulous in their dress, furnish their houses with European-type furniture, eat European-type foodstuffs, possess radios, read newspapers, talk English to each other, drink bottled beer instead of the traditional brew, patronize ballroom dancing instead of tribal dances, and so on. They strive in fact to take over the European way of life, as they see it, as fully as they can.

The upper stratum of this prestige continuum tends to despise those who are unable to achieve a 'civilized' standard of living and tend to associate with those who share their own standards. There are not many who are able to share these standards. On one mine, for example, in a random sample of 1,779 men 55.5 percent had had no schooling at all and only 2.1 percent had completed primary school education. In another mine in a sample of 527 men 70.9 percent had had no schooling while only 1.4 percent had completed their primary school education. It is clear, therefore, that the proportion who can achieve a 'civilized way of life' is really very small. Our analysis of the social structure in urban areas had not proceeded far enough for us to say whether those high in the prestige scale are drawn from different tribes or not. Preliminary results seem to suggest that certain tribes predominate in certain occupations so that it is possible that divisions tend to coincide with those based on socioeconomic criteria (McCulloch, 1956). We should not assume too readily that so-called 'class' divisions are cutting across tribal divisions, so causing a rearrangement of the social structure of urban African communities.

Like tribalism these 'class' divisions do not provide a barrier to African unity in issues which involve relationships with Europeans. Instead, the position seems to be that because of their education, the fact that they can speak English, and their relatively better understanding of the European way of thinking, those at the top of the prestige scale tend to become accepted by all Africans as their leaders to represent their interests to the European authorities. The present-day African National Congress, for example, arose out of an amalgamation of various welfare societies which from the beginning recruited their members from the 'intelligentsia'

(Coulter, 1933). They have also filled the positions on the Urban Advisory Council since free elections were introduced (Epstein, 1956).

It seems likely that in the future 'class' will supersede tribal affiliations, but whether 'class' differences will ever become strong enough to divide the African community in situations involving Europeans depends on developments in a social field which is much larger than merely the industrial towns.

16 . . . .

Nigerians: The Dream
Is Unfulfilled[1]

LEONARD PLOTNICOV

The country boy goes to the city. He is looking for fame and fortune — or at least a job. But the farm remains "home" — his family, his roots, and possibly even his heart are there. He swears he will not desert the old people or the old ways: he will send back money; he will write; he will visit; he will renew his ties; and when he has made his fortune he will return to spend the remainder of his life in the bosom of his family.

It seldom works out that way in the industrial nations of the world. And now, even in developing nations of Africa, many people are finding that they can't go home again.

From late 1960 to mid-1962 I did anthropological field work in Jos, a city of over 50,000 in Northern Nigeria. Almost every ethnic group in Nigeria is represented, and in approximately the same proportions as for the nation as a whole. Most of the people I spoke to — those who had come originally from the country — stated emphatically that they felt that the small towns or farms they came from were their "real" homes. They were in the city to make money. Someday they would return.

Their descriptions of these real homes were lyrical and idyllic. The contrast to the city was strong. They did not merely *hope* to return; already retirement houses were being built for them (with money they sent) and they were able to describe the houses and the states of construction in considerable detail.

They were so persuasive and specific that for a long time I believed them — as, undoubtedly, they believed themselves. I believe now that "return home" is merely a widely-held myth — a golden dream that cannot be fulfilled completely and may never be fulfilled at all.

The ties to home are real enough, psychologically and economically. The migrant is entitled to share in the benefits from family land and property, and he is expected to return for important family events and ceremonials, especially funerals. Even if he cannot attend on these occasions, he is expected to help pay their costs, which can be large. Gifts are frequently exchanged, including food stuffs. Immigrants particularly like to receive familiar foods unobtainable in the cities — especially those actually grown on the home farmland.

Why then can't the dream be fulfilled?

One major reason is that the natures and demands of the home ties themselves make friction easy and the accumulation of wealth difficult. Since first loyalty must be to homeland and family, requests for money cannot be easily refused — and they start early. Money that might become investment in a business or savings in a bank is spent instead on traditional gifts to chiefs, and elders, gifts or support for relatives (some rather distant), help during illness or for lawsuits, and educational expenses for young male relatives.

The heaviest requests from home fall on those with most apparent success — professionals, traders, clerks, skilled workers. The wealthier of those I spoke to took pride in their ability to meet their obligations, even if it meant financial strain. The poorer complained of "family parasitism" and stated defensively that they preferred to live at a distance. But even they kept writing to the family and tried to meet at least some of the requests.

What happens if a city dweller doesn't send money home? It becomes obvious that he has abandoned his people and the simple rural virtues and been corrupted and seduced by that Babylon, the city. Pleading poverty is not a good defense: anybody who can't make money in the city must obviously be weak in character, dissolute, lazy, spendthrift, incompetent, and generally useless.

EATING BUSH MONEY

Unfortunately the urban people foster the naive beliefs of greenhorn immigrants and old folks at home that city streets are practically paved with gold. Costs are high by rural standards, and wages melt away on essentials — but city dwellers either can't make this clear or don't try. When they come home on visits they almost invariably reinforce the belief that they are doing well. Naturally, they want to impress relatives and "put on the dog" a little. In addition, according to custom they must be generous and distribute money, tobacco, and beer. Stay-at-homes take advantage of the situation to put the squeeze on the city cousin. This form of milking and exploitation is called "eating bush money." If the city dweller ever really hopes to come back he must put up with this, because if he doesn't he will be humbled. To live in the country, one must respect country judgements and standards. Also, in Southern Nigeria, loyalty to home and proof of intention to return must be visibly expressed, by erecting an expensive European-design retirement home. Coming home with dignity is not cheap.

And even the emigré who does return will not find ready acceptance. He has been in alien territory, he has acquired strange customs and viewpoints, he is a threat to the local orthodoxy and the local elite. He can sweeten such a reception usually only at the price of joining that conservative elite himself — defending the old ways, scornful of the outsider, and making the *parvenu* unwelcome.

So only a relative handful actually return. Valdo Pons found a similar situation in Stanleyville, indicating that the same pattern may be present in the Congo. Many men told him that, whatever their feelings, they knew they could not go back to the rustic life to stay:

> . . . the village people are . . . distrustful and jealous of those who have "followed the Europeans." One may return home to visit, and most . . . do so, but to return home permanently is . . . courting disaster. "They like you to come back for a few months," one man explained, "but if you stay for good they will poison you."

The changing use of land also makes return very difficult. Southern Nigeria, with government encouragement, has turned more and more to cash crops — palm oil, cocoa, rubber, and bananas for export; palm oil, yams, plantains, rice, maize, and kola nuts for local markets. The larger farms necessary for cash cropping become available precisely because some heirs give up their rights to divided plots and go to the city. They do not, of course, give up their claim to a share of family income from the land.

HOME IS ALWAYS ELSEWHERE

Distance does not always make the heart grow fonder; it may foster distrust. Many of my informants complained that they were dunned for money too often — they could not understand exactly what was going on at home, or how their money was being used. They were suspicious that they were not being told everything. One man told me that when he was asked for forty or fifty pounds he sent one or two, "just to keep them quiet." This in turn apparently roused resentment from those at home.

Commonly, the city people complain that their kinsmen — "brothers" — don't repay loans and even cheat them, that they make false reports of family income and "eat" all the profits. Some said that if they left a kinsman in charge of building the retirement house he falsified costs and embezzled funds. Sometimes a wife might be sent back to supervise the remaining construction — but in case of dispute, the house usually remained incomplete.

Perhaps the kinfolk accused were really innocent; but just as they had trouble understanding or believing stories of hardship and poverty in the city, the city dwellers in their turn had trouble believing that crops had been *that* poor, hired labor troubles *that* bad, market prices had fallen *that* far. A city worker could express his displeasure and distrust by withholding money, or by staying away from family ceremonials. But that might cause a country relative to feel that he would be justified in retaliating by cheating.

Disputes are inevitable. What is a fair share? Is it fair to share and share alike on a jointly owned farm when the city "brother" does not work on it?

Some city dwellers try to cover up their grievances, meet only minimal obligations and make only brief appearances at home. Those who do visit often avoid open discussion of disputes, either to keep the visit "pleasant" or to keep up a front before outsiders. But avoidance can be interpreted as guilt — and the longer grievances remain covered, issues are dodged, accusations not challenged, the greater the chances of revenge. In Jos, some old people were pointed out to me who, I was told, were afraid to go home because they might become victims of sorcery; others feared being poisoned. Some retired people intended to go home eventually — but meanwhile they didn't feel well, the climate in Jos was better, and so on. Some even went home, gave up after a while, and came back to Jos.

The reasons given for not returning are many, but most of them mention lack of money — and the shame and fear that causes. "When my business was good, I had planned to go home. . . ."

A retired motor mechanic kept delaying his return — he said he did not have enough money to finish his retirement house. "It's a shameful thing to go home before the building is finished. People'll say, 'What kind of man is this who lives in his father's house and hasn't built his own?'" When after one year I suggested that Jos was really his home because he had lived there longer than on the farm, the real reason came out: "Jos is not my home. I stay here because I fear poison at home. I don't have enough money to satisfy them now. If I go home they'll be expecting me to be rich and give them plenty. Some might have an evil mind if I don't give enough. If I don't satisfy them they'll try by all means to take my life. Those people will come around day after day and I will have to entertain them with plenty of drinks and food. They think that when anybody goes to 'bush' he gets rich — so they want to eat 'bush' money That's the only reason I stay so long."

Since so few return to the farm to stay and probably even fewer will do so in the future, why is there still a pretense? There are two major reasons:

Even if the city Nigerian will not go home, he does not want to cut his ties completely. As long as the idea and the hope are maintained, the lines of communication stay open, relationships and loyalties are observed, and gifts are exchanged (even if the flow is mostly one way).

"Home is elsewhere." This legend reconciles the immigrant to the loneliness and to the absence of family in the faceless city. Also, if he achieves little success, he has a ready psychological compensation and retreat: he belongs and he has value in a better place — back home.

NOTES

1. This article is one of the results of three years of research (twenty months spent in Nigeria) conducted by Leonard Plotnicov under the sponsorship of the National Institute of Health. His current writing and research focuses on the development of modern, urban Africa. He is assistant professor of anthropology at the University of Pittsburgh.

17 ....

Onitsha Market Literature

DONATUS I. NWOGA

A vast reading public exists in Nigeria and a large body of literature is addressed to this public that has not been much acknowledged in serious discussions on African literature. Sociological and economic factors have concentrated in certain centres a big collection of people who have left school after the minimum period of six to eight years with enough knowledge to be interested in reading novels, but not enough interest, or time, or even reading ability, to tackle the major novelists who were, in any case, in most of the novels available in the markets, talking of an environment that was most unfamiliar to the people under consideration.

Tutuola was published in 1952 and was acclaimed in Europe and America but was not known in Nigeria. Ekwensi's *People of the City* came out in 1954. A few more novels have been published, Tutuola, Ekwensi, Achebe, Nzekwu, Aluko etc. But the people have had their reading matter from the 1940's. It started with cheap, popular Indian novelettes. These came in large quantities, with flashy "romantic" pictures of glamorous women being kissed by he-men on the covers, and large scale advertisements for talismen for all occasions — love, examinations — at the back. Then Nigerians started to supply their own material. One of the first titles to appear was Ekwensi's *When Love Whispers* which came out about 1947 with three others, published by Tabansi Bookshop in Onitsha. By 1963 there were more than 250 titles extant. And this, I am sure, is not the total. These books go quickly out of print. As with much popular art, there is no sense of preservation or continuity. Books are often not reprinted because they would be "out of date." One of the authors, Momoh Aroye of Aba, showed me twenty-six titles that he had had published. Only five of these were available in the markets. The others had had their run and disappeared. When the readers finished with a book they used it for toilet paper or rolled their tobacco in it to make cigarettes or just threw it away.

This lack of a sense of continuity has led the publishers not to put dates of publication on their books. One of them explained to me that if the date indicated that a book was up to a year old nobody would buy it. This lack of dating presents a problem to an interested person who wants to trace the development of theme — but I suppose that is not the concern of the people engaged in the business of publishing and selling. The point here is that many of the titles are lost. But there are about 250 current titles, which gives an impression of the prolific output of the authors and the volume of the audience.

The bulk of this production is concentrated in Onitsha. Onitsha has always had the largest number of students in secondary and commercial schools, approved and unapproved, of any town in Nigeria, if not in West Africa. The Onitsha Market is also one of the biggest in Africa. Students and market traders make up the largest audience for this type of literature, and that is one reason for the concentration. Another is that Onitsha has a vast number of printing presses, and they are ready to print anything.

Unfortunately, many of these printing firms are staffed with compositors so poorly educated that they produce spellings so extraordinary that a reader has to work to extract the writer's words. Within three pages of a novel like *Rosemary and the Taxi Driver,* for example, we are told that Rosemary "had packed all her suitcases like sardines and noisted (hoisted?) her headtie on her onboards shaving (a hair-style)," that "her voilet (violet? violent?) gown with vibrant colours and heavenly colours vested (rested?) below her knees," that she "gestriculated" (gesticulated) and that she said that "Lagos is a neautiful (beautiful) town." Sometimes, of course, the mistakes are the author's. Printers also present another problem. It appears that an established printer, for a price, will help to popularise a new enterprise by sending out his own products in the name of the new. It takes a lot of searching, and one is suspected for doing this, to discover who actually did print some of the books.

One thing that has to be realised from the start is that the authors of these pamphlets are serious in their intentions and with their art. In May 1962, the authors, through their Union, launched a magazine called *The Nigerian Author Magazine*. Unfortunately, this was a failure, especially a financial disaster for the editor, Momoh Aroye. Only the first issue ever came out. But what is important here is the moral purpose expressed in the editorial column:

> In the verdict of a prolific writer, literature is supposed to reflect the time we live in — and that kind of literature being more prevalent than anything else, we are compelled and study it as "The Mirror of the Age."
>
> In spite of harassing difficulties which are often inevitable at the initial stage of any set-up, the fact remains clear that we obviously have explored new educational grounds by digging the well of knowledge with a needle, and by offering sacrificial efforts to launch this magazine — to serve as a desirable asset to the community. That in theory and practice is indubitable. That too, as is here evident, is a colourful exhibition of latent powers unpurchaseable in the literary field; and a material contribution to the national progress of this country. In the main, let's call it a bold venture of a significant educational value — that which exceeds much expectation.
>
> 'Author' is, in our own candid opinion, and in the opinion of those who matter in the literary field, a prouder title than 'king' . . . (p. 3)

The emphasis is on educating the people. Education in the limited sense has produced pamphlets like *How to Write Good English and Compositions, How to Write Better Letters, Applications and Business Letters, How to Succeed in Life, How to Conduct Meetings, How to Write Love Letters*, and there are five different pamphlets on *How to Know Hausa, Ibo, Yoruba and English Languages.*

Mostly, however, education is taken in its broader sense and these authors are trying to teach people to live a more moral life. One of the more serious concerns of the Union of Authors was to eradicate what they called "immoral, immaterial, aching, unartistic and flowery manuscripts" and they claimed that "all literary productions bearing our 'certificate of suitability for publishing' are censored and polished." And in the prefaces to many of the pamphlets we read, "It is to satisfy the romantic, offend the callous lover, redress the selfish principles of the monopolistic admirer that the novel is written"; "This is a story about a married couple who had spent most part of their time in playing 'High Life'. This afterwards brought trouble into their domestic set-up," and again, "This is a way through which the public can learn good and bad."

More than three quarters of the extant titles aim at the education of the readers, and more than half of these have to do with the relationship between men and women, boys and girls. This, in a way, is inevitable because when there is a break-up of established moral conscience, sex is the most common direction of expression of the new freedom. And so we have titles like *Beware of Harlots and Many Friends: The World is Hard* by Okenwa Olisa; *About Boys and Girls* by R. Obonkwo; *Rose Only Loved My Money* by H. O. Ogu; *Our Modern Ladies' Characters towards Boys* by Highbred Maxwell,(?)[1] *Why Men Never Trust Women, The Sorrows of Love, Money Hard But Some Women Don't Know* by Okenwa Olisah, *Why Harlots Hate Married Men and Love Bachelors* by Money-Hard, and most explicitly *Beware of Women* by Nathan Njoku. One of the authors declares in his preface:

> I have declared a wordy war with girls and ladies of nowadays and warn them to stop deceiving and telling lies to boys and also stop demanding much money from their boy friends.

There are many titles in this vein, warning men against the pitfalls they could fall into in their dealings with women, the dangers of bankruptcy in trade due to overspending on extravagant girls, the possibilities of students failing their exams because of chasing girls.

On the other hand, there are novels warning girls of what they let themselves into when they go with certain men. There are pamphlets like *The Broken Heart* by E. Uba, *How a Passenger Collector Posed and Got a Lady Teacher in Love* by H. Ogu, *The Sorrows of Love or Why Maria Killed Her Husband* and *John in the Romance of True Love* both by Thomas O. Igu. The danger expressed here is that girls are the ones that get pregnant and ruined. They might be going with boys who will leave them anytime, especially when there is trouble, and who will even go sometimes with the girls' own friends. One of the Prefaces reinforces the point:

> This drama . . . will serve as a warning to some of our girls who are often carried away by some fantastic never-to-come promises made to them by men.

In spite of these titles, there is really no balance and the greater bulk of the pamphlets is addressed to the masculine section of the population. The writers are men and most of their readers, after all, are men. And women, since the time of Eve, have caused most of the troubles in life. It appears they haven't yet paid for it in the volume of derogatory literature addressed against them. In most places, and Africa is no exception, the man is always right.

These writers produce an image of a new type of African girl. The girls are no longer the traditional quiet, modest, playthings of their parents.

They write love letters. They are coy. They demand presents from their boy friends and victims. They even deceive men. Thy are no longer the dumb creatures to be won through their parents — *Miss Comfort's Heart Cries for Tommy's Love* by C. N. Aririguzo (?). They are sometimes too proud for the suitors that come to them either because they consider themselves too educated to accept the common suitor — *Miss Appolonia's Pride Leads Her To Be Unmarried* by C. N. Aririguzo (?) or they think themselves too beautiful — *Beauty is a Trouble* by R. I. M. Obioha. The beautiful ones are the most dangerous. A popular record in Nigeria was a song by "Lord" Kitchener of the West Indies — "Never marry a woman prettier than you." The novelists make a point of this in *Stella at a Beauty and Fashion Parade, Nancy in Blooming Beauty* by Momoh Aroye; *Susanna 'The One in Town'* by G. H. A. Obi Nwala and *Jonny the Most Worried Husband* by H. O. Ogu.

The girls have changed and the boys need a new technique to tackle the new situation. Many authors have offered their prescriptions: Felix N. Stephen has supplied many means in his novels and plays — *The School of Love and How To Attend It. A Journey Into Love, How To Play Love, How To Make Love, How To Get a Lady in Love,* and he also offers a warning in one of his titles *Be Careful! Solution Is Not Love.*

Others prefer to approach the problem through letters and so we have titles like *How to Write Love Letters* by N. Njoku (?), *Our Modern Love Letters* by R. I. M. Obioha. A lot of guides have been produced to help the young men — *How to Make Friends With Girls* by R. Okonkwo, *A Guide to Marriage* by N. Okonkwo (?), *Guide for Engagement* by High-bred Maxwell (?), *How to Fall in Love With Girls* by H. O. Ogu. To some, love is a game — *The Game of Love* by R. Okonkwo. To others it is an art — *The Art of Love in Real Sense* by Speedy Eric. All are agreed that it is something to be approached with technique and caution. Many point out that the boys have to pretend that they are poorer than they really are in order to test the girl's love and find out whether it is for the person or for his money. All are agreed that the moment the girl starts making demands for presents is the time for the boy to draw back. They recommend however that the boy should make presents within his ability to his girl friend.

I mentioned earlier that these novelists present the image of change among the girls. Many times they do not disapprove of a certain type of change. One of the most serious problems that young men encounter is that of finding enough money to afford the bride price. Sometimes fantastic sums like £ 300 are asked from young men who are struggling to make £ 100 a year in the lower ranks of teaching or in trade. A law was passed sometime ago in Eastern Nigeria (and most of the writers are from Eastern Nigeria) limiting the bride price to £ 30. This law is practically impossible to enforce as the father of the bride can refuse to allow his daughter to marry. Normally private agreements are arrived at and a receipt for £30 is given though more than £150 could have gone into fulfilling a variety of customs. This concerns the young writers intimately and they take their opportunity to raise to heroic proportions the girl who stands against her father in favour of the young man she has chosen to marry.

Ogali A. Ogali was one of the first to use this theme and he established the pattern that has become typical of the treatment of this topic. His play *Veronica, My Daughter* achieved immense popularity and sold up to 60,000 copies. The dramatis personae include a girl and her confidante: Veronica and Alice here, Alice and Caroline in *Alice in the Romance of Love,* Agnes and Beatrice in *Agnes the Faithful Lover,* Maria and Teresa in *Beautiful Maria in the Act of True Love.* Then there are the parents: the father, wicked and half illiterate, the mother more educated and on her daughter's side; then there are the two men, the suitor approved by the father — usually old, rich and half-illiterate, and the unapproved suitor — young, handsome, educated, but above all poor and unable to pay anything beyond the government sanctioned price of £30.

The story usually starts with a discussion between the heroine and her confidante in the parlour of the wicked father's house. It is soon disclosed that the heroine is unhappy because she is in love with a young man and her father has provided her with a rich old friend of his own. But the girl is determined to marry her young man even if she should die for it. Agnes declares in *Agnes the Faithful Lover* that she will die and "Then my name will go into history as having died like Julliet (sic) for the cause of true love." Then comes the ogre of a father shouting for his "Mi-si-si-o" and talking in pidgin English as evidence of his half-illiteracy. The wife arrives and her support for the daughter leads to a beating that brings the neighbours in. These neighbours normally support the husband who has a right to dispose of his daughter without interference from a wife who thinks herself superior. But a meeting is called of the relations and the father is normally terrified by the threat of law into submitting.

Ogali created an exciting dialogue situation out of the discrepancies in the standard of spoken English. In *Veronica, My Daughter,* Chief Jombo, feeling that Veronica, his daughter and Pauline, his wife, were trying to browbeat him with their superior knowledge of the English language, sent for Bomber Billy, reputed for the word bombs he could throw. The following dialogue then ensued when Bomber Billy arrived:

> CHIEF JOMBO: My pikin, you hear how my Misisi and Veronica my
> daughter dey talk grammarian for me?
> BOMBER BILLY: Madam, what's the meaning of all the hullabaloo that

disturbed my capillary and tonsorial artist from discharging his duty efficiently, thus compelling me to have a pedestrian excursion to this place?

PAULINA: (?) [sic] My husband does not want Vero to marry the man of her choice and I feel he is making a sad mistake.

BOMBER BILLY: You are the person labouring under a delusion and not your husband.

VERO: What are you after? Are you hired to disturb us now?

BOMBER BILLY: If you talk to me again, I simply order your father to put you in a coffin of ostracism.

CHIEF JOMBO: Yes, make una talk grammarian. My pikin, talkam I dey hear.

PAULINA: You must know, Billy, that I am at least older than you and (you) MUST stop talking nonsense now.

VERO: Don't mind him. Does he know more than Mike (the man of her choice) who has his Inter B.A.

BOMBER BILLY: Look here! Are you promulgating your exorditation or articulating superficial sentimentality and amicable philosophical observation, beware of platitudeness and ponderosity and learn to respect my integrity.

CHIEF JOMBO: Here! Here! [sic] (he claps and laughs) I hear you! Talkam, my pikin, for dem moth don closs.

VERO: My Mike will answer you well when he meets you.

PAULINA: Never mind that hopeless boy who is rather irresponsible.

BOMBER BILLY: Your statement, Veronica, indicates nothing but a psychological defeatism because you do not take into account the spirit of dynamism in my cerebrium and cerebellum.

PAULINA: I assure you that you are rather miscocopic [Microscopic?] to be noticed. A negligible pocket radio that utters useless words.

BOMBER BILLY: I must advice [sic] you madam, to let your conversational communications possess a cherified [clarified?] consciousness and cogency, let your entamporaneous discernment and unpermitted expectation have intangibility, veroness and versity. Avoid pomposity, proticity, verbocity and rapacity.

CHIEF JOMBO: Talk now misiss! My pikin, go your way and when they talk too much again, I go callam you.

BOMBER BILLY: Thank you, Chief. Before I go, I must make your wife know that she, as a woman, is expected to maintain perfect tranquility whenever you talk to her. Well, goodbye all. I'll see you again.

CHIEF JOMBO: Salute your papa for me — O!

EXIT BOMBER BILLY

There are various things of interest in this passage. There are Pauline's appeal to the traditional respect due to older people, Veronica's equation of Mike's Inter B.A. to the peak of academic prowess (it used to be!), and Bomber Billy's appeal to the traditional place of woman in the society, and his choice of words. This concatenation of bombasts would be greatly effective on stage in Nigeria where big words do make an impact. One shares Chief Jombo's enthusiastic asides. Achebe points at this love for big words in the speech of the President of the Umuofa Progressive Union at the reception for Obi Okonkwo in *No Longer at Ease;* Bambulu, in Henshaw's *This is Our Choice,* says of himself and his medicine:

> This is the child of my brain, the product of my endeavour and the materialization of my inventive genius. It is an anti-snakebite vaccine. Western science has not succeeded in producing anything so potent, but I, Bambulu, have, without any laboratories, without any help, produced this medicine from the herbs of this village. I am a Scientist, I am an Analyst, I am a Catalyst. You may one day find this anti-snakebite vaccine very useful. It is a remedy not only for snakebites and various insect stings, but also for various canine and reptilian contingencies.

And Wole Soyinka's teacher, Lakunle, talks of the custom of paying bride price in *The Lion and the Jewel* as

> A savage custom, barbaric, out-dated,
> Rejected, denounced, accursed,
> Ex-communicated, archaic, degrading,
> Humiliating, unspeakable, redundant,
> Retrogressive, remarkable, unpalatable.

and only stopped because he had only the Shorter Companion Dictionary — the longer edition which he had ordered hadn't arrived.

Many of the words of Bomber Bill are nonsense words, coined on the spur of the moment. Others appeal to various groups. "Capillary and tonsorial artist" for barber is common among students of Latin; "a coffin of ostracism" was popular among the early politicians who also would not "fraternise" with the imperialist; "integrity" is used frequently to mean ability and "cerebrum" and "cerebellum" were very popular terms in biology classes.

Okenwa Olisah, using the same theme in *My Wife, About Husband and Wife Who Hate Themselves,* concentrates the attention on the father's inability to understand why, after he had spent so much to bring up his daughter, he should accept £30 as compensaion. He increases the immediacy of the speech by using pidgin English. Victoria breaks up her marriage with the rich Mark to whom she has been forcibly married by her father and falls in love with young but poor Bontus. When her father, Chief Monger[2] asks Bontus to pay a bride price of £180 and Bontus explains that the law puts the limit at £30, Chief Monger exclaims to his gathered relations:

> Israel, Rufus, Mrs. Una,[3] hear the law this boy de quote for me I no go givam my daughter again. Bontus go, go now, now.

When his relatives try to pacify him he continues:

> Law makers, I de hear you people. I go go prison because my daughter
> marry. How much I take train my daughter for school and the cost of
> other maintainance? The other man paid me £ 120. I go prison for that?

At a certain stage, his wife interjects a remark and he turns on her: "Mrs.,
I no want your mouth again."[4] Chief Monger tries to make a private
arrangement:

> If Bontus pay me £ 180 for my daughter, who go tell Goverment that I
> received above £ 30?

When this fails, he reluctantly yields his consent:

> You see trouble, man takes all his money train his daughter, after any man
> come pack those training and pay only £ 30. Wetin I go do. Nobi this
> my daughter takes my foot out.[5] If she agree stay with the former hus-
> band, who and me go de talk with. Now if I receive £ 30 from Bontus
> I will add it £ 90 to settle the former husband. Wetin I will do. Bontus
> alright bring the smallest sum of £ 30.

The success of many of these authors lies in their closeness to their
subject and their audience. They know what their audience wants. They
too are part of that audience and they share the same problems, and in
the mode of expression, they also know how to put things to catch the
interest of that audience — bombastic words, pidgin English and the point
of view. In supporting Victoria in the above play, Olisah also does manage to preserve some sympathy for Chief Monger. After all, he belonged
to a tradition in which parents decided who their daughters married, and
he had spent more than £ 30 on his daughter and, if he was to get compensation, £ 30 was a ridiculous sum. Justice demands that he be given
some sympathy.

A certain sense of justice appears in the organisation of many of the
pamphlets. *My Wives Are in Love With My Servants* by Okenwa Olisah
is a bold attack on one of the more popular sins of the new affluent society
of Nigeria — that husbands, with even two wives of their own, go around
with other women and harlots. Okenwa Olisah, like others, is interested
in the processes of law administration. He has written a pamphlet on *Ibo
Native Law and Custom*. In *My Wives Are in Love With My Servants*,
old relatives, called in by Obiakaja to settle a dispute between him and his
wives over extramarital love-making, follow the established processes of
examination and cross-examination and use expressions like: "Your wives
will make statements one by one before we ask questions . . ." This is time
for judgement. Naturally, when there is dispute, the parties concerned
would be asked to go out after giving "evidence" so that their judges will

be at every liberty to review their "evidence" and then give judgement. ". . . I am directed by my co-judges to deliver this most impartial judgement."

The play itself suggests a cure for the evil of the "womanizing" husband — expressing a feminist egalitarian attitude that not many men will find appealing. Ubiakaja comes home one afternoon to find his wives half naked and playing with his servants. To his angry outburst one of the wives replies:

> We must continue to please ourselves with Joe and Emma [the servants]. We warned you time without number to abandon your love-making with other females but you did not heed the warning. We know many of your lovers. Some of them used to visit you here without being afraid of us. It is because you told them that your wives are nothing and this is why they are not afraid of us.

> If you know how you felt when you met us with Joe and Emma playing, it was the same feeling when we see you playing and making love with other women. If you are annoyed, then imagine what might have been our feelings long ago you started to mess up with other women. Human beings have similar feelings no matter the sex. Therefore we *will never* stop being in friendship with other men until we are satisfied that you have stopped to love other women.

I found this a rather alarming statement. It does something to the traditional male prerogative of infidelity — but it is justice. And that was what the judges called by Ubiakaja, all men, thought. Their "impartial judgement" was:

> We are satisfied that Ubiakaja is a womanizer. He messed up very much and we appreciate the resentment which you his wives showed to him. You are human beings with feelings. You are not beasts. You are not blamed at all.

The case of the unfaithful husband also produced the poetic justice in *Why Some Rich Men Have No Trust in Some Girls* by H. O. Ogu. Again this is an attack on a rather common social practice — rich men having young girls whom they maintain in greater luxury than their wives. I might mention here that this play-novel gives an inkling of an answer to the problem of a kind of African (?) sense of humour that has cropped up over a few occasions. A group of Nigerian students watching a production of Antigone laughed in the last scene when the grief-stricken Cleon came on stage weeping over his dear son. Joyce Cary, in *The African Witch*, describes the laughter of the crowd watching Akande Tom, who had denied the power of Elizabeth, the witch, creeping back to her on his knees to receive his punishment. I thought when I read this that Cary's explanation of the laughter with the proposition that the crowd was hysterical with fear was wrong. I would suggest that laughter in such situations has to do with the irony of fate with the sense of relief at the re-establishment of order, with the bringing to line of the one that had dared to claim a new morality to himself. The comedy, with a purpose, of *Why Some Rich Men Have No Trust in Some Girls* is based on the irony of the situation produced, with poetic justice.

Nwankwo, a rich Lagos trader, is returning from a visit to Eastern Nigeria, and picks up a young girl, Rose, who had run away from home because she did not want to go through the fattening ceremony. He is going to keep Rose as his mistress but is not afraid to take her to his house when they arrive in Lagos. When his first wife asks "Master, who is this lady with you? Have you married another wife without our information?" He replies with a burst of laughter:

> Oko-ko ko-kono! This my wife go kill me. How I go go marry a third wife put for house, when you two wey I get at present no allow me rest. This lady na Rose, him father be my tight, tight friend. Him father ben see me for home and giam me say make I sendam to him brother wey de work for N.B.C. for this Lagos. Make una prepare chop foram. We don hungry tire for lorry.

So the wives entertain Rose generously. Later Nwankwo finds a house for Rose, keeps her lavishly, and spends most of his nights with her. But then Rose tires of doing nothing and when Nwankwo has bought her a job, she promptly falls in love with Eddie, one of her young co-workers. One evening Nwankwo catches them walking hand in hand and is enraged and explodes.

NWANKWO: Rose! you again? you again for this Lagos? Who bi this man wey you and him dey walk like husband and wife? Eh?

ROSE: Please try to control your temper whenever you are annoyed.

NWANKWO: Control my temper! how, when I don see this with my eyes?

ROSE: What? See what with your eyes? What you should have done is to ask me whom the man whom I am walking with is.

NWANKWO: O.K., who bi na man now?

ROSE: Yes, this what I expect from you. You see this man here, his name is Eddy, he is from the same family with me. His father and my father are from the same parents. He is my first cousin. I met him here today in Lagos and he was to surprised to see me. I am just coming home with him so as to introduce him to you. I have already told him all about you — your kindness and your love to me.

And so Nwankwo is deceived just as he had deceived his wives, and he not only entertains Eddy but gives him money. Later, Eddy gives him a thrashing and pays the court fine with only a minor part of the money he and Rose had saved from Nwankwo's lavish generosity.

Another aspect of justice is exhibited in Ogali A. Ogali's *Caroline the One Guinea Girl*.[6] This has to do with what one might call the graph of African justice. One of the objections raised against Cyprian Ekwensi's

Jagua Nana is that Jagua has too easy a relief from the consequences of her evil life. Ogali's explanation might help to create a calmer atmosphere for its discussion. Ogali's story is about a girl who chose to lead what may be euphemistically called an irregular life. She leaves her family and rises from the lower rank of prostitution to become a highclass "society lady," she commits a series of abortions, something abhorred by a people that value children rather highly. She reaches an apex of vice and wealth. Then things begin to happen to her. She comes back from a night of revelry to discover all her property stolen. In her poverty she is rejected by all erstwhile admirers. Then she is struck down by a foul disease and is jeered at. Her parents take her back home and for a time she is village gossip. But she begins to mend, becomes religious, and is finally married by a prosperous lawyer whom she makes happy and gives two sons and a daughter.

It was suggested to Ogali that if he had any intentions of advising girls not to follow his heroine's way of life he had spoilt it by giving her a happily married life. His reply was that the girl had suffered for her evil ways and that at the end of punishment and disgrace comes salvation and forgiveness. It appears that many of the women who read the pamphlet, though they seriously disapproved of the girl's behaviour, pitied her enough in her sufferings to feel quite happy at her good fortune at the end. This rather clashes with the Christian notion of an eternal hell for the evil-doer. The graph that goes down should go up again or balance is overthrown. I am tempted to throw in Senghor's theory of rhythm as an element of the African consciousness — but it is probably too high-sounding for the present discussion.

I have been trying to establish that the best of the pamphleteers take their sense of mission as educationists seriously. I also suggest that they take their art seriously. There are a few writers centred in Port Harcourt and they complain of the way in which their art is being degraded by some of the pamphlets published in Onitsha. One of the contributors to *The Nigerian Author Magazine* expresses concern over the existence of "fake" authors of whom he writes:

> Fake authors do themselves great disservice when they refuse to stoop down to learn. This class of authors, from point of experience, often take special delight in copying the works of others, since it is obvious that they cannot rely on their own individual literary efforts. Such offense, if proved in a court of law means 'PLAGIARISM.' Apt quotations used with the names of such authors are permissible however . . . (Ikpoto, 1962).

There is something perhaps naive in the way the statement is made but it shows the author's serious concern with the dignity and the nature of his art. In the Introduction to his novelette, *Surprise Packet,* Sigis Kamalu comments on the poor quality of some of the literature on the market and attempts a critical analysis of his own novel. Most of these writers end their prefaces by inviting serious criticism of their works and express ready willingness to accept correction.

Grey Ikpoto starts the above-mentioned essay with the assertion that "The 'born' or 'fair' authors are naturally thirsty for reading, hungry for learning . . ." There is no doubt that the better writers of the group do read whatever is available to them and try to bring their reading into their writing — sometimes to show off their learning (one remembers many school boy debates where the most applauded speakers were those who could roll out a string of quotations), at other times in a serious effort to improve their writing.

A dictum among the Ibos is to the effect that to make a speech without using proverbs is like trying to climb a palm tree without the climbing rope. I suggest that the tendency towards supporting one's statements with proverbs might have carried over into this market literature in the form of using quotations. *In Veronica My Daughter,* between pages 20 and 23, there are quotations from Richard Whately, William Shakespeare, G. A. Gallock, Rudyard Kipling, Benjamin Harrison, William Ernest Henley and Henry Longfellow; and before the end of the story there are further quotations from Johann Wolfgang Von Goethe and some unknown poet. Momoh Aroye's *Nancy in Blooming Beauty* opens with a quotation "culled from 'GOOD WIVES' edited by Louisa M. Alcott."

Incidentally, the mania for quotations is not determined by the standard of education. Onuorah Nzekwu's *Wand of Noble Wood,* for example, contains its fair share of quotations. Snatches of poems and songs keep running through the mind of Peter Obesie, the hero, and in one conversation in the story there are quotations from Sir Walter Scott, Southey, Reynold's *The Will,* and from Shakespeare. And on the day on which I first thought of this issue I glanced through one Nigerian newspaper and the leader article started its second paragraph with a quotation from Edmund Burke. This is impressive where breadth of knowledge of English is not only a prestige factor but also a guide to social and employment status. In *Veronica My Daughter,* Veronica looks down on her father's intelligence and wisdom because he had not attended "even infant school as to be able to read and write simple English." But one has to admit that sometimes quotations are used for the genuine purpose of giving to the opinion of the speaker or writer an extra and higher authority.

Nancy in Blooming Beauty reveals another kind of influence from reading. Momoh Aroye's English in this novel is stilted and so is the framework in which he puts his story. Nancy says that she "was born and bred in the little Cottage of Funland along the shores of the Rio De La Plata on the 1st day of April." The setting gets all mixed up, some fantastic situations mingling with the customs of that part of Nigeria where Momoh Aroye was brought up. The author appears to be so intent on reproducing the tone and style of the romances he has read that he comes out with affected and pompous impossibilities and flourishes of style that may impress the semi-illiterate but sound rather ridiculous to the enlightened reader, even admitting the robustness of the experiment with words. And this is a pity because he has a story that supports his theme that "Contentment can't be got by seeking."

Another type of influence is interestingly portrayed in Thomas O. Igu's *Agnes the Faithful Lover*. Agnes declares that she is ready to die for her love and "then my name will go into history as having died like Julliet [sic] for the cause of true love." At the end of the play Agnes and her lover commit suicide in true Romeo and Juliet fashion and are mourned by all those who had opposed them. *Romeo and Juliet* also provides the inspiration for Igu's other play *Alice in the Romance of Love*. Alice's confidante warns her against being in love with Fidelis, the boy "with whose family yours have been engaged in a series of court actions over a piece of land." The feud had to be about a piece of land in Nigerian terms. Later in the "drama" there is the following scene obviously influenced by *Romeo and Juliet* Act II, Scene ii.

ALICE: It is alright; good night.
(Fidelis leaves).

ALICE: Come back darling for I can't afford to let you go without a kiss; (She kisses him again).

FIDELIS: Sweet heart I shall be here again to see you tomorrow.

ALICE: Is tomorrow not too far? O! don't you know I find it difficult to control my sentimental emotions when I don't see you for a single hour.

FIDELIS: Alright darling, but for the memory of this great night, have this ring and wear it always on your fingers.

ALICE: In fact I have now agreed you love me and that being the case, always count me first among those that love you dearly for I don't think anybody loves you more than myself. Oh sweet heart hurry out for my dad is coming.

FIDELIS: Alright good night; (he leaves).

ALICE: Don't go please without a kiss for it is one of the pleasures of being in love with some one of the opposite sex. (They kiss themselves again.)
(EXIT FIDELIS)

ALICE: Oh this boy is really sweet. I don't know why I have within a short space of time loved him so much. He is my morning star and has ultimately stolen my heart away. No I must call him back.
(She goes to the window)

ALICE: Fidelis! Fidelis! Fidelis, sweet heart! (she shouts for him). Oh! you're gone far, but how do I stay alone without you. Can't you listen and answer my call? I am Alice calling you. (At this stage she turns back). He has gone far. Oh! he doesn't hear me (she cries).

Reading, learning, taking expressions from here and there, sometimes borrowing settings, at others borrowing scenes, always interested in improving their vocabulary and technique, these writers are providing literature for the audience ready to take their works. They are read by traders and students, and I have seen some of these pamphlets in the hands of village children. Many of these writers are serious with their work. Their interests vary from love to politics. (There is a large body of political writing which, for purposes of brevity, I have not discussed.) They are interested in social problems — prostitution, drunkenness, bribery, bride price, the taking of brain pills by students; they are interested in the customs of the land.

Some, of course, are interested in nothing but catching the market. Miller O. Albert, for example, has produced an extravaganza called *Rosemary and the Taxi Driver,* all fantasy and word exuberance. To illustrate, this pamphlet opens with

> If there was a prize to be awarded for falling in love at first blush, Rosemary should be given the richest golden medal. She has been chasing around the romantic sea port of Lagos, with her flareful glush of romance. Her violet gown with vibrant colours and heavenly patterns vested below her knees. She wore a dazzling gold necklace, shiny ear rings and a botanical veil, stained all over with jet colours.

Occasionally there is an interesting word play resulting from the extravagance of the imagination, as when Rosemary muses: "I know I'm Rosemary. Mary is the last tail of it, Yes! But I will one day, add an "R" after a letter, from the last spelling, to make it a vital gut that's Yes the much sought after treasure 'Marry'." But most of the book is in the vein of the following extraordinary passage, describing the sensation caused by Rosemary on entering the train:

> Soon she entered into the train rolling the sleeves of her gown, getting ready for any strange eventuality. All the mask faced odd boys were soaring on the air, for her cheerful romance because of her saucy red lips. The character they presented, necame very lhicky to happiness and some, were savouring insubordination, mostly the odd concomitant type, of immoral stimulation, which provoked the impetus of glaring at sexual menace, below the belt, leading to excessive giving back of daily toping and night time tipples of dry gin and whiskey.

There is much Onitsha market literature that is below the standard of even its own audience. The best of its examples do not attain a high literary standard. The English is rather poor though sometimes exciting, and is made worse by printing. Most of the characters are undeveloped types. Themes are treated much too superficially. Some of the authors know this and explain the handicaps under which they work. The publishers dictate to them about subject matter and number of pages. Some of the writers have no other source of income and since they do not receive much for a manuscript they have to produce rather fast.

The audience dictates to them. For example Love is the most popular theme and sometimes titles are distorted to attract interest. Okenwa Olisah's *My Seven Daughters Are After Young Boys,* for example, has a deceptive title. The play deals with the attempts being made on a king's life by his three wives whom he had 'sacked' following the evidence of his servant Godwin that they had tried to make love to him. The title only comes in at the end when the king, in rewarding Godwin for his services, says to him.

> My servant, Godwin, you are a very faithful servant, you serve me very well. You gives me informations. I trust you more than my wives and children. My wives want me to die. My children are stupid things. MY DAUGHTERS ARE AFTER YOUNG BOYS! They only know how to play love and nothing more again. But Selinah will make a good wife. She is not after young boys as others; she is different from my daughters. Selinah will be your wife as from Thursday next week.

And Thursday, the following week Selinah became Godwin's wife. But this is not enough to justify the title and one must accept the existence of some outside pressure that led to the choice of that title.

The audience also demands vigorous action in love or crime or politics. It also demands big words. There is a middle group of better educated writers who try to psychologise in good but simple English and they are finding it difficult to make any impact or money.

With these handicaps it is surprising that so many books of definite interest are produced. And these books are significant both as literary efforts and in their revelation of the popular attitudes to socio-cultural phenomena. We have a new life and a new language. In the unassuming simplicity and directness of Onitsha Market literature we find authentic evidence of what these new elements mean to the common man and what are his reactions to them.

NOTES

1. Where I put a question mark after the author's name, the author has denied authorship. I found that there are many authors who sell their manuscripts outright for £20 to £30 and the publisher then brings out the book under his own name.

2. Those who are considered to follow money too eagerly are called money mongers.

3. The plural for "you" in Ibo is Unu.

4. This is a translation from Ibo and is something equivalent to "I don't want your cheek."

5. Again a translation from Ibo. Traditionally corpses are carried out feet first. To have one's feet taken out [last] has come to mean to be exposed or disgraced, or generally to be a cause of public gathering and concern. Chief Jumbo is saying therefore that it is his daughter that has made him cause of public commotion. This is the power of pidgin English that, because it has no standard form, the speaker has the freedom to adopt whatever he chooses into it.

6. Unfortunately this is out of print. The information that follows about the novel is the outcome of an interview with the author.

Bibliography

ABRAMS, CHARLES
1965   Man's struggle for shelter in an urbanizing world. Cambridge, MIT Press.

1966   Squatter settlements: The problem and the opportunity. Washington, D.C., Department of Housing and Urban Development.

ABU-LUGHOD, JANET
1967.   Migrant adjustment to city life: The Egyptian case. *In* Peasant society, Jack Potter et al., eds. Boston, Little, Brown and Co.

ADAMS, RICHARD N.
1953   A change from caste to class in a Peruvian sierra town. Social Forces 31:3:238–244.

ADAMS, RICHARD N. AND CHARLES C. CUMBERLAND
1960   U.S. university cooperation in Latin America: A study based on selected programs in Bolivia, Chile, Peru, and Mexico. East Lansing, Michigan State Institute of Research on Overseas Programs.

ADORNO, T. ET. AL.
1952   The authoritarian personality. New York, Harper and Row.

AFRICAN HOUSING DEPARTMENT
1956   Annual report, government printer, Entebbe, Uganda.

ALEGRÍA, CIRO
1941   El mundo es ancho y ajeno. Santiago de Chile, Ediciones Ercilla.

ARGUEDAS, JOSE MARIA
1952   El complejo cultural en el Peru y el primer congreso de Peruanistas. American Indigena 21:131–139.

AUSTIN, ALLAN
1964   Research report of Peruvian local government. New York, Institute of Public Administration.

BAILEY, F. C.
1958   Caste and the economic frontier. Oxford, Oxford University Press.

BEALS, RALPH L.
1951   Urbanism, urbanization and acculturation. American Anthropologist 53:1.

1953   Social stratification of Latin America. American Journal of Sociology 58:327–339.

193

BELLIN, SEYMOUR
1960   Co-residence and family structure. Report of Mental Health Research Unit, New York State Department of Mental Hygiene, Syracuse.

BERGER, PETER L.
1963   Invitation to sociology. Garden City, New York, Doubleday, Inc.

BOCK, PHILIP K.
1969   Peasants in the modern world. Albuquerque, University of New Mexico Press.

BOOTH, CHARLES
1902   Labour and life of the London poor. New York, Kelley Co.

BOUGLE, C.
1908   Essais sur les regimes des castes. Paris.

BOURRICAUD, FRANCOIS
1954   Algunas caracteristicas originales de la cultura mestiza en el Peru contemporaneo. Revista del Museo Nacional 23:162–173.

BROWN, CLAUDE
1966   Manchild in the promised land. New York, Signet.

BRUNER, EDWARD M.
1959   Kinship organization among the urban Batak of Sumatra. Transactions of the New York Academy of Science 22:118–125.

1961   Urbanization and ethnic identity in North Sumatra. American Anthropologist 63:508–521.

BRYCE-LAPORTE, ROY S.
1968   Family adaptation of relocated slum dwellers in Puerto Rico: Implications for urban research and development. The Journal of Developing Areas 2:533–540.

BUECHLER, HANS C.
1967   A social game and its transformations: The Aymara fiesta system. Paper presented at the 66th annual meeting of the American Anthropological Association, November 1967, Washington, D.C.

1968   The reorganization of countries in the Bolivian highlands: An analysis of rural-urban networks and hierarchies. In Urban anthropology, Elizabeth Eddy, ed. Proceedings of the Southern Anthropological Society, No. 2. Athens, University of Georgia Press.

BUECHLER, JUDITH-MARIA
1967   To market, to market: An evaluation of changing market relations of Aymara women in La Paz. Paper presented at the 66th annual meeting of the American Anthropological Association.

BUTTERWORTH, D. S.
1962   A study of the urbanization process among Mixtec immigrants from Tilantongo in Mexico City. America Indigena 22:257–274.

CANCIAN, FRANK
    1965   Economics and prestige in Zinancantan. Stanford, Stanford University Press.

CAPLOW, THEODORE
    1949   The ecology of middle American cities. Social Forces 28:2.

    1952   The modern Latin American city. *In* Acculturation in the Americas, Sol Tax, ed. Chicago, University of Chicago Pr., ICA, 29th.

CARTER, WILLIAM
    1968   Secular reinforcement in Aymara death ritual. American Anthropologist 70:238–263.

CASTILLO, HERNAN, TERESA CASTILLO, AND ARCENIO REVILLA
    1964   Caracas: The forgotten community. Ithaca, Cornell Peru Project.

CAUDILL, HARRY M.
    1963   Night comes to the Cumberlands. Boston, Little Brown.

CLINARD, MARSHALL
    1966   Slums and community development. New York, Free Press.

COHEN, ALBERT
    1955   Delinquent boys. Glencoe, Free Press.

COLES, ROBERT
    1965   There's sinew in the Negro family. Washington Post, October 10.

    1968   Life in Appalachia — the case of Hugh McCaslin. Transaction, June:23–33.

COLLIER, JOHN, JR. AND ANIBAL BUITRÓN
    1949   The awakening valley. Chicago, University of Chicago Press.

COULTER, G. C.
    1933   The sociological aspects. *In* Modern industry and the African, M. Davis, ed. London, Macmillan & Co.

CROOKE, PATRICK AND CARLO DOGLIO
    1960   Scuole e comunita. Comunita 84:28–57.

CRUMRINE, N. ROSS
    1969   The function of ritual and sacred symbolism in acculturation and pluralism with special reference to Mayo Indian ceremonialism. Paper presented at the 28th annual meeting of the Society for Applied Anthropology, Mexico, April 1969.

CUMMING, ELAINE AND DAVID M. SCHNEIDER
    1961   Sibling solidarity: A property of American kinship. American Anthropologist 63:498–507.

DAVIS, KINGSLEY AND ANA CASIS
    1946   Urbanization in Latin America. The Milbank Memorial Fund Quarterly 24, 2.

DEGEZ, A.
    1961   Aspects d'un urbanisme a Fes. Bull. Econ. et Soc. Maroc. 89:31–39.

DEVERDUN, G.
1959   Marrakesh, des origines a 1919. Rabat.

DIRECCIÓN GENERAL DE ESTADÍSTICA
1940   Sexto censo general de población. México.
1950   Séptimo censo general de población. México.
1960   Octavo censo general de población. México.

DOUGHTY, PAUL
1967   La bebida, la cultura y el trabajo en un distrito andino mestizo. America Indigena 27:4:667–687.

1968   Huaylas: An Andean district in search of progress. Ithaca, New York, Cornell University Press.

DUBOIS, P.
1958   Enquete par sondage sur Pemploi a Casablanca. Bull. Mensuel Statist. 5.

ECOCHARD, J.
1955   Casablanca, le roman d'une ville. Paris.

EPLING, D. J.
n.d.   Ethnographic notes on the Venice Negro community, 1964–1966. (Unpublished)

EPSTEIN, A. L.
1956   Politics in an urban African community. Rhodes-Livingstone Institute. Manchester, Manchester University Press.

ERASMUS, CHARLES J.
1967   Upper limits of peasantry and agrarian reform: Bolivia, Venezuela, and Mexico compared. Ethnology 6:349–380.

ERICKSEN, E. GORDON
1954   Urban behavior. New York, Macmillan.

ERIKSON, ERIK H.
1965   The concept of identity in race relations: Notes and queries. Daedalus, Winter:145–171. 1966.

ESCOBAR, GABRIEL
1967   Organización social y cultural del Sur del Perú. (Instituto Indigenista Interamericano) Serie Antropologia Social:7, Mexicó, D.F.

FANON, FRANZ
1963   The wretched of the earth. New York, Grove Press.

FOSTER, G.M.
1960/1 Interpersonal relations in peasant society. Human Organization 19, Winter

1961   The dyadic contract: A model for the social structure of a Mexican peasant village. American Anthropologist 63:1173–1192.

1965a   Cultural responses to expressions of envy in Tzintzuntzan. Southwestern Journal of Anthropology 21:1, 24–35.

1965b   Peasant society and the image of a limited good. American Anthropologist 67:293–315.

FRAZIER, E. FRANKLIN
1939   The Negro family in the United States. Chicago, University of Chicago Press.

FREILICH, MORRIS
1961   Serial polygyny, Negro peasants and model analysis. American Anthropologist 63:955–975.

FRIED, JACOB
1959   Acculturation and mental health among Indian migrants in Peru. *In* Culture and mental health: Cross cultural studies, Marvin K. Opler, ed. New York, Macmillan.

1960   Enfermedad y organizacion social en Vicos. Etnolgia y Arqueologia 1:1:38–49.

FRIEDEN, BERNARD J.
1965   The search for a housing policy in Mexico City. Town Planning Review 36, July.

FROMM, E.
1947   Man for himself. New York, Rinehart.

GANS, HERBERT
1962   The urban villagers. New York, Free Press.

GEDDES, PATRICK
1918   Town planning towards city development. A report prepared for the Durbar of Indore, India, Vol. 1:85.

GILLIN, JOHN
1951   The culture of security in San Carlos. Middle American Research Institute, Tulane University Publ. 16.

GLAZER, NATHAN
1965   Slum dwellings do not make a slum. New York Times Magazine, November 21:55–68.

GOLDKIND, VICTOR
1961   Sociocultural contrasts in rural and urban settlement types in Costa Rica. Rural Sociology 26, 4.

GOLDRICH, DANIEL
1965   Toward the comparative study of politicization in Latin America. *In* contemporary cultures and societies of Latin America, D. Heath and R. Adams, eds. New York, Random House.

GOMES CONSORTE, JOSILDETH
1959   A crianca favelada e a escola publica. Educacao e Ciencias Sociais 5:11, August.

GORER, GEOFFREY
1948   Japanese child-rearing patterns. *In* Personal character and cultural milieu, D. G. Haring, ed. Syracuse, Syracuse University Press.

GOULD, HAROLD A.
1959   The peasant village: Centrifugal or centripetal? Eastern Anthropologist 13:1.

GUTKIND, P. C. W.
1963   The African administration of the Kibuga of Buganda, Mouton. The Hague.

HAMMEL, EUGENE
1961a   Wealth, authority and prestige in the Ica Valley. New Mexico Press.

1961b   The family cycle in a Peruvian slum and village. American Anthropologist 63:989–1006.

HANDLIN, OSCAR, (ED.)
1959   Immigration as a factor in American history. New York, Prentice Hall.

HARRINGTON, MICHAEL
1962   The other America. New York, Macmillan.

HARRIS, MARVIN
1964   Patterns of race in the Americas. New York, Walker.

HERZOG, ELIZABETH
1966   Is there a 'breakdown' of the Negro family? Social Work, January 2:3–10.

HOBSBAWM, E. J.
1965   Primitive rebels, studies in archaic forms of social movements in the 19th and 20th centuries. New York, Norton.

HOLMBERG, ALLAN R.
1955   Participant intervention in the field. Human Organization 14:23–28.

1958   The research and development approach to the study of change. Human Organization 17:1:12–16.

1960   Changing community attitudes and values in Peru: A case study in guided change. In Social change in Latin America today. New York, Harper & Brothers.

HOLMBERG, ALLAN R. ET AL.
1965   The Vicos case: Peasant society in transition. American Behavioral Scientist 8:7:3–33.

HUTCHINSON, BERTRAM
1960   Mobilidade e trabalho. Rio de Janeiro: Centro Brasileiro de Pesquisas Educacionais.

IKPOTO, GREY
1962   The field of authorship. The Nigerian Author Magazine, May, p. 7.

INDONESIA
1960   Statistical pocketbook of Indonesia, Djakarta, Biro Pusat Statistik.

JOLY, F.
1961   Casablanca, elements pour une etude de geographie urbaine. Cah.
        d'Outre-Mer 1, 2:119–148.

JOSEPHINE
1964   Tell me, Josephine. Edited by Barbara Hall. New York, Simon and
        Schuster.

KAHL, JOSEPH
1960   Three types of Mexican industrial workers. Economic Develop-
        ment and cultural change 8:164–169.

KUBLER, GEORGE
1946   The Quechua in the colonial world. *In* The Andean civilizations,
        Julian Steward, ed. Washington, Smithsonian, BAE, Bulletin 143,
        Handbook of South American Indians.

KVARACEUS, WILLIAM C. AND WALTER B. MILLER
1959   Delinquent behavior: Culture and the individual. National Edu-
        cation Association, Washington.

LANDAU, R.
1956   Moroccan drama. Robert Hale.

LANDSBERGER, HENRY A.
1968   The role of peasant movements and revolts in development: An
        analytical framework. *In* Latin American peasant movements,
        Henry A. Landsberger, ed. Ithaca, Cornell University Press.

LAQUIAN, APRODICIO
1968   Slums are for people. Manila, DM Press.

LEACH, E. R.
1960   Introduction: What should we mean by caste? *In* Aspects of
        caste in South India, Ceylon and Northwest Pakistan, E. R. Leach,
        ed. Cambridge, University of Cambridge, Cambridge Papers in
        Social Anthropology No. 2.

LEE, DOROTHY
1959   Freedom and culture. Englewood Cliffs, New Jersey, Prentice-
        Hall.

LEONARD, OLIN E.
1948   La Paz, Bolivia: Its population and growth. American Sociological
        Review 13:4.

LE TOURNEAU, R.
1952   Les ville musulmanes de l'Amerique du Nord. Algiers.

LEWIS, OSCAR
1951   Life in a Mexican village: Tepoztlan revisited. Urbana, University
        of Illinois Press.

1952   Urbanization without breakdown: A case study. The Scientific
        Monthly 75:31–41.

1957   Urbanización sin desorganización. Les familias tepoztecas en la
        ciudad de Mexico. American Indigena 17:231–246.

1959   Five families. New York, Basic Books.

1961   The children of Sanchez. New York, Random House.

1962   Further observations on the folk-urban continuum and urbanization with special reference to Mexico City. Paper presented at 35th Congress of Americanists, Mexico City.

1965   Urbanization without breakdown. *In* Contemporary cultures and societies of Latin America, D. B. Heath and R. N. Adams, eds. New York, Random House.

1966a   La Vida: A Puerto Rican family in the culture of poverty — San Juan and New York. New York, Random House.

1966b   The culture of poverty. Scientific American, October, 19–25.

LINTON, R.
1936   The study of man. New York.

LITTLE, KENNETH
1965   West African urbanization: A study of voluntary associations in social change. London, Cambridge University Press.

LITWACK, EUGENE
1960a   The use of the extended family groups in the achievement of social goals: Some policy implications. Social Problems 7:177–186.

1960b   Geographical mobility and extended family cohesion. American Sociological Review 25:385–394.

LOPREATO, JOSEPH
1967   Peasants no more. San Francisco, Chandler Publishing Company.

MAJUMDAR, D. N.
1959   Caste and communication in an Indian village. Bombay, Asia Publishing House.

MALCOLM X
1965   Malcolm X. speaks. George Breitman, ed. New York, Merit Publishers.

1966   The autobiography of Malcolm X. New York, Grove Press.

MANGIN, WILLIAM
1954   The cultural significance of the fiesta complex in an Indian hacienda in Peru. Ph.D. dissertation, Yale University.

1955a   The role of regional associations in the adaptation of rural population in Peru. Berlin, Germany, Sociologus 9:21–36.

1955b   Estratificatión social en el Callejón de Huaylas. Lima, Peru, Revista Del Museo Nacional 24:174–189.

1957   Haciendas, comunidades and strategic acculturation in the Peruvian sierra. Sociologus 7:2:142–146.

1959   The role of regional associations in the adaption of rural population in Peru. Sociologus 9:1:23–35.

1960a   Mental health and migration to cities. Annals of the New York Academy of Sciences 84:17:911–917.

1960b   Organization social en Vicos. Etnologia y Arqueologia 1:1:24–37.

1963   Urbanization case history in Peru. Architectural Design, August.

1965   The role of social organization in improving the environment. Environment Determinants of Community Well-Being-Scientific Publications, PAHO, 123: (Dec.) 41–51.

1967a   Las comunidades altenas de America Latina. Institute Indegenista Interamericano, Serie monografico, Mexico, D.F.

1967b   Latin America squatter settlements: A problem and a solution. Latin American Research Review 2:3:65–98.

1967c   Squatter settlements. Scientific American, October 21–29.

Mangin, William and John C. Turner
1968   The barriada movement. Progressive Architecture May: 154–162.

Marris, Peter
1960   Slum clearance and family life in Lagos. Human Organization 19:123–128.

Martinez, Hector
1963   Vicos: Las fiestas en la integración y desintegración cultural. Lima, Ministerio de Trabajo y Asuntos Indigenas, serie monografica, no. 15.

Mas, P.
1962   Tanger une ile. Rev. Geogr. Maroc. 1–2:153–155.

McCulloch, M.
1956   A social survey of the African population of Livingstone. Rhodes-Livingstone Paper No. 26.

Meillassoux, Claude
1968   Urbanization of an African community: Voluntary associations in Bamako. Seattle, University of Washington Press.

Merton, Robert and Alice Kitt
1950   Contributions to the theory of reference group behavior. In Studies in the scope and method of "The American Soldier," Robert Merton and Paul Lazarsfeld, eds. Glencoe, Free Press.

Miller, Eric J.
1954   Caste and territory in Malabar. American Anthropologist 56:3.

Miller, S. M. and Martin Rein
1964   Poverty and social change (Mizruchi). The American Child, March.

Mills, C. Wright
1943   The ideology of social pathologists. American Journal of Sociology 59:165–180.

MITCHELL, J. C.
1951   A note on the urbanization of Africans on the copperbelt. Human Problems in British Central Africa 12:20–27.

1954a   African urbanization in Ndola and Luanshya. Rhodes-Livingstone Communication No. 6.

1954b   Urbanization, detribalization and stabilization: A problem of definition and measurement. Paper presented to the UNESCO Conference on the Social Impact of Industrialization and Urban Conditions in Africa. Abijan, September.

MONTALVO, ABNER
1967   Las relaciones de trabajo entre los indígenas peruanas. Perú Indígena, No. 26, 238–253.

MOORE, ALEXANDER
1966   Social and ritual change in a Guatemalan town. Ph.D. dissertation, Columbia University.

MOYNIHAN, DANIEL P.
1965   The Negro family: The case for national action. Washington, U.S. Department of Labor.

MURDOCK, GEORGE
1949   Social structure. New York, Macmillan.

MYRDAL, GUNNAR
1944   An American dilemma. New York, Harper.

NASH, JUNE
1968   The passion play in Maya Indian communities. Comparative Studies in Sociology and History 10:3:318–327.

NASH, MANNING
1964   Capital saving and credit in a Guatemalan and a Mexican Indian peasant society. *In* saving and credit in peasant society, R. Firth and B. S. Yamey, eds. Chicago, Aldine Press.

NEIRA, HUGO
1964   Cuzco: Tierra y muerte. Reportaje al Sur. Problemas de Hoy, Lima.

NESPOLA, H.
1960   Kenitra, historique et analyse du developpment de l'agglomeration et du port et ses incidents sur l'evolution et l'economie du Gharb. Bull. Econ. Soc. Maroc. 24:85:25–89.

NIDDRIE, D.
1954   The road to work: A survey of the influence of transport on migrant labor in central Africa. Human Problems in British Central Africa 4:30–42.

NÚÑEZ, THOMAS A., JR.
1963   Tourism, tradition, and acculturation: Weekendism in a Mexican village. Ethnology 2:347–352.

NUÑEZ DEL PRADO, OSCAR
1951   Aspecto economico de Viru, una comunidad de la costa norte del Peru. Cuzco.

OHLIN, LLOYD AND RICHARD CLOWARD
1960   Delinquency and opportunity. Glencoe, Free Press.

PADILLA, ELENA
1958   Up from Puerto Rico. New York, Columbia University Press.

PAREDES, RIGOBERTO
1949   El arte folklorico de Bolivia. La Paz, Talleres graficos Gamarra.

PARSONS, TALCOTT
1951   The social system. Glencoe, Free Press.

PARSONS, TALCOTT ET AL.
1953   Toward a general theory of action. Cambridge, Harvard University Press.

PATCH, RICHARD W.
1957   An hacienda becomes a community. Peru, American Universities Field Staff Letter.

1964   Vicos and the Peace Corps. American University Field Staff Report, West Coast South America, 11:2.

1967   La parada, Lima's market: Part 1: A villager who met disaster. American Universities Field Staff Reports, West Coast of South America Series 14:1, Peru.

PEARSE, ANDREW
1958   Notas sobre a organizacao social de uma favela do rio de Janeiro. Educacao e Ciencias Sociais 3:7.

PEATTIE, LISA
1968   The view from the barrio. Ann Arbor, University of Michigan Press.

POCOCK, DAVID F.
1957a   Inclusion and exclusion: A process in the caste system of Gujerat. Southwestern Journal of Anthropology 13:1.

1957b   "Difference" in East Africa: A study of caste and religion in Indian society. Southwestern Journal of Anthropology 13:4.

POTTER, JACK M., MAY N. DIAZ, AND GEORGE M. FOSTER
1967   Peasant society: A reader. Boston, Little, Brown.

REDFIELD, ROBERT
1941   The folk culture of Yucatan. Chicago, University of Chicago Press.

1953   The primitive world and its transformations. Ithaca, Cornell University Press.

REINA, RUBEN E.
1964   The urban world view of a tropical forest community in the absence of a city, Petan, Guatemala. Human Organization (Winter) 23:4:265–277.

RICHARDS, A. I. AND P. REINING
   1954   Report on fertility surveys in Buganda and Buhaya. *In* Culture and human fertility, Frank Lorimer, ed. UNESCO.

RIESMAN, DAVID
   1950   The lonely crowd. New Haven, Yale University Press.

RIIS, JACOB A.
   1957   How the other half lives. American Century Series. New York, Sycamore Press.

RODMAN, HYMAN
   1963   The lower class value stretch. Social Forces 42:205–215.

   1964   Middle class misconception about lower class families. *In* Blue collar world, Arthur B. Shostak and William C. Gomberg, eds. Englewood Cliffs, New Jersey, Prentice-Hall.

ROTONDO, HUMBERTO ET AL.
   1959   Estudios de psiquistria social en areas urbanas y rurales. No. 1, Mendocita. Lima, Peru, Ministry of Public Health, Department of Mental Hygiene.

ROWE, JOHN H.
   1947   The distribution of Indians and Indian languages in Peru. Geographical Review 37:2:202–215.

   1957   The Incas under Spanish colonial institutions. Hispanic American Historical Review 37:2:155–199.

SAFA, HELEN
   1964   From shantytown to public housing: A comparison of family structure in two urban neighborhoods in Puerto Rico. Caribbean Studies 4:1:3–12.

   1965   The female-based household in public housing: A case study in Puerto Rico. Human Organization 24:135–139.

SAPIR, EDWARD
   1924   Culture, genuine and spurious. American Journal of Sociology 29:401–429.

SCHULMAN, SAM
   1966   Latin American shanty town. New York Times Magazine, January 16.

SEDA-BONILLA, EDUARDO
   1965   Dependence as an obstacle to growth: Puerto Rico. New World Quarterly 2:13–18.

SEWELL, GRANVILLE H.
   1964   Squatter settlements in Turkey: Analysis of a social, political and economic problem. Ph.D. dissertation, MIT. (Monograph)

SIMMEL, GEORG
   1957   The metropolis and mental life. *In* Cities and society: The revised reader in urban sociology, Paul K. Hatt and Albert J. Reiss, Jr., eds. Glencoe, Illinois, Free Press.

SIMMONS, OZZIE G.
1952   El uso de los conceptos de aculturacion y asimillacion en el estudio del cambio cultural en el Peru. Peru Indigena 2:40–47.

1955   The Criollo outlook in the mestizo culture of coastal Peru. American Anthropologist 57:107–177.

SMITH, RAYMOND
1956   The Negro family in British Guiana. London, Routledge & Kegan Paul.

SOUTHALL, A. W.
1956   Determinants of the social structure of African urban populations. *In* Social implications of industrialization and urbanization in Africa South of the Sahara. UNESCO.

1961   (Ed.) Social change in modern Africa. Oxford, International African Institute.

1966   The growth of urban society. *In* The transformation of East Africa, S. Diamond and F. G. Burke, eds. New York, Basic Books.

1967   Kampala-Mengo. *In* The city in modern Africa, Horace Miner, ed. New York, Praeger.

SOUTHALL, A. W. AND P. C. W. GUTKIND
1957   Townsmen in the making — Kampala and its suburbs. Kampala, East African Institute of Social Research, East African Studies No. 9.

SRINIVAS, M. N.
1957   Caste in modern India. The Journal of Asian Studies 4:529–548.

STEIN, WILLIAM
1961   Hualcan: Life in the highlands of Peru. Ithaca, Cornell University Press.

STEWARD, JULIAN H.
1960   Evolutionary principles and social types. *In* Evolution after Darwin, volume 2, Sol Tax, ed. Chicago, University of Chicago Press.

STORM, HANS OTTO
1948   Of good family. New York, William Morrow Company.

STOWE, LELAND
1963   Miracle at Vicos. Reader's Digest, April, 222–228.

SUSSMAN, MARVIN B.
1962   Kin family network: Unheralded structure in current conceptualization of family functioning. Marriage and Family Living 24:231–240.

TSCHOPIK, HARRY, JR.
1947   Highland communities of Central Peru. Institute of Social Anthropology, Smithsonian, Pub. No. 5.

1952   On the identification of the Indian in Peru. *In* Acculturation in the Americas, Sol Tax, ed. Chicago.

TUMIN, MELVIN
1952   Caste in a peasant society. Princeton, Princeton University Press.

TURNER, JOHN C.
1965   Lima's barriadas and corralones: Suburbs versus slums. Ekistics 112, March.

1966a   Uncontrolled urban settlement: Problems and policies. Paper prepared for the United Nations Seminar on Development Policies and Planning in Relation to Urbanization. Pittsburgh, Pennsylvania (Fall).

1966b   A new view of the housing deficit. A paper prepared for the seminar on a Housing Policy for a Developing Economy. University of San Juan, Puerto Rico (April).

UNITED NATIONS
1957   Report on the world social situation. New York, Bureau of Social Affairs.

1962   Report of the ad hoc group of experts on housing and urban development. New York, United Nations.

1965   Methods for establishing targets and standards for housing and environmental development. E/C, 6/31.

VALENTINE, CHARLES A.
1968   Culture and poverty. Chicago, University of Chicago Press.

VAN ZANTWIJK, R.
1967   Servants of the saints: The social and cultural identity of a Tarascan community in Mexico. Assen, Van Gorcum & Co.

VASQUEZ, MARIO
1952   La antropogia cultural y nuestro problems del Indio. Vicos: Un caso de antropologia aplicada. Peru Indigena 2, 5, 6:7–158.

1955   Cambios en la estratificación social en una hacienda Andia del Peru. Revista del Muzeo Nacional 24:190–209.

VOGEL, WILLIAM M.
1968   Is labor migration of decreasing significance in the economics of East Africa? Occasional Paper, Program of Eastern African Studies, Syracuse University.

WAKEFIELD, DAN
1959   Island in the city. Boston.

WALLACE, ANTHONY
1966   Religion: An anthropological view. New York, Random House.

WALLIS, ETHEL EMILIA
1953   Problemas de aculturacion implicitas en la educacion indigena del Otomi del Mezquital. America Indigena 13:234–258.

WEISSMANN, ERNEST
1966   Statement made at the 403rd meeting, April 25, United Nations, Economic and Social Council, Social Commission, U. N. Bulletin No. E/CN 5/L, 313.

WHETTEN, NATHAN L. AND ROBERT G. BURNIGHT
   1956   International migration in Mexico. Estudios antropologicos pub-
             licados en homenaje al Doctor Manuel Gamio. Mexico.

WHITE, LESLIE A.
   1959   The evolution of culture. New York, McGraw-Hill.

WHYTE, WILLIAM FOOTE
   1943   Street corner society. Chicago, University of Chicago Press.

WILSON, G.
   1942   An essay on the economics of detribalization in northern Rhodesia.
             Rhodes-Livingstone Paper No. 6.

WIRTH, LOUIS
   1938   Urbanism as a way of life. The American Journal of Sociology 44.

WITHINGTON, WILLIAM A.
   1962   Medan: Primary regional metropolis of Sumatra. Journal of Geog-
             raphy 61:59–67.

WOLF, ERIC R.
   1955   Types of Latin American peasantry. American Anthropologist
             57:452–471.

   1966   Peasants. Englewood Cliffs, New Jersey, Prentice-Hall.

   1969   Peasant wars of the twentieth century. New York, Harper and Row.

ZBOROWSKI, MARK AND ELIZABETH HERZOG
   1952   Life is with people: The Jewish little-town of eastern Europe. New
             York, International University Press.

ZIMMER, BASIL G.
   1955   Participation of migrants in urban structures. American Sociological
             Review 20:219–224.

ZUIDEMA, R. T.
   1964   The ceque system of Cuzco. Leiden, E. J. Brill.